ESSAYS IN
MUSICAL ANALYSIS

By

DONALD FRANCIS TOVEY

IN SIX VOLUMES

CONTENTS

ESSAYS IN
MUSICAL ANALYSIS

By

DONALD FRANCIS TOVEY

REID PROFESSOR OF MUSIC IN THE
UNIVERSITY OF EDINBURGH

Volume I

SYMPHONIES

LONDON
OXFORD UNIVERSITY PRESS
HUMPHREY MILFORD

OXFORD
UNIVERSITY PRESS
AMEN HOUSE, E.C. 4
London Edinburgh Glasgow New York
Toronto Melbourne Capetown Bombay
Calcutta Madras
HUMPHREY MILFORD
PUBLISHER TO THE
UNIVERSITY

FIRST PRINTED	1935
SECOND IMPRESSION	1936
THIRD IMPRESSION	1938
FOURTH IMPRESSION	1940
FIFTH IMPRESSION	1942

PRINTED IN GREAT BRITAIN

To

ROBERT CALVERLEY TREVELYAN

Dear Poet

These volumes must be dedicated to you. The dedication is the only part of them that has not profited by your suggestions as to grammar, syntax, punctuation, spelling, logical form, discoverable meaning, and such other negative decencies of prose as may be attained by a writer concerned only with music.

You have added much to your labours by your meticulous care not to interfere with anything that could charitably be construed as a feature of my style. The scholiast will (alas!) find these pages as unenlightened by Trevelyanese as he will find your poems free from any tendency to sink into musical analysis.

Now that I have profited by your help, my nobler instincts impel me to beg you not to give to the correction of other people's prose too much of the time that the Muses (at least five of them, for Terpsichore controls song as well as dance—I have just looked her up in Enc. Brit.) *intend you to devote to your*

*own poetry. That is the claim which the General
Reader has upon you. But to him I commend your
example in that you have enabled (if not know-
ingly permitted) me to advertise that these volumes
have been read with unremitting attention by one
who has not learnt musical notation, plays no
instrument, and has not been heard by close friends
of a quarter of a century to sing even in his bath.*

Yours while these habits endure,

DONALD FRANCIS TOVEY

CONTENTS

MOZART

SCHUBERT

MENDELSSOHN

I. INTRODUCTION

THESE essays are programme notes written for the concert room. The reader will know better than to expect from such things a complete system of criticism. The duty of the writer of programme notes is that of counsel for the defence. If the defects of the works analysed are too notorious to be ignored, he must find what can be said in favour of keeping the work in the concert repertoire. A series of essays produced under such conditions cannot have a good cumulative effect. The writer cannot even vary his optimism by praising the work in hand at the expense of something he dislikes; that procedure often irritates the reader and may become extremely inconvenient when the writer has to change his point of view. (*Vide* Ruskin, *passim*.)

The present series of essays is then certainly not designed for continuous reading. Nor, on the other hand, can it pass for a work of reference. Here again its range is limited. Programme notes need not be confined to what can be digested in the concert-room, but they cannot take the form of a work of research. I have not, in fact, made any researches beyond occasionally verifying my quotations, where they are not better unverified.

The reader of these volumes will not find that works of equal importance always receive equivalent treatment, nor will he find any system in the selection of works. Some of the analyses, e.g. that on the Eroica Symphony, were written on occasions where there was no opportunity for musical quotations, which accordingly have been added afterwards, though the letterpress has not been expanded. Others again, such as the essays on the Ninth Symphony and the B minor Mass, were published some time before the concerts for which they were written, and have accordingly taken advantage of the opportunity for a fuller treatment of their subjects.

The essay on the Ninth Symphony has been reprinted several times, and I have accordingly thought fit to supplement it by a radically different kind of analysis, the sort of précis-writing, which, as a result of my early experience as a pupil of Sir Hubert Parry, I expect from students of musical form. Its method underlies most of what I have written in these volumes, and I have used it elsewhere in my *Companion to the Art of Fugue* (Oxford University Press) and in my *Companion to Beethoven's Pianoforte Sonatas* (Assoc. Board of R.A.M. and R.C.M.). If such précis-writing constituted the whole of the contents of the present volumes, they would certainly amount to a work of reference; but I have no intention of producing such a work. It would defeat the object

B

I have in view in including my précis of the Ninth Symphony: the object of inducing lovers of music to get at the bare musical facts by doing such précis-writing themselves; and so, by their own efforts and such other guidance as they can obtain, learning what is knowable about music as music, instead of indulging in abstruse fancies which can never be matters of knowledge.

The necessary optimism of these essays, monotonous though it be, is at all events honest. The programmes were those of my own concerts, where I had no reason to produce any music I disliked. No doubt my prejudices will appear in spite of my most diplomatic efforts. It will be evident that I do not like certain kinds of oiliness and slickness, however admirable the technique with which they are often associated. But nevertheless, like Sir Charles Stanford, I simply cannot help producing *Le Rouet d'Omphale* and *Phaëton*; 'they are so damned clever'. On the other hand, I do not consider clumsiness and other results of a defective technique as inherently noble. But my views as to musical form are unorthodox in some matters; and I am quite certain that the musical orthodoxy of my young days had no means whatever of knowing how far such composers as Schubert and Dvořák were right or wrong in their 'heavenly lengths'. I was not brought up in that orthodoxy. Parry's method of analysis taught me that no piece of music can be understood from *a priori* generalizations as to form, but that all music must be followed phrase by phrase as a process in time. It is very unlikely that this principle has been essentially violated in these volumes.

Few technical terms are used here, and those few are not used consistently. In my *Companion to Beethoven's Pianoforte Sonatas* I have discarded the term 'second subject', which has worked such havoc in our notions of sonata form and sonata themes. There is no prescribed number of subjects to a movement in sonata form; and the only correct description of what theorists mean by the 'second subjects' of such movements is 'second group', which has the merit of not necessarily implying themes at all. But these essays would need a thorough recasting before I could achieve a consistent substitution of the term 'second group' for 'second subject' throughout the volumes; and the use of the old-fashioned term has not been allowed to vitiate the analysis.

With the exception of the précis of the Ninth Symphony, none of these essays assumes any more technical knowledge than is likely to be picked up in the ordinary course of concert-going by a listener who can read the musical quotations or recognize them when played. But even the simplest musical terminology is in a very unscientific state in all languages, and the legal profession itself is not richer than music in terms that have a meaning in ordinary language widely different from their technical meaning. Accordingly I add here an explanation of the terms that are used in a musical sense in these volumes. A musical dictionary will hardly serve the reader's purpose, for my terms are apt to bear a Pickwickian sense as well.

Key, key relations, and tonality. 'Key' is a term primarily applicable to the music of the eighteenth and nineteenth centuries, and to such later music as has not revolted from what the term implies. When it is possible to say that a piece or passage of music is in a certain key, the statement is aesthetically equivalent to saying that the perspective of a picture is related to a certain vanishing-point. 'Tonality' is the art or system of such key perspective; and 'key relations' are facts concerning areas of the whole composition which are large enough to have a key of their own. Statements about the character of a key in itself are of interest mainly to psychologists, and the psychologist is at the mercy of a large mass of nonsense and malobservation thrust upon him by obsolescent musical theories. The true interest in the character of a key taken by itself is of the same order as that of number-forms and colours— the various ways in which people visualize the letters of the alphabet and the Arabic numerals. Beethoven thought B minor a 'black' key; I find it a rather light brown. Beethoven said that the key of A flat was 'barbarous'; yet he used it often, and almost always in a particularly amiable lyric vein. The strongest subjective fancy as to the character of a key in itself is annihilated by the slightest contact with other associations or with actuality. Most of Beethoven's work in the key of A flat is in the character that key assumes in relation to C minor. If you know enough about keys to name them at all you can hardly escape relating them to C. Key relations are among the most powerful and accurate means of expression in music. The reader who wishes to test these essays by closer technical inquiry will find the facts on which I rely in two publications: my article on 'Harmony' in the fourteenth edition of the *Encyclopaedia Britannica*, and my Introduction to the *Companion to Beethoven's Pianoforte Sonatas.*

I will attempt to summarize the theory in more popular style here, at some loss to cogency and accuracy. Readers who play any instrument will have encountered the names of keys and the dogmas of theorists often enough to welcome any chance of relief from a load of traditional mystification. Other readers may skim lightly over what may or may not convey a meaning to them. I cannot be sure how far the facts of tonality can become as vivid to the listener who does not know the names of keys as they are to musicians. The difficulty of describing them is no ground for doubt as to their value for the layman. It is not the difficulty of describing red to the colour-blind: it is the difficulty of describing red to anybody; you can only point to red things and hope that other people see them as you do. It is even more like trying to describe the taste of a peach; and, as a person with no pretensions to an expert palate, I doubt whether my most thorough researches in tonality can approach the august indefinables and incommunicables of the expert wine-taster.

The *tonic* is the horizon, or vanishing-point, of any piece of music that can be said to have the harmonic perspective which we call key. There are two modes of key, major and minor. The reader may rest satisfied with his familiar experience of these modes; the scientific definition of familiar sensations may prevent those who can follow it from talking nonsense, but does not make the sensations more vivid. Let us therefore keep this discussion on the plane of descriptive analogy. The kind of tonality which we are now discussing is not that of mere melody, but is the result of a long history of harmony, or rather counterpoint: that is to say, the combination of several simultaneous melodies. The chords produced at each moment of such a combination will differ in their acoustic and physiological effects. If the listener takes no interest in the sequence of events, his estimate of each chord will have purely physiological and acoustic criteria; all chords that irritate the ear by their acoustic 'beats' will be classed as discords, and the absence of beats will be the only criterion of concord. This primitive criterion survives to the present day in the terms 'perfect' and 'imperfect' concords, though for the last four centuries the naïve Western listener would find the bareness of a music confined to perfect concords harsh to a degree hardly surpassable by constant discord. The art of counterpoint took some five centuries to evolve into maturity; and the criteria of its Golden Age, the sixteenth century, differ so widely from those of the eighteenth and later centuries that it is inconvenient to base our theory of tonality on their foundation. Palestrina's modes are not quite what we call keys, though musicians are beginning to realize that a study of them is essential to a correct view of tonality. They are like paintings in which the draughtsmanship of figures and details is often impressively solid, but the horizon is different for each item.

Note, however, throughout this argument, that there is a radical difference between pictorial perspective and musical tonality. Perspective is a science which exists whether art chooses to use it or not; whereas tonality is wholly the product of musical art. This makes it all the more remarkable that classical tonality, including that of the musical primitives, should by its purely artistic coherence have dominated classical music almost as long as perspective has dominated Western painting. Musical theorists can hardly be blamed for the wish to found a system of classical harmony on an acoustic basis equivalent to the scientific basis of perspective. It is a hopeless task; and the failure of all such attempts may serve to convince us that the foundations of an art can never be identical with those of a science, however much works of art may use material which is capable of scientific analysis. But the truth about a work of art cannot be contrary to scientific truth. The facts of musical harmony cannot contradict the facts of acoustics, though the terms concord and discord soon show themselves to have acquired musical implications which pure acoustics can give no means of knowing. Optical perspective is a comparatively simple region of science, concerned with sensations which we have learnt to regard as immediate, but which are in reality quite interesting intellectual habits. And such a compound of immediate sensations with intellectual analysis already amounts to an aesthetic pleasure. The modern painter who refuses to let his art be dominated by optical science may find in the history of music moral support for his revolt. The atonal composer may get into trouble when, finding his atonal resources lacking in contrast, he tries to effect a harmonious relation between the twentieth century and the sixteenth. The difficulty lies in the nature of his art, not in any external nature; and the painter who finds that he must be careful how he mixes a scientific with an unscientific perspective is probably in no essentially different position from the modern composer.

Whatever reservations may be necessary in comparing tonality with perspective, I can find no other analogy equally clear or equally trustworthy, and I shall continue to use it without scruple.

The *dominant* of a scale is its fifth note reckoned upwards from the tonic, as G from C. With harmonized music, its chord is normally major, even when the mode of the key is minor. This major chord is the normal penultimate chord of a full close. Consequently, if a major triad has not been previously established as a tonic, you cannot harp very long upon it without arousing a suspicion that it is really a dominant to the key a fifth below—a suspicion which becomes certainty when a seventh is added to the chord. Hence the almost proverbial importance of the 'dominant seventh'. The dominant governs the tonic as a transitive verb governs its object. 'Dominant preparation' is a convenient term for the process of arousing expectancy by harping upon the dominant of a key; and one of the most important lessons that students of music, whether scholars or composers, need to learn is that which will teach them to recognize when a major key is really a key and when it is only a dominant. On this point most text-books are uninformative, and many widely accepted commentaries definitely unsound. The analogy of perspective may be made to give further light on tonality if we leave the art of painting and bring in the elements of time and movement which are so essential to music. A picture with more than one vanishing point is out of drawing as a whole; but in real life the vanishing point moves with the movements of the spectator. Most compositions in classical tonality end in the key in which they began; this being the obvious way to secure unity and finality in that category. But they often visit other keys, and this not merely by the way but in such a fashion as to carry the listener's tonal sense away from the original tonic and establish a new tonic with a complete set of relations of its own. The harmonic perspective is not that of a 'primitive' painting in which different objects, each solidly drawn in itself, have different horizons; it is that of a space in which we ourselves move from object to object. On this analogy you may call the tonic the listener's point of view and the dominant the vanishing point. This gives a good idea of the effect of harping on the dominant as a means of fixing the position of an expected tonic.

In these essays the term 'dominant' sometimes means the dominant of a key, and sometimes an established key on a tonic which is the dominant of the main tonic. Latterly I have found the terms 'home dominant' and 'home tonic' useful for showing when I am referring to the main key of the work or movement.

The 'subdominant' is usually described as the note or chord below the dominant. Historically and harmonically, the correct notion is that of the fifth below the tonic, as F downwards from C; and the illuminating term would be 'anti-dominant'. As a foreign key, it is the key to which the home-tonic is dominant; and beginners in composition are apt, like some seventeenth-century pioneers of tonality, to upset their tonic by a top-heavy subdominant introduced too early in a short piece. The effect of the subdominant is inevitably the opposite to that of the dominant. Stepping on to or into the dominant is an active measure like walking towards the vanishing point; subsiding into the subdominant indicates recession and repose. When the tonic is minor, the change of key to the subdominant means changing the home-tonic chord from minor to major, with an effect necessarily pathetic, since the bright major chord instantly shows itself as an illusion, being no tonic, but the threshold of a darker minor key. The subdominant has a solemn effect as penultimate chord in 'plagal cadences'. In all probability it was the Lost Chord which the weary and uneasy organist failed to find again after stumbling upon the Sound of a Great Amen. One chord does not make a cadence any more than one syllable makes an Amen; and perhaps the organist often played the Lost Chord in the wrong context without recognizing it again.

As a technical term in music, the word 'modulation' means change of key, and is used in these essays in no other sense. From your home tonic you can modulate easily to five directly related keys. The direct relation between two keys consists in the fact that the tonic triad of the one is among the triads of the others. This definition is carefully worded so as to avoid troublesome details in reckoning from a minor tonic. By way of summarizing a troublesome grammatical affair in a simple, comprehensive, and concrete illustration I give here the series of direct relations of C major and C minor, with their particular names above and their generic names and numeral symbols below.

* i.e. mediant between tonic and *lower* subdominant.

It will be seen that with A minor as home tonic the table of relations to a minor tonic is that of the relations to a major tonic read backwards. Probably this is why the terms 'relative minor' and 'relative major' are applied to (vi) and (♭III) respectively. Both terms are misleading; these relations are no more direct than the others.

Major and minor keys on the same tonic are identical in spite of their vivid emotional contrast; that is to say, a composition in C minor has not ended in another key if it ends in C major. The brightening to the major mode is a fact that strikes literally home, and is thus far more powerful than any change of key. Compositions beginning in a major key and ending in its tonic minor are more rare and represent some unusual emotional conflict.

Bach normally moves within the range of these direct key-relations. When he goes outside them, his purpose is always to astonish or mystify, except in a few cases of unnoticed drift a little beyond and back again. And he never fails in his purpose of astonishing, because all his extraordinary modulations go at once to the extremes of the harmonic universe, avoiding the regions which later music has annexed to the scheme of key-relations. These regions Haydn, Mozart, and Beethoven extended so enormously that many theorists have jumped to the conclusion that all keys are equally related and that Bach's miracles are miracles no longer. This is the negation of all harmonic sensibility. It is a hasty reaction from old orthodoxies which regarded unrelated keys as forbidden, and recognized none but direct relations.

The wider key-relations used by Haydn, Mozart, and Beethoven were first exploited by Domenico Scarlatti as paradoxes. To Haydn they were true mysteries; and the dark ones, but not the bright ones, make an almost systematic feature in some of Mozart's procedures. When we come to Beethoven we find the whole range of key-relationships expressible in musical notation rationally mapped out, with an exact knowledge of each degree of remoteness and each possibility of relation. The governing principle of the extension is based simply upon accepting the fact that major and minor keys on the same tonic are identical, so that the modes of either member of a pair of keys may be changed and the resulting pair still accepted as related. There is also a group of relations which I sometimes call Neapolitan, consisting of the flat supertonic and its converse, the sharp seventh, which are derived from an intensification of the minor mode. There are many complicated details in the aesthetics and technique of these wider relations, and I have treated of them in the works and articles mentioned above. For the present purpose the reader should understand that when I talk of key-relations as remote, dark, or bright, I am describing not subjective impressions but facts. I cannot promise always to have used the word 'key-relation' instead of 'key', but if I say that A flat is a dark key or E major a bright key I mean dark or bright according to the direction from which the key is approached. If a composer chooses to make a brilliant modulation from C to A flat, or a gloomy modulation from C to the bright key of E, then there is an element of conflict (imaginative or unimaginative) between his manner and his matter. If he modulates from C major to D major in such a manner that the D major does not explain itself away as a mere dominant of the dominant, then he has either achieved a stupendous stroke of genius, like that of Beethoven in a famous passage in the Eroica Symphony, or he has shown that this juxtaposition of keys means no more to him than similar accidents in the key-sequence of dances in a ball-room.

Music-lovers should not load their consciences with alarming ideas as to what great composers expect of the listener in recognizing key-relations. It is one thing to recognize what is addressed to the ear, but quite another matter to recognize the causes of weakness in a structure. This is where these programme notes are debarred from giving help, except in cases so weak that counsel for the defence can only plead 'confession and avoidance'. But the reader may be glad to know that great composers quite consistently refrain from basing definite effects of key-relations on the assumption that the ear will recognize them otherwise than in juxtaposition or, if at a distance, by collateral evidence. By far the most important effect of tonality at a distance is that of returning to the home tonic. Not only can I recall no case where the importance of recognizing this does not coincide with the return of matter that is already associated with the tonic, or expected to appear in it; but I find that in every case where no such aid is given to the listener there is a definite aesthetic value in the fact that we do not recognize the tonic immediately. Of course, if a composition returns to the tonic without any purpose at all, it is simply wasting its opportunities, and its key-relations will neither surprise nor interest. But the reader may safely disregard any criticism or theory which assumes that the ear assigns definite values to two tonics as being connected through the medium of a third tonic, or as perceptible across intervening matter without some element of recapitulation.[1]

Often the purport of a modulation is to obliterate the sense of key-relationship. This is most typically effected by 'enharmonic' modulations, where a chord changes its intonation by a minute interval lost in the compromise of the pianoforte's 12-semitone octave, but expressible by voices and stringed instruments; as when the diminished 7th C♯ E G B♭ is changed to D♭ F♭ G B♭ and so swings from the dominant of D minor to that of A♭ minor. The mastery of the composer determines whether the effect is that of a bad pun or a sublime mystery: the listener needs no theoretic knowledge to experience the proper degree of surprise in each case. Though the actual change of intonation is lost in the tempered scale the ear has no more difficulty in appreciating it than in appreciating puns.

Art-Forms. Some technicalities are defined as they arise in each essay; and in volumes so little calculated for continuous reading I have not avoided repetition. But the reader may find it convenient to have the terms of sonata form defined here once for all.

In the first place, the classical use of the word 'sonata' implies a group of pieces called movements. It will, I hope, be always clear from the context when I am using the word 'movement' in its English sense, whether extended metaphorically or not, and when

---

[1] It would be ungracious not to acknowledge the service the tonic-solfa system has done in awakening the sense of local tonality in the young and the musical laity; but if it can inculcate any larger grasp of tonality, I have been unfortunate in the examples I have seen of its treatment of keys and key-relations.

I mean a member of a sonata. By some curious accident, the word 'sonata' is not applied to compositions for more than two instruments. This has tiresome results. In *Grove's Dictionary of Music and Musicians*, Parry felt so bound by the usages of language that his article on 'Sonata Form' was actually cramped by a conscientious objection to quote from any of the larger works which display sonata forms in a normal full size. He was able to refer to Brahms's Quintet in F minor because the composer, in arranging it for two pianofortes, was able to call it a sonata. In these essays it is assumed that the trios, quartets, quintets, &c., of composers from Haydn onwards are sonatas, and that a symphony is a sonata for orchestra.

A 'concerto' is a sonata for one or more solo instruments in concert, contest, or contrast with an orchestra.

The normal movements of a full-size sonata are four, viz. an important and more or less dramatic first movement in a form hereafter to be summarized; a slow movement, which may take any form ranging from lyric forms to that of the first movement; a minuet or scherzo, representing to some extent the forms of dance music in contrast to the more lyric style of slow movements; and a finale, generally lively, often in the same form as the first movement, but typically in rondo form.

The normal form of a first movement has earned the title 'sonata form' *par excellence*. Its evolution can be easily traced as originating in the so-called 'binary form' of a certain kind of melody. Melodies that consist of more than one phrase naturally fall into two classes: that in which the first phrase is complete, and that in which it is incomplete. If the first phrase is complete, it, or the end of it, may also be used as the end of the whole melody; with the result that the middle portion tends to become detached from the first phrase, if not also from the last. Hence, the shape of such melodies may often be summarized as A B A. This is what is commonly meant by 'ternary form'. Melodies in binary form are supposed to fall into only two parts because, the first part being incomplete, the middle portion does not stand out so distinctly. Now these terms, 'binary' and 'ternary', not only miss the essential grounds of classification, but are thoroughly misleading in all that they imply. The essential distinction is that between a form in which the first member is complete in itself and a form in which the first member is incomplete. Musical experience shows that if the melody, or form, is small enough to make the repetition of its portions desirable, the division always falls into two, and never into three. One of the best-known ternary melodies in classical music is that of the slow movement of the Kreutzer Sonata. Nothing could be clearer than its division into a complete 8-bar strain A, an 11-bar middle portion B, mainly in the dominant, and a complete da capo of strain A. But it is worth while trying the experiment of repeating these three strains in the order A A B B A A, so as to see how impossible it is to regard the whole structure as divisible otherwise than into A, BA. The experience of this test would justify us in concluding that all melodic forms are binary. On the other hand, Sir Henry Hadow in his primer on *Sonata Form* found himself driven by the facts of form on a larger scale of developed movements to conclude that sonata form was essentially ternary: that is to say, that its main divisions of exposition, development, and recapitulation were comparable rather with the A B A form than with anything that could reasonably be called binary.

But his difficulties are forced on him not by a system of mere cross-classification, but by an irrelevant terminology. For one thing, any musical terminology must be wrong if it assumes a map-like or space-like view of music instead of a time-like view. Whether a composition is divisible into three or four sections is a fact that can be ascertained only when we have heard the whole, and even then it is not the kind of fact that 'vibrates in the memory'. But it is a vital and immediately impressive event in time that the first clearly marked division of a piece of music should impress the listener as complete in itself or incomplete. Obviously, the kinds of form in which the first section is incomplete will tend to be more highly organized than those in which it is complete. To take an extreme case, if in your A B A form the B is as complete as the A, the total form is a mere symmetrical arrangement of detachable objects, like a picture with a vase of flowers to the right and another vase of flowers to the left of it. Such a case is the classical scheme of minuet, trio, and minuet da capo. On the other hand, when the first member of a musical form is incomplete, it creates a strong presumption that the rest will be more or less highly organized. The most highly organized of all musical forms is that of the first movement of a sonata in the miscalled 'binary' form. Externally, its mature examples are not easily distinguishable from its earlier evolutionary types as shown in the dance forms of suites; and inextricable confusion will result if we try to follow the orthodox lines according to which the distinction depends on the number of themes. I regret that in all but the latest of these essays I have used the current English terms 'first subject' and 'second subject' for the materials of sonata-form movements. In my *Companion to Beethoven's Pianoforte Sonatas* I have introduced the unobjection-able terms 'first group' and 'second group', which commit the analyst to no propositions as to themes or subjects. You may find dance movements by Bach with several beautifully distinct themes and full-sized first movements by Haydn with only one, but you will find no movement by Bach with the essentials of sonata style

and hardly even an early first movement by Haydn without signs of
them. The typical features of sonata form are these: the 'exposition', which contains a first group which asserts the tonic key, and
a second group which not only asserts, but firmly establishes,
another key, usually the dominant if the tonic was major, and the
mediant major or dominant minor if the tonic was minor; a section
of 'development' which treats the materials of the exposition dis-
cursively, wandering through various keys; a 'recapitulation' of
the whole exposition giving both groups in the home tonic, and,
if this recapitulation does not give an effect of finality, a coda or
peroration. By firmly establishing another key, we understand some
process which causes the original tonic as it were to sink below the
horizon. In Bach the tonic cannot thus sink out of sight unless in
some series of remote modulations, the object of which is to startle
and bewilder. From most points in movements by Bach or Handel
it would be possible to drop back into the tonic without much ado;
and the establishment of a key did not become a dramatic, or even
important, event until Haydn and Mozart brought to maturity the
style that could make it so.

There are no rules as to the number of themes the exposition of
a sonata movement may contain; nor, indeed, is it worth while to
define what we mean by a 'theme', still less what we mean by a
'subject'. One theme may be derived from another in all sorts of
ways, and a group of a few notes may be detachable as a 'figure',
and shared by several otherwise contrasted themes. The sonata
form, even on the largest scale, retains so much of the primitive
character of the melodic form in which it originated that huge
movements, like the first movement of the Eroica Symphony and
the first movement of Brahms's Second Symphony, can afford to
repeat the exposition.

These repetitions sometimes present a curious problem in
musical aesthetics. In their total effect they undoubtedly become
recognized by the ear as mere encores, even though, as in Brahms's
Second Symphony, the composer has effected them by a specially
beautiful joint. In suite movements and early sonatas the custom
was for both parts to be repeated; and the second repeat survives
in certain quite late and important works of Beethoven, where one
object is the effect produced by the special joint that sinks back
to the beginning of the development, and the other is the effect
upon the coda. In modern performances there is a natural tendency to sweep away all these repeats. In many cases this is
justified and would not be objected to by the composer. But we
must not overlook the cases in which the composer has vividly
imagined the moment at which the repeat begins. Nor must we
consider the whole question settled if we lose nothing obviously

thrilling by omitting the repeat. The objections to which repeats
are most liable are: first, that they make the work too long; and
secondly, that 'we don't want to be told the same thing twice
over'. The question of length is partly a question of programme
making. Spacious works notorious for their repeat marks, such as
Beethoven's last three trios and the Quartet in E minor, op. 59,
no. 2, are all the better for being placed in programmes where
there is room for them to be displayed in full. The dramatic point
of their repeats will prove surprising if we are given a chance of
appreciating it. The objection that we don't want to be told the
same thing twice is based on a radical misapprehension of the
nature of music. It obviously does not apply to symmetrical
repetition, which has the same kind of function in music as it has
in architecture. But the repeats we are here discussing are not
symmetries. They are peculiar to an art that moves in time, and
their nearest analogy in architecture would be opportunities, more
or less charmingly contrived by a guide, for going over part of a
building twice. To enjoy this you must of course be in the best
mood for enjoying every feature of the work. The practical musician is seldom able to consult his palate and digestion in these
matters, and he is naturally most dyspeptic with the best-known
works.

After the exposition comes the 'development'. As its name
implies, its function is to develop the resources already in hand.
Not only will it tend to avoid the tonic and the complementary
key already established, but it will be apt to range widely over
many keys, establishing none until the time comes for the recapitulation. Many illustrations of the processes of development will
be found in these essays. The essential idea of sonata development
is the break-up of the themes as originally phrased, and the re-
building and recombining of their figures into sentences and
sequences of a different kind. There are no rules for the conduct
of a development, but of course it is possible to say that such-and-
such a procedure more or less enhances or reduces the energy of
a development. Thus, Schubert is apt to weaken and lengthen
his expositions by processes of discursive development where
Beethoven would have had a crowd of terse new themes; while,
on the other hand, Schubert's developments are apt indeed to
develop some feature of one of his themes, but by turning it into
a long lyric process which is repeated symmetrically. Dvořák is
apt to be dangerously discursive at any point of his exposition, and
frequently loses his way before he has begun his second group,
while his developments often merely harp upon a single figure
with a persistence not much more energetic or cumulative than
that of the Dormouse that continued to say 'twinkle, twinkle' in

its sleep. But none of these matters can be settled by rule of thumb. If a short development contains an entirely new theme, the whole tends to become a detached episode, though the enormous development of the Eroica Symphony contrives to introduce a new lyric melody in two places in the course of executing its own energetic voyage round the harmonic world. On the other hand, if you find that the development of some mature work by Mozart or Beethoven consists almost wholly of an irresponsible episode, you have no reason to suppose that the composer has made a mistake.

After the development comes the 'recapitulation', which consists, as its name implies, of a restatement of the material of the exposition. Both groups are restated, and it is more important to restate the second group fully than the first, for the restatement of the second group will not be in the complementary key, but, with rare exceptions, in the home tonic. Three points in the recapitulation present dramatic possibilities. Those of the return to the opening are obvious. Then there is the process by which the original complementary key of the second group was established. Some alteration must evidently happen here if the second group is to appear in the tonic. Lastly, there is the end of the exposition, which now will have either to end the whole movement satisfactorily with its own momentum, or to lead into the 'coda', or peroration.

For the construction of the coda there are many possibilities and no rules but common sense. Clearly, if the coda departs from the home tonic, it must spend a due proportion of its later energies in re-establishing it.

If the form of a first movement is applied to a slow movement, the composer must not lose sight of the fact, frequently pointed out in these essays, that in music 'slowness' means 'bigness'. If the orthodox reader is inclined to be shocked at me for describing the slow movement of Beethoven's D major Trio, op. 70, no. 1, as in full sonata form, when the portion which I describe as its development is only 8 bars long, I can justify myself by pointing out that those 8 bars contain two distinct lines of development passing through several different keys, and that, as measured by metronome, they come to a considerably greater length than the unquestionably orthodox development of the finale. So long as the reader finds a consistent meaning in my use of terms, he need not worry about musical terminology. I am concerned only to convey clear impressions of musical facts without adding a new terminology to the confusions of an old one. In spite of the limitations of a slow tempo, Beethoven has several times achieved a sonata-form slow movement with quite a long development. One example is the slow movement of the Quartet, op. 59, no. 1, where Beethoven has actually found room for an independent episode, and others are the slow movements of the Second and Sixth Symphonies, fairly fully analysed in the present volume. If the composer wishes to get a sonata-like breadth of effect in a smaller space, there is always the possibility of a movement consisting of exposition, recapitulation, and (*ad libitum*) coda, without development at all. On the other hand, there are many varieties of the A B A form; and a slow movement may economize space and yet attain a high degree of development by making B an elaborate and discursive affair. Or the whole movement may be predominantly lyric, with A as one tune and B as another.

Next in importance to the sonata form is the 'rondo', which is typical of finales. As its name implies, it consists essentially of a melody that comes round again and again after contrasted episodes. In its early forms, as in the suites of Couperin and Bach, it shows its derivation from the *rondeau* of the sixteenth-century French poets. Orlando di Lasso set many such poems to music which faithfully reflects the poetic form. Couperin, again, shows the identity between the poetic and the musical form by calling the episodes of his rondos 'couplets'. In the rondos of sonatas the main theme is usually more than a single strain; though Beethoven in his early works (up to the Quartet, op. 18, no. 4) took over from Haydn a development of the older kind of rondo in which the main theme is a single epigram and the episodes are highly sectional, with a final accumulation of coda-episodes in the tonic. Mozart developed to its fullest extent the type of rondo which is usually ascribed to Beethoven. In this the main theme is a complete tune, possibly 'binary' or 'ternary', and evidently designed for recurrence rather than for development. The first episode behaves like the second group of a sonata-form movement, being recapitulated in the home tonic at the penultimate stage of the rondo. The second episode may be a new tune-like structure fixed in another key, or it may be a process of development on material new or old. It is obvious that, if the first return of the main theme has been curtailed and made to lead quickly to an elaborate development, the line which distinguishes such a rondo from a first movement will become so faint that disputes as to classification will be inconclusive. The only important criterion is that of style. Mozart is not particular. If a movement begins with a square-cut tune, he may call it a rondo, even when it has exactly the repeat marks and shape of a first movement; and for some obscure reason it is seldom that a movement will be labelled as a rondo unless it happens to be a finale.

The full-sized scheme of a sonata includes a movement which

does not normally admit of development at all, but is typically a dance movement, consisting of two complete members arranged in the form A B A; as minuet, trio, and minuet da capo. Why the minuet alone of the suite dances should have been taken over into the sonata scheme nobody knows. Perhaps it was eminently fitted to survive in the early stages of the sonata style by being lively enough to contrast with the slow movement and not so lively as to foreshadow the finale. In Haydn's hands it became surprisingly energetic, and developed to considerable length without losing its character as a dance movement. When Beethoven expanded it into the scherzo, he took pains and pleasure in preserving and enhancing that character. Only twice, and that in early works, did he enlarge the minuet by giving it a second trio. His notion of the way to expand the form is at once more dramatic and more preservative of its character as a dance. It consists in going twice round the alternation of scherzo and trio, with no variation except perhaps a damping-down to pianissimo at the second or third recurrence of the scherzo. The listener is caught up in the unceasing round and is extricated only by some drastic intervention when the trio seems about to recur a third time. Of all Beethoven's repeats, these most arouse the impatience of modern performers and critics. But they are among the most vividly imagined subtleties of Beethoven's invention, and music-lovers are well advised who keep their musical digestions in a fit state to enjoy them.

The scheme of a sonata admits among the four movements, either in the position of the slow movement or finale, two other forms which are radically different from those of a movement of development. 'Variations' are restatements of a theme complete in itself, and a set of variations is fairly often to be met with as a sonata movement. In that position, its range, and more especially its depth, are limited by the fact that the sonata style trains the ear to recognize themes by their melody, whereas the deeper type of variation is often not concerned with the melody at all. In any case, variations are not developments of the theme. To develop a theme is practically to break up and re-arrange its figures into different structures. To make a variation in the classical sense of the word is to take the whole structure of a theme and build a similar structure with a different exterior. The proper effect of a set of variations is cumulative. The theme may or may not be recognized by the listener, though in the sonata style melodic resemblance will not long be absent; but, whether the theme be recognized or not, its momentum will become powerful through all changes of tempo and emotion. The composer's main difficulty will be to stop this momentum or bring it to a climax in a natural and conclusive way. Post-classical variations depend upon a much more superficial view of the theme, and they take no account of this factor of momentum at all. Recent criticism shows a mistaken idea as to what the listener is expected to hear in a classical set of variations. Such variations may depend on the composer's profoundest insight into the form of his theme, but this is to the ear what the painter's or sculptor's knowledge of anatomy is to the eye. Without it the figure becomes a sack stuffed with straw and the variations lose their momentum.

More rarely than variations, but still often enough to need description at this point, the 'fugue' may figure as a sonata movement. If 'discussion' were equivalent to 'development' in the dramatic sense, a fugue might be said to be all development, but in fact it is neither more nor less amenable to the sonata idea of development than a prolonged argument on the stage is to the development of a drama. The first fact to realize about fugue is that it is a medium, like blank verse, not a thing, like a rondo. You should not think of 'fugues' but of passages or pieces written 'in fugue'. A piece written entirely in fugue is 'a fugue', and the rules for its composition are many, vexatious, and largely the result of malobservation and of early nineteenth-century Italian generalizations that meticulously exclude Bach. The essentials of fugue consist in the discussion of a compact melodic idea by a definite number of voices. The melodic idea is called the subject; the number of voices is definite in this respect, that the voices employed in the discussion are supposed to be self-sufficient, and that any further accompaniment is outside the scheme. 'Fugato' is the term used for passages in fugue. A fugue normally begins with a single voice announcing the subject, though 'double fugues' may begin with two voices and two subjects. A second voice announces the answer, which is a reproduction of the subject *in* or *on* the dominant. The distinction between *in* and *on* is important; and being *on* the dominant has the obvious aesthetic advantage of not involving a stiff change of key to and fro as the subject enters in the successive voices. An answer *on* the dominant usually avoids being *in* the dominant by slightly altering the subject in certain ways vexatious to codify and analyse, but very satisfactory to the ear when properly achieved without pedantry. Far be it from me to vex any reader with grammatical minutiae, but the essential principle of the so-called tonal answer is a self-evident musical fact of which you can convince yourself by striking in succession the notes G C (upward or downward) and noticing the effect of answering them by C G instead of by D G. The 'tonal' answer is a reflection at an angle; the exact, or 'real', answer is a mere transposition. But it is absurd to found upon this feature a solemn distinction between real fugues and tonal fugues, especially as the rules for producing a tonal answer happen as often as not to give an exact transposition.

The 'countersubject' is normally the matter with which the voice that announced the subject accompanies the answer, if that matter is preserved on later occasions; and in the same way the first voice may proceed to a second countersubject when the third voice enters. But the term is also used for new subjects introduced at later stages of a fugue. Such a new subject, if stated by itself and vividly contrasted with the main subject, will produce a brilliant effect when, as is probably its purpose, it afterwards enters into combination with it.

The term 'episode' is used for those portions of a fugue during which the complete subject is not being heard. It thus has a wholly different sense from its use in sonata forms and rondos. Generally speaking, the devices of fugue, though argumentative, are entirely unlike those of the sonata style and contribute nothing except contrast to the idea of sonata development.

'Augmentation' is the delivery of a subject or countersubject in consistently slower notes; 'diminution' the delivery in quicker notes.

The term 'inversion' has two meanings: first, inversion in double counterpoint, a device essential to polyphonic music if the bass is to have its fair share of subjects and countersubjects. A combination of themes is said to be in 'double', 'triple', &c., counterpoint, when each theme is equally capable of being a bass to the others. This implies transposition by octaves, and therefore double counterpoint is normally said to be at the octave. But sometimes a combination of themes can be so designed that one of them will bear transposition by some other interval, and this will produce a quite new set of harmonies. Some fairly vivid illustrations of these facts appear in the present essays, and my *Companion to Bach's Art of Fugue* illustrates fully from that work the aesthetic purpose of these matters. 'Inversion' has another sense: the melodic sense of the reversal of every interval in a melody, replacing each upward movement by an equal downward movement, and vice versa.

A 'stretto' is the overlapping of the subject with one or more answers. The term should not be applied to mere sketchy allusions to the first figure of the subject, such as might occur in any episode, but only to episodes where the subject and answers survive more or less completely in each voice.

Other technical terms will be found defined in the glossary provided in the Index-volume.

In conclusion, I once more beg to reassert my first article of musical faith: that, while the listener must not expect to hear the whole contents of a piece of music at once, nothing concerns him that will not ultimately reach his ear either as a directly audible fact or as a cumulative satisfaction in things of which the hidden foundations are well and truly laid. Whatever the defects of these essays, they do not contain speculative and fanciful thematic derivations which exist only to the eye, nor do they rest on theories which imply a *coup d'œil* view of music. I have myself often been fascinated by the theory that classical music, like classical sculpture, measures its proportions in 'golden sections', that is to say, that unequal divisions follow the law that the smaller part is to the larger as the larger is to the whole. Possible illustrations of this are innumerable; there is one by no means hackneyed quartet of Haydn (op. 50, no. 5 in F) where the first movement falls into golden sections in every way, from point to point, and backwards and forwards, with one of Haydn's characteristic silent bars falling beautifully into place. Yet I have become sceptical; there are so many ways of taking your sections that I doubt whether any musical composition can avoid golden ones somewhere. And I see no means of allowing for 'who time gambols withal, who time trots withal, who time gallops withal, and who he stands still withal.'

I should retain more interest in such speculations if the deeper researches in them did not so often show an inability to recognize the most obvious musical facts. Such inability is far more serious than any failure to recognize subtleties. The obvious musical facts, when they are facts at all, lead of their own accord to the profoundest subtleties; and it is my hope that the lines of analysis indicated in these volumes may lead in the right direction.

BEETHOVEN

II. FIRST SYMPHONY IN C MAJOR, OP. 21

1 *Adagio molto, leading to* 2 *Allegro con brio.* 3 *Andante cantabile con moto*
4 MENUETTO: *Allegro molto, e vivace.* 5 *Adagio, leading to*
6 *Allegro molto e vivace.*

Beethoven's first symphony, produced in 1800, is a fitting farewell
to the eighteenth century. It has more of the true nineteenth-
century Beethoven in its depths than he allows to appear upon the
surface. Its style is that of the Comedy of Manners, as translated
by Mozart into the music of his operas and of his most light-
hearted works of symphonic and chamber music. The fact that it
is comedy from beginning to end is prophetic of changes in music
no less profound than those which the French Revolution brought
about in the social organism. But Beethoven was the most con-
servative of revolutionists; a Revolutionist without the R; and in his
first symphony he shows, as has often been remarked, a characteristic caution in handling sonata form for the first time with a full
orchestra. But the caution which seems so obvious to us was not
noticed by his contemporary critics. We may leave out of account
the oft-quoted fact that several Viennese musicians objected to his
beginning his introduction with chords foreign to the key; such
objectors were pedants miserably behind the culture not only of
their own time but of the previous generation. They were the kind
of pedants who are not even classicists, and whose grammatical
knowledge is based upon no known language. Carl Philipp
Emanuel Bach, who, much more than his father, was at that time
regarded as a founder of modern music by persons who considered
the lately deceased Mozart a dangerous person, had gone very much
farther in this matter of opening in a foreign key than Beethoven
ever went in the whole course of his career. Where the contemporary critics showed intelligent observation was in marking,
though with mild censure, the fact that Beethoven's first symphony is written so heavily for the wind band that it seems almost
more like a 'Harmoniemusik' than a proper orchestral piece. This
observation was technically correct. Beethoven had at that time
a young composer's interest in wind instruments, which he handled
with a mastery stimulated by the wind-band ('Harmonie') masterpieces of Mozart. His handling of the strings was not less masterly,
though his interest in their possibilities developed mightily in later
works.

The position then is this: that in his first symphony Beethoven
overwhelmed his listeners with a scoring for the full wind band

almost as highly developed as it was ever destined to be (except that
he did not as yet appreciate the possibilities of the clarinet as an
instrument for the foreground). The scale of the work as a whole
gave no scope for an equivalent development of the strings. Even
to-day there is an appreciable difficulty in accommodating the
wind band of Beethoven's first symphony to a small body of
strings, and consequently an agreeable absence of the difficulties
of balance which have become notorious in the performance of
classical symphonies by large orchestras without double wind.

The introduction, made famous by pedantic contemporary
objections to its mixed tonality, has in later times been sharply
criticized by so great a Beethoven worshipper as Sir George Grove
for its ineffectual scoring. With all respect to that pioneer of
English musical culture, such a criticism is evidently traceable to
the effect of pianoforte arrangements, which often suggest that a
chord which is loud for the individual players of the orchestra is
meant to be as loud as a full orchestral passage. When two pianists
play these *forte-piano* chords in a duet, they naturally make as much
noise as they can get out of their instrument. This sets up an impression in early life which many conductors and critics fail to get
rid of. Hence the complaint that the pizzicato chords of the strings
are feeble, a complaint that assumes that it is their business to be
forcible.

I am delighted to find myself anticipated by Mr. Vaclav Talich
in the view that the opening is mysterious and groping, and that
the first grand note of triumph is sounded when the dominant is
reached.

For the rest, a list of the principal themes will cover the ground
of the work, leaving but little need for comment.

The first theme of the allegro con brio is a quietly energetic,
business-like proposition, moving in sequences from tonic to supertonic, and thence rising through subdominant to dominant.

It is the opening of a formal rather than of a big work. If you wish to see the same proposition in a loftier style, look at Beethoven's C major String Quintet, where the same harmonic plan is executed in a single eight-bar phrase.

The transition-theme needs no quotation. Not only is it extremely formal, but, instead of establishing the key of the 'second subject' (G major) by getting on to its dominant, it is contented with the old practical joke, which Mozart uses only in his earlier or lighter works, the joke of taking the mere dominant *chord* (here the chord of G) as equivalent to the dominant *key*, and starting in that key with no more ado.

It is solemn impertinence to suppose that there is anything early or primitive in Beethoven's technique in this symphony. In at least twenty works in sonata form he had already been successful in a range of bold experiments far exceeding that covered by Haydn and Mozart: and it now interested him to write a small and comic sonata for orchestra. After Ex. 3 he strikes a deeper note; and the passage in which that theme descends into dark regions around its minor mode, while an oboe sings plaintively above, is prophetic of the future Beethoven in proportion as it is inspired by Mozart. Several other themes ensue. The development is terse and masterly, and the coda is more brilliant and massive than Mozart's style would have admitted.

The slow movement begins, like its more enterprising twin-brother, the andante of the C minor String Quartet, op. 18, No. 4, with a kittenish theme treated like a fugue.

Here again, as in the first movement (and *not* as in the C minor Quartet), the second subject follows with no further transition than a taking of the old dominant chord for the new dominant key.

Two other themes follow; the second being notable for its under-lying drum-rhythm. Beethoven got the idea of using C and G drums in this F major movement from Mozart's wonderful Linz Symphony.

Dr. Ernest Walker has well observed that the minuet is a really great Beethoven scherzo, larger than any in the sonatas, trios, and quartets before the opus fifties, and far more important than that of the Second Symphony. I quote the profound modulations which lead back to the theme in the middle of the second part.

Ex. 6.

The trio, with its throbbing wind-band chords and mysterious violin runs, is, like so many of Beethoven's early minuets and trios, prophetic of Schumann's most intimate epigrammatic sentiments. But, as Schumann rouses himself from romantic dreams to ostenta-tiously prosaic aphorisms, so Beethoven rouses himself to a brilliant forte before returning to the so-called minuet.

The finale begins with a Haydnesque joke; the violins letting out a scale as a cat from a bag.

Ex. 7.

The theme thus released puts its first rhythmic stress after the scale, as shown by my figures under the bars. It has a second strain, on fresh material.

Ex. 8.

The transition takes the trouble to reach the real dominant of the new key. The second subject begins with the following theme.

Ex. 9.

and, after a syncopated cadence-theme, concludes with a development of the scale figure.

The course of the movement is normal, though brilliantly organized, until the coda in which an absurd little march enters, as if everybody must know who it is.

Ex. 10.

As it, like every conceivable theme, can be accompanied by a scale, the Organic Unity of the Whole is vindicated as surely as there is a B in Both.

III. SECOND SYMPHONY IN D MAJOR, OP. 36

1 *Adagio molto, leading to* 2 *Allegro con brio.* 3 *Larghetto.*
4 SCHERZO, *Allegro.* 5 *Allegro molto.*

The works that produce the most traceable effects in the subsequent history of an art are not always those which come to be regarded as epoch-making. The epoch-making works are, more often than not, merely shocking to just those contemporaries best qualified to appreciate them; and by the time they become acceptable they are accepted as inimitable. Even their general types of form are chronicled in history as the 'inventor's' contribution to the progress of his art, only to be the more conspicuously avoided by later artists. Thus Beethoven 'invented' the scherzo; and no art-form has been laid down more precisely and even rigorously than that of his dozen most typical examples. Yet the scherzos of Schubert, Schumann, Mendelssohn, and Brahms differ as widely from Beethoven's, and from each other, as Beethoven's differ from Mozart's minuets. The nearest approach to a use of Beethoven's model is to be found where we least expect it, in the grim and almost macabre scherzos of Chopin.

Far otherwise is it with certain works which immediately impressed contemporaries as marking a startling advance in the art without a disconcerting change in its language. Beethoven's Second Symphony was evidently larger and more brilliant than any that had been heard up to 1801; and people who could understand

the three great symphonies that Mozart had poured out in the six
weeks between the end of June and the 10th of August 1788, would
find Beethoven's language less abstruse, though the brilliance and
breadth of his design and the dramatic vigour of his style were so
exciting that it was thought advisable to warn young persons
against so 'subversive' (*sittenverderblich*) a work. What the effect
of such warnings might be is a bootless inquiry; but Beethoven's
Second Symphony and his next opus, the Concerto in C minor
(op. 37), have produced a greater number of definite echoes from
later composers than any other of his works before the Ninth Symphony. And the echoes are by no means confined to imitative or
classicist efforts: they are to be found in things like Schubert's
Grand Duo and Schumann's Fourth Symphony, works written at
high noontide of their composers' powers and quite unrestrained in
the urgency of important new developments. Indeed, Beethoven's
Second Symphony itself seems almost classicist in the neighbourhood of such works as his profoundly dramatic Sonata in D minor,
op. 31, no. 2; while we can go back as far as the C minor Trio,
op. 1, no. 3, and find Beethoven already both as mature and as
sittenverderblich in style and matter.

The Second Symphony begins with a grand introduction, more
in Haydn's manner than in Mozart's. It is Haydn's way to begin
his introduction, after a good *coup d'archet*, with a broad melody fit
for an independent slow movement, and to proceed from this to
romantic modulations. Mozart, on the rare occasions when he
writes a big introduction, builds it with introductory types of
phrase throughout. Beethoven here makes the best of both
methods; and the climax of his romantic modulations, instead of
ending in one of Haydn's pauses in an attitude of surprise, leads
to a fine quiet ('dominant-pedal') approach, in Mozart's grandest
style, that finally runs without break into the allegro. Contemporaries were probably the last to feel, as we feel, the 'influence' of
Haydn and Mozart in all this; for this is in all respects the real
thing, and Beethoven was the only survivor of Haydn and Mozart
who could do it.

The main theme of the first movement—

Ex. 1.

has often been quoted thus far as an example of complacent formal-
ism; but if you get to the end of the paragraph you will not accept
that view. The sentence fills eighteen bars (overlapping into the
next sentence), and takes shape, not as a formal sequence, but as

an expanding melody by no means easily foreseen in its course or
stiff in its proportions.

The main theme of the second subject—

Ex. 2.

has a certain almost military brilliance, which is in keeping with the
fact that nobody wrote more formidably spirited marches than
Beethoven.

Towards the end of the exposition, the semiquaver figure (*a*) of
the 'complacently formal' first theme (Ex. 1) gives rise to one of
Beethoven's most *sittenverderblich* dramatic incidents.

The whole course of the movement is normal, but its brilliance
and energy were quite unprecedented in orchestral music at the time;
nor could Beethoven himself have surpassed the choral grandeur
of the climax of his coda until he had revolutionized the language
of music. The choral quality comes from 'The Heavens are telling'
in Haydn's *Creation*.

The larghetto is one of the most luxurious slow movements in
the world; and there is small wonder that the discursive Schubert
ran away with large slices of it in his Grand Duo (see Ex. 6). Beethoven begins with a leisurely tune in two strains, of which Ex. 3
shows the first figures.

Ex. 3.

Both strains are repeated; the repetitions being almost the only
passages in this symphony in which the clarinets emerge from
an archaic state of servitude. To many a musical child, or child
in musical matters, this movement has brought about the first
awakening to a sense of beauty in music. A binary melody with
repeats is a bulky affair to work into sonata form in a slow
tempo; and so, in spite of the direction *larghetto*, the tempo is
not really very slow. Beethoven later on arranged this symphony
as a pianoforte trio (astonishingly badly too); and it is significant
that he added to the slow movement the direction *quasi andante*.

The music flows along with a reckless opulence of themes. In the
second subject three are well worth quoting; the opening theme—

Ex. 4.

for the sake of its influence on the jaunty second subject of the
finale of Schumann's Fourth Symphony; its continuation—

Ex. 5.

on account of its dramatic urgency in the most lofty vein of Italian
opera seria; and its debonair cadence theme—

Ex. 6.

which so completely captivated Schubert in his Grand Duo.

In spite of all this luxury the movement achieves its career in
perfect form, and at no unreasonable length.

The tiny scherzo—

Ex. 7.

s not as large as Haydn's later minuets, but is typical Beethoven of
any period, early or late: that is to say, he would not have been
ashamed to write a movement on similar lines even in his last
quartets. But when we come to the trio there is a notable contrast
between the young man of 1802 playing with children, and the seer
of 1824 revealing intimations of immortality. (Compare the trio
of the scherzo of the Ninth Symphony.)

Ex. 8.
1802.

Brahms, in his Serenade, op. 11, exercised himself in small
classical forms by an amusing combination of the scherzos of
Beethoven's Septet and Second Symphony.

With the finale we find ourselves unquestionably in Beethoven's
'second period'. It is a rondo on a powerfully humorous theme
as original as any that Beethoven invented.

Ex. 9.

The transition-theme, with its almost ecclesiastical tone, strikes a grand note of contrast which will be very useful in the coda.

Ex. 10.

Just before the second subject a figure requires quotation—

Ex. 11.

as being afterwards put to dramatic use in effecting the returns to the main theme.

The second subject expands in more leisurely rhythms.

Ex. 12.

The coda is pure Beethoven in full power.

IV. THIRD SYMPHONY IN E FLAT MAJOR (SINFONIA EROICA), OP. 55

1 *Allegro con brio.* 2 *Marcia Funebre : Adagio assai.* 3 SCHERZO: *Allegro vivace.* 4 FINALE : *Allegro molto.*

Every one knows the story of how Beethoven's admiration for Napoleon inspired this symphony, and how the news of Napoleon's coronation infuriated Beethoven almost to the point of destroying the finished work. A copy with an autograph title-page is in the musical archives of Vienna; and where Bonaparte's name once stood, a ragged hole attests the truth of the story.

Much comment has been wasted on the position of the funeral march, and on the scherzo and finale which follow it. One very useful treatise on composition actually cites the Eroica Symphony as an example of the way in which the sonata form loads the composer with inappropriate additions to his programme. Such criticism has two aspects, the literary, which concerns the programme, and the musical, which concerns the form. In order to be literary, it is not necessary to be unmusical. Beethoven does not think a symphony a reasonable vehicle for a chronological

biography of Napoleon; but he does think it the best possible way
of expressing his feelings about heroes and hero-worship. Death
must be faced by heroes and hero-worshippers, and if what heroes
know about it is of any value to mankind, they may as well tell
us of their knowledge while they are alive. And the mere courage
of battle is not enough; it is the stricken nations whose sorrow
must be faced. Afterwards the world revives, ready to nourish
more heroes for happier times.

I. *Allegro con brio.* After two strong introductory chords the
violoncellos state the principal theme. It is simply the notes of
a common chord swinging backwards and forwards in a quietly
energetic rhythm. Then, as the violins enter with a palpitating high
note, the harmony becomes clouded, soon however to resolve
in sunshine. Whatever you may enjoy or miss in the Eroica
Symphony, remember this cloud: it leads eventually to one of the
most astonishing and subtle dramatic strokes in all music.

Ex. 1.

Long afterwards, when the vast 'second subject' has displayed its
procession of themes, beginning with one which, though of cardinal
importance, has escaped the notice of analysts—

Ex. 2.

and when the still more vast development has twice introduced an
entirely new lyric passage—

Ex. 3.

we are waiting on the threshold of the original key in breathless suspense for the return of the first theme. At last the suspense becomes too much for one of the horns, who, while the echoes of the dominant chord are still whispering, softly gives out the tonic chord of the theme. The orchestra instantly awakens and settles down to recapitulate the opening. (Let us hope that the days are past when any one could doubt the sanity of Beethoven's genius in that famous collision of shadowy harmonies; but even Bülow corrected the passage into exactly the sort of lopsided platitude that creeps into a classical text through the mediation of a 'gloss'.) Soon the theme reaches the little cloud that we noticed in the beginning. The cloud 'resolves' in a new direction, and the sun comes out in one of the two keys whose only characteristic is that of complete contradiction to the tonic which has been regained after all that suspense.

Ex. 4.

The other contradictory key follows, by way of restoring the balance; and then the main key proves strong enough to stand the shock, and the design finishes its normal course and expands freely in its huge peroration.

The other surprises and strokes of genius in this movement may safely be left to speak for themselves; with the exception of the last of all, which, together with the unobtrusive but cardinally important theme it concerns (Ex. 2), has singularly contrived to escape the notice of all the best-known commentators, including even Weingartner. It need not escape the notice of any listener, for it is marked by a sudden and impressive lull at the very height of the final climax.

II. *Marcia Funebre.* The great length of the funeral march results mainly from the size of its principal theme. This is a broad melody in two portions, each of which is given out by the strings and repeated (in the first case with a close in a new key) by the wind. This takes time; and in addition there is a series of afterthoughts

which brings this main theme to a close on a scale almost large
enough for a complete movement. Yet Beethoven's purpose is
to work out the whole in rondo form; that is to say, a form in
which the main theme recurs like a choral refrain alternating with
at least two contrasted episodes. It is obvious that such a purpose
can here be carried out only by a miracle of concentration and
terseness; but such miracles are Beethoven's normal form of
action, and this funeral march broadens in its flow as it develops.
The first episode is a regular trio in the major mode, beginning in
consolation and twice bursting into triumph. Then the light fails
and the mournful main theme returns. Its energy cannot carry it
even through its first phrase; and the second episode breaks in.
It is a solemn double fugue which Weingartner has well called
Aeschylean.

Ex. 5.

This comes to a climax and ends with a solemn slow close in the
dominant. Upon this a fragment of the main theme rises upwards
with a sigh which is suddenly answered by a roar from the depths,
and an upheaval fit for a setting of the *Dies Irae*. 'Never' (says
Weingartner) 'has a fearful catastrophe been described with simpler
means.' The tumult subsides in the weeping of a *lacrimosa dies*,
and through the sound of weeping the entire theme of the march
is heard in both its portions and with its whole series of afterthoughts. These close in a change of harmony; and then some
moments are measured only as it were by the slow swing of
a pendulum. Above this enters at last, in a distant key, the
beginning of a new message of consolation, but it dies away and
the movement concludes with a final utterance of the main theme,
its rhythms and accents utterly broken with grief.

III. This scherzo is the first in which Beethoven fully attained
Haydn's desire to replace the minuet by something on a scale
comparable to the rest of a great symphony. Its characteristics
are unmistakable, and we need only mention the long, subdued
whispering of the opening, blazing out so suddenly into a fortissimo;
the trio with its three horns, whose classical imperfections of technique Beethoven has exploited to poetic ends, which the perfectly
equipped modern player has to rediscover by careful research; and
the mysterious coda with its menacing drums.

IV. The finale is in a form which was unique when it appeared,
and has remained unique ever since. This has given rise to a widespread notion that it is formless or incoherent. It is neither; and its

life, which is its form, does not depend upon a label. The best way
to understand it is not to think of the important earlier pianoforte
Variations and Fugue on a theme from Prometheus, on which its
material is based, but simply to identify its material under three
headings, a Bass, a Tune, and a Fugue. But first there is a short
and fiery introduction which asserts a foreign key. It abruptly
corrects this as if it had found it to be a mistake. Then the Bass is
solemnly given by the strings, pizzicato, and echoed by the wind.
Its first part happens to make a grotesque but presentable theme,
and many a later composer has owed Beethoven a grudge for thus
indelibly stamping his name on one of the most unavoidable basses
a simple melody can have. But the second part is quite absurd,
and we can almost see Beethoven laughing at our mystified faces
as it digs us in the ribs. However the whole Bass proceeds to put
on clothes, of a respectable contrapuntal cut; and by the time we
are almost ready to believe its pretensions, the Tune comes sailing
over it in full radiance and we think no more of the Bass, though
it faithfully performs its duty as such. The vision of dry bones is
accomplished.

Ex. 6.

So far Beethoven's design has been exactly that of his *Introdu-
zione col basso del tema* in the *Prometheus* variations; but now,
instead of making variations, he leads in a few argumentative steps
to a new key and then proceeds to the Fugue. The subject of the
Fugue comes from the Bass, and is worked up to a vigorous climax
which suddenly breaks off into a rich double variation (i.e. a variation in which the repeats are themselves varied) of the Tune in
a remote key. In the second part of this variation the flute is very
brilliant, and the orchestra repeats the part with rough energy,
leading to a high-spirited episode in a dance-rhythm, with the first
four notes of the Bass sturdily marking time throughout. After
this the first part of the Tune reappears and soon leads to a

D

resumption of the Fugue with new features—inversion of its subject; combination with part of the Tune in a new accentuation, &c. The Fugue, which is here throughout in the main key, now comes to a grand climax ending with an anticipatory pause. Then, like the opening of the gates of Paradise, the Tune enters slowly (*poco andante*) in a glorious double variation, the richness of which has led some analysts to think that much of its material is gratuitously new, whereas in fact the slightness of the second part of the Tune is expressly designed to give scope for the utmost freedom in variations. Then (as in the parallel finale to the pianoforte variations, though with incomparably more solemn pomp) there is a tremendous fortissimo variation with the Tune in the bass. The original Bass had finally disappeared with the last Fugue.

After this climax all is coda, and one of the most profound codas Beethoven ever wrote. With a passing hint at a new variation, the music modulates with some passion through a distant key to a point where it suddenly melts into a mood we have not found before in the whole symphony. It is the mood of that mysterious and true humour that is not far from tears; and without it the greatest of heroes is but a demigod with powers alien to humanity and therefore less than divine. Here, just upon the close of his heroic symphony, Beethoven holds us for the last time in suspense, until the orchestra blazes out in a larger version of the fiery introduction and brings the work to its triumphant end.

V. FOURTH SYMPHONY IN B♭ MAJOR, OP. 60

1 *Adagio, leading to* 2 *Allegro vivace.* 3 *Adagio.* 4 *Allegro vivace.*
5 *Allegro ma non troppo.*

As in later years Beethoven followed his gigantic Seventh Symphony by the terse and unshadowed comedy of his Eighth, so he followed his Eroica Symphony (the longest of all his works except the Ninth) by a symphony the proportions and scope of which are, except for three powerful passages, almost within the range of Mozart and Haydn. Yet the exceptional passages are in no way 'out of the picture'; and the contemporary critics who accused Beethoven's Fourth Symphony of every fault a symphony could have, would have had more difficulty than we in picking them out. The solemn introduction, which excited Weber's derision for its few notes spread over five minutes; the dramatic hush and crescendo leading to the recapitulation in the first movement; the astonishing middle episode of the slow movement, and the double alternating repetition of scherzo and trio; these are the features we recognize as peculiarly Beethovenish in this work. To contemporaries they were mere additional eccentricities in a work in which the whole style,

being Beethoven's, was notoriously extravagant; and the chances
are that if the work had been produced under the name of Mozart
or Haydn, the outstanding features would not have been noticed at
all, and the work would have been sleepily accepted as a masterpiece at once. As it was, people listened whether they liked it or not.

The Fourth Symphony is perhaps the work in which Beethoven
first fully reveals his mastery of movement. He had already shown
his command of a vastly wider range of musical possibilities than
that of Mozart or Haydn. And he had shown no lack of ease and
power in the handling of his new resources. But now he shows that
these resources can be handled in such a way that Mozart's own
freedom of movement reappears as one of the most striking
qualities of the whole. The sky-dome vastness of the dark introduction is evident at the outset; but it is first fully understood in
the daylight of the opening of the allegro; for which reason I give
the connecting passage.

Ex. 1.

Note how the new quick tempo asserts itself with the muscular
strength of real bodily movement. Ordinary writers of Italian
opera buffa, and some ambitious modern composers, would think
they were asserting the quick tempo if they began the allegro with
the pianissimo passage (with figure (b) in the bassoons) which
follows the tutti counterstatement of the present theme, and which,
put where Beethoven puts it, has the settled vital energy of a top
that has 'gone to sleep'. The 'spin' of the whole movement,
tremendous as it is, depends entirely on the variety, the contrasts,
and the order of themes and sequences, varying in length from odd
fractions of bars (e.g. the exciting three-minim staccato sequence
early in the second subject) to the 32-bar and even longer processes
in the development. This statement may seem self-evident; but, of

all the arts that have been lost since 'classical' times, this art of movement is the most characteristic, the most universally necessary, and the most immediately successful in its results. A composer who could keep up the spin, as Beethoven keeps it up in the most ordinary levels of his Fourth Symphony, would have no difficulty in tackling the most powerful inspirations when they occurred to him.

The second subject begins with a conversation between the bassoon, the oboe, and the flute, which leads to the 3-minim sequence I mentioned above, and to a number of other themes, ending with a syncopated cadence-theme which gathers up a thread started in the transition between first and second subject.

The development keeps up the spin by moving on lines far broader than any yet indicated by the exposition. The delightful cantabile added as a counterpoint to the entries (in various keys) of the main theme, is one of the salient features. Nearly half the whole development is occupied by the wonderful hovering on the threshold of the remote key of B natural major in order to return therefrom to the tonic B flat, by a process resembling, more subtly and on a higher plane, the return in the first movement of the Waldstein Sonata (written about a year earlier). The recapitulation is quite normal, and the coda is no longer than one of Mozart's usual final expansions.

The slow movement is a full-sized rondo, a form which is extremely spacious when worked out in a slow tempo. I need only quote its main theme, with the stroke of genius achieved in the all-pervading rhythmic figure of its introductory bar—

Ex. 2.

and the opening of its first episode or second subject, a still more subtle melody—

Ex. 3.

The main theme returns in a florid variation; and the middle episode, which follows, is one of the most imaginative passages anywhere in Beethoven. From its mysterious end arises the return of the main theme in its varied form, this time in the flute; whereupon follows a regular recapitulation, including the transition and the second-subject episode (Ex. 3). The coda consists of a final allusion to the main theme, dispersing itself mysteriously over the orchestra, till the drums make an end by recalling the opening stroke of genius.

For the scherzo no quotations are needed: the double repetition of scherzo and trio makes everything as clear as any dance, in spite of the numerous rhythmic whims. The final repetition of the scherzo is abridged (in other cases Beethoven prefers to make full repetition aggressively the point of the joke). Never have three short bars contained more meaning than the coda in which the two horns blow the whole movement away.

The finale represents Beethoven's full maturity in that subtlest of all disguises, his discovery of the true inwardness of Mozart and Haydn; a discovery inaccessible to him whenever, as in a few early works (notably the Septet), he seemed or tried to imitate them, but possible as soon as he obtained full freedom in handling his own resources. Everything is present in this unsurpassably adroit and playful finale; and it is all pure Beethoven, even when, by drawing out its opening theme into quavers with pauses, it borrows an old joke of Haydn's, the excellence of which lies in its badness. Lamb would have understood it—in spite of the Essay on Ears.

I quote the main themes of the first subject—

and of the second—

To do justice to the boldness and power that underly all the grace and humour of this finale, it would be necessary to go into details. It is a study for a lifetime; but, once begun, it is in many ways more directly useful to the artist than the study of things the power of which is allowed to appear on the surface. Those who think the finale of the Fourth Symphony 'too light' will never get nearer than Spohr (if as near) towards a right understanding of the Fifth, however much they may admire it.

VI. FIFTH SYMPHONY IN C MINOR, OP. 67

1 *Allegro con brio.* 2 *Andante con moto.* 3 *Allegro, leading to*
4 *Allegro, ending with* 5 *Presto.*

This work shares with Beethoven's Seventh Symphony the distinction of being not only among the most popular but also among the least misunderstood of musical classics. It has not failed to inspire 'roaring cataracts of nonsense' from commentators, but the nonsense has, for the most part, been confined to technical matters of little concern to the naïve (or ideal) listener; though one heresy I shall discuss here, since on it depends one's whole view of the difference between real composition and mere manufacture. Another immensely lucky fact conducive to the popular appreciation of this symphony is that the famous phrase (made still more famous by Robert Louis Stevenson in *The Ebb Tide*)—the phrase which describes the theme of the first movement as 'destiny knocking at the door'—is no mere figment of a commentator, but is Beethoven's very own words. Mistakes and misreadings in this mighty work have been as frequent as anywhere; the very band-parts issued under the auspices of the 'critical' edition have some scandalously stupid editorial alterations; but not even the notorious old trick of changing the first three quavers into crotchets has been able to make any headway against the overwhelming power and clearness of the whole.

Some good, however, may be done by denouncing the heresy which preaches that 'the whole first movement is built up of the initial figure of four notes'. It is well worth refuting, for it has led to most of the worst features of that kind of academic music which goes furthest to justify the use of the word 'academic' as a term of vulgar abuse. No great music has ever been built from an initial figure of four notes. As I have said elsewhere, you might as well say that every piece of music is built from an initial figure of *one* note. You may profitably say that the highest living creatures have begun from the single nucleated cell. But no ultra-microscope has yet unravelled the complexities of the single living cell; nor, if the spectroscope is to be believed, are we yet very fully informed of the complexities of a single atom of iron: and it is quite absurd to suppose that the evolution of a piece of music can proceed from 'a simple figure of four notes' on lines in the least resembling those of nature. As far as I know, Weingartner is the first writer who has pointed out the truth that the first movement of the C minor symphony is really remarkable for the length of its sentences; that the first sentences, instead of being 'built up' from a single figure, *break up* into other sentences of even greater variety and breadth; and that the composer who first really 'built up' symphonic movements out of short figures was not Beethoven but Schumann, whose handling of the larger forms became sectional, diffuse, and yet stiff for this very reason.

Obviously the same argument applies to the whole theory of Wagnerian *Leitmotif*. Wagner attained full mastery over the broadest sweep of sequence that music has yet achieved. This alone suffices to refute the orthodox Wagnerian belief that his music is 'built up' from the scraps of theme to which it can be reduced by its dramatic associations, and by the general possibility of articulating big phrases into small figures.

In the first fine careless rapture of Wagnerian analysis it was discovered that the 'four taps', with which 'destiny knocks at the door' in the first movement, recur elsewhere; once (quite accidentally, though in an impressive passage) in the slow movement, and very prominently in the second theme of that dream of terror which we technically call the scherzo (Ex. 4). This profound discovery was supposed to reveal an unsuspected unity in the work; but it does not seem to have been carried far enough. It conclusively proves that the Sonata Appassionata, the G major Pianoforte Concerto, the third movement of the Quartet, op. 74, and, with the final consummation of a fifth tap, the Violin Concerto, all belong to the C minor Symphony; for the same rhythmic figure pervades them too. The simple truth is that Beethoven could not do without just such purely rhythmic figures at this stage of his art. It was absolutely necessary that every inner part in his texture should assert its own life; but at the same time it was equally necessary that it should not cause constant or rapid changes of harmony by doing so. Figures that can identify a theme while remaining on one note are the natural response to these requirements. In his later works Beethoven used more and more polyphony in Bach's sense; and rhythmic figures no longer pressed into the foreground of his invention, though he could still use them when he wanted them. It is astonishing how many of Beethoven's themes can be recognized by their bare rhythm without quoting any melody at all.

Here are some specimens, not including those mentioned above:

In selecting the following illustrations for the C minor Symphony I have been guided mainly by the purpose of counteracting the effects of the 'short figure' heresy, and secondly, by the chance of removing by numerals a misconception which is likely to arise from the notation of long sentences in such very short bars. Thus Ex. 1 evidently comprises only the first half of a big sentence. (The crotchet tails and the small added notes show the pathetic new light in which it appears at the very end of the movement.)

Ex. 1.

Ex. 2, which gives the opening of the second subject, shows first the way in which the famous rhythmic figure (a) pervades the whole movement, and secondly, with the aid of my numerals, the scansion of the four-bar rhythm.

Ex. 2.

From the second and third bars of this quotation (marked 1 and 2 in the rhythmic periods) are derived, first, the famous diminuendo of chords in dialogue between strings and wind near the end of the development, and secondly, the furious opening of the coda, one of the most powerful tuttis ever written, and written with incredibly few notes for its weight. Of the recapitulation two observations may here be made: first, that, as Weingartner points out, the pathetic cadenza for the oboe at the end of Ex. 1 is the outcome of a melodic line which it has been tracing for the last sixteen bars; and secondly, that it is really a mistaken reverence for Beethoven which puts up with the comic bassoon instead of horns when we have Ex. 2 in C major. Beethoven had not time to change the horns from E flat; but now that the modern horn has all the notes that were missing in Beethoven's day, there is no reason why his spirit should continue to put up with an unmitigated nuisance, even if we are sure that he put up with it in a mood of Shakespearian humour. The continuation of the passage has a bitter note that was not in the original statement.

The andante I have left without illustration. Shakespeare's women have the same courage, the same beauty of goodness, and the same humour. In form the movement is unique, if dimly suggested by Haydn's special form of variations on two alternating themes. But here the themes are of quite peculiar types. Violas and 'cellos (it is curious that Beethoven never uses orchestral 'cellos for melody without doubling them by violas) state the first theme in a single broad phrase, the end of which the higher instruments echo and carry on into a series of echoing afterthoughts. Then the second theme begins, very simply, pauses on a wistful note, and suddenly bursts into a blaze of triumph in a remote key, C major, the tonic of the whole symphony. The triumph dies away into a passage of profound mystery and pathos, which leads back to the key of the movement (A flat). The first theme now returns varied in notes twice as rapid as the time-beats (the kind of variation which in the eighteenth century would be called a double). A clarinet holds a sustained note above, with a boldness which led early critics to suspect a blunder. (Dvořák did not think so when he reproduced it in the slow movement of his first symphony.) Again the second theme follows, likewise with a quicker accompaniment, and leads to its blaze of triumph, which again dies out in the recognition that its day is not yet come. A second double of the first theme follows in due course, but, instead of getting beyond the first phrase, is given three times, the last time forte, leading to a climax and a pause. Then there is an astonishing series of meditations and adventures, on which the second theme breaks with its full note of triumph. The reaction from this (in one of those profound passages which early critics found quite ridiculous because they listened with ears attuned to the proportions of a Mozart symphony) leads to an exquisite treatment of the first theme smiling through tears in the minor mode. Then, after more meditative delay, it comes fortissimo, for the

first and only time, on the full orchestra. Note the imitation by
the wood-wind, if you can hear it through the far from evenly-
balanced scoring. This time the echoing afterthoughts follow;
and nothing in music is bolder and more convincing than the
profusion with which these afterthoughts give rise to others, until
the whole movement is rounded off in perfect proportions which
at no point have revealed to us what they are going to be until the
last note has been heard.

The third movement I will not describe seriatim; but there
is one piece of information which is very interesting historically,
and which commentators, including Sir George Grove, have failed
to make as clear as it might be. My quotations are again furnished
with numerals which show where the pulses of four-bar rhythm
begin. The movement has often been scanned wrongly from
beginning to end, and the writer in *Grove's Dictionary* who cites
the trio as an unacknowledged case of three-bar rhythm has
blundered straight into the trap.

Ex. 3.

Ex. 4.

Ex. 5.

TRIO.

Now it is well known that in the early editions there were two
superfluous bars where the first theme (Ex. 3) returns after the trio.
The second and third full bars (marked 1 and 2 in my rhythmic
numbers) were written twice, at first legato as in Ex. 3, and then
in crotchets with rests, as they ought to be after the trio. Beethoven
wrote to his publishers to correct the redundancy; but it still
remained upheld as a stroke of genius forty years after his death.

How did it originate? The answer is that this movement was,
until after its first performance, meant to be of the same form as
the scherzos of the Fourth, Sixth, and Seventh Symphonies (compare also the Pianoforte Trios, op. 70, no. 2, and op. 97, and the
String Quartets, op. 59, no. 2, opp. 74, 95, and 132)—that is to say,

the whole movement, trio and all, was to be given twice; and the breathless pianissimo da capo was to be the third presentation of the main theme. The redundant bars were for the *prima volta*, and they led back to bar four of Ex. 3 (here marked 3 in my rhythmic periods). The double-bar and $ that must have stood there at the time would have had the effect of making it impossible to misread the rhythm; and Beethoven had actually chosen this point for marking his repeat, though it forced him to write out those two bars which afterwards became redundant when the repeat was abandoned. That it was abandoned shows how Beethoven's own special form of the round-and-round scherzo, alternating twice over with its trio, had to yield to the terrific impressiveness of the emotions created by these themes. Probably the long repeat proved detrimental, not to the great darkness that leads to the finale (nothing could weaken that), but to the reappearance of the 'scherzo' in the development of the finale.

In the finale trombones appear for the first time in symphonic music. I quote a part of the first theme in order to show that it is again a case of a magnificently long sentence, weighted with repetitions even more powerful than those of the first movement, inasmuch as they are not sequential repetitions, but plain reiterations on the same position in the scale.

Ex. 6.

The main theme of the second subject (Ex. 7) I quote in order to point out that the minims in the 'cellos form an important figure (*c*) turned to powerful account in the development.

Ex. 7.

The final theme of the second subject (Ex. 8) is destined to be worked up in the presto coda.

Ex. 3.

Spohr, who thought the theme of the first movement scrappy and undignified, and the whole finale an orgy of vulgar noise, admitted that the reappearance of the 'scherzo' in the middle of the finale was a stroke of genius for which the rest of the work might be forgiven. It is indeed a stroke of genius. Spohr liked it because it was interesting as a feature of form. He evidently disbelieved or disapproved of anything that could be said about emotional values in this symphony, and so he can hardly have realized where the genius really lay in the stroke. Let us remember that the 'scherzo' had a tremendous emotional value, and then consider how it is to be reintroduced into the sustained triumph of the finale. Any one would think that there were only two ways of working the problem: first, to reproduce the mood just as it was. Of course this is impossible. We cannot forget that the terror is passed. Secondly then, could we recover the mood by elaborating the details? This would betray itself as fictitious. If you cannot recover the sensations you felt during an earthquake, it is not much use telling as your own experience things about it that you could not possibly have known at the time. We can easily see, now that Beethoven has shown us, that his is the one true solution which confirms the truth of the former terror and the security of the present triumph; but no lesser artist could have found it. Beethoven recalls the third movement as a memory which we know for a fact but can no longer understand: there is now a note of self-pity, for which we had no leisure when the terror was upon our souls: the depth and the darkness are alike absent, and in the dry light of day we cannot remember our fears of the unknown. And so the triumph resumes its progress and enlarges its range until it reaches its appointed end.

VII. SIXTH SYMPHONY IN F MAJOR (SINFONIA PASTORALE),
OP. 68

1 *Awakening of happy feelings on getting out into the country. (Allegro ma non troppo.)*
2 *By the brook side. (Andante molto mosso.)*
3 *Merry gathering of the country folk. (Allegro), leading to*
4 *Thunderstorm. (Allegro), leading to*
5 *Shepherd's Song: Happy and thankful feelings after the storm. (Allegretto.)*

The first and the last word of common sense about programme music in general was said by Beethoven on this symphony in particular. He said it was 'the expression of feelings rather than painting'. This has not prevented the usual 'roaring cataract of nonsense' from descending upon this intensely musical work and swamping it in volumes of literature; sometimes praising Beethoven for his intelligent anticipation of the true functions of music as a purely illustrative art, but more often blaming him for leading music into so dangerous a bypath by sacrificing musical form to the demands of his external musical programme. The passage which has given most offence in this symphony is the representation of the cuckoo, the nightingale, and the quail at the end of the slow movement. That passage is a master-stroke of pure musical form. It differs from a dozen earlier examples in Beethoven's works (and about a hundred in Haydn's) only in one essential respect, that it is by far the ripest in style; and in one unessential respect, that persons who can tell the difference between the birdcalls of cuckoos, quails, and nightingales can recognize something rather like them here. But for this unessential detail the passage would never have been supposed to be abnormal at all. No treatise on musical form enters into enough detail to make its analysis of this passage distinguishable from its errors of observation. As for the thunderstorm, it is a monumental introduction, dramatically cutting short a very typical Beethoven scherzo, and leading equally dramatically into a serene and spacious rondo. The only unusual thing about it is that it is in a quick tempo, whereas most introductions are slow. The kind of objection that is raised against the thunderstorm is the assertion that 'the thunder comes first and the lightning afterwards'; as if anybody were quite sure that he had seen the first flash which preceded the first loud thunderclap. Authorities on scoring have remarked that the use of the piccolo in this movement does not show that instrument at its best, since sustained notes are not highly characteristic of it. In other words, a real thunderstorm would be an expensive and inefficient substitute for the piccolo. Beethoven, then, should have used the piccolo to imitate, not the whistling of the wind, which it does exceedingly well, but the more characteristic whistle of the railway guard. Let us be quite fair, then, and call it the bos'n's whistle, which might be in place in a storm; but then let us remember that this is not a storm at sea, but a thunderstorm that has interrupted something like a dance round the maypole, and which, far from being a danger, gives rise to 'happy and thankful feelings' afterwards. In the whole symphony there is not a note of which the musical value would be altered if cuckoos and nightingales, and country folk, and thunder and lightning, and the howling and whistling of the wind, were things that had never been named by man, either in connexion with music or with anything else. Whether we have words for common objects and events of the countryside, or whether we have no words, there are feelings evoked by these objects in proportion to our intelligent suscepti- bility; and the great master of any language, whether that language be music, painting, sculpture, architecture, or speech, can invoke the deepest part of these feelings in his own terms. And his art will always remain pure as long as he holds to Beethoven's dictum; which may be philosophically re-translated 'more the expression of feelings than the illustration of things'.

There is one more mare's-nest over which we may stumble at the very beginning of this symphony. It has been alleged that large tracts of it are transcribed from Rhenish folk-songs. It would take too long to investigate this matter thoroughly; but it will all even- tually come to this, that the symphony is a composition in large and diversely coherent paragraphs, and that when Beethoven is writing under the inspiration of country life, he uses appropriate types of melody.

We have then to deal with a perfect classical symphony. Like every one of Beethoven's symphonies, some forty of Haydn's, and at least seven outstanding ones of Mozart's, this symphony contains features that are not to be found in any other. Otherwise it would not be a classic. But Beethoven has told us, with certain very broad particulars (themselves more like universals), that this symphony expresses his love of country life. If it does not express ours, so much the worse for us.

The first movement opens at once with a quiet melody full of lively figures.

Ex. 1.

The harmonization throughout the first movement, the scherzo, and the finale, is of a rustic simplicity, asserting, with primitive directness, the tonic, dominant, and subdominant of whatever key it is in. There are very few definite drone-bass effects, but the possi- bility of them is never far off, and each figure of each theme is apt to be piled up in a long series of bird-song repetitions. Much time has been wasted in identifying other birds than those Beethoven has mentioned in that famous place in the slow movement. Schindler, a solemn Boswell without the genius, who used to inscribe 'Ami de Beethoven' on his visiting-card, bored Beethoven so fearfully with silly questions that Beethoven generally put him off with

answers of the same quality. These answers have been faithfully
transmitted to posterity. And so Beethoven's 'yellow-hammer'
comes down to us as a bird with a compass of two octaves
consisting of the arpeggio of G major; and it is a regrettable
anachronism that has prevented the Jub-Jub bird and the Orient
Calf from the Land of Tute from helping Beethoven to satisfy
Schindler's curiosity. The real meaning of these bird-song repetitions is not that they represent birds in particular, but that birds
themselves repeat their songs continually when they are happy and
have nothing else to do. The Pastoral Symphony has the enormous
strength of some one who knows how to relax. The strength and
the relaxation are at their highest point in the slow movement, as
we shall see when we come to it; but they are already gigantic in the
first movement, which is in no respect but externals less powerful
than that of the C minor Symphony. Nothing could be easier to
follow, and yet nothing could be more unexpected than its course.
The transition, in which the first figure (a) of Ex. 1 is built up into
phrases punctuated by subdued chuckles in the wood-wind, leads
in three indolent strides to a second subject which slowly stretches
itself out over tonic and dominant as a sort of three-part round.

The cadence-theme of the second subject also needs quotation
for the sake of a delicious variation of it in the coda.

The development sets out in the subdominant, B flat, and
therein proceeds slowly to pile up a long passage out of bird-song
repetitions of figure (b). An immense stretch of the chord of B flat
is followed by a still bigger stretch of the bright chord of D major
with a slow crescendo to a fortissimo. This dies away, and the last
two notes of the figure (b) are broken off in a comic dialogue
between the bassoon and the violins. Then the first theme is given
out again in G, and here again figure (b) is piled up into an immense

crescendo. This time the change of harmony is in the opposite direction, from G to E, with the same climax and the same decline. A third time the theme starts in A major, and is now allowed to proceed to its second phrase, figure (*d*). This is then developed fluently in broad steps, moving simply through D and G minor to the dominant of F, where a fortissimo climax leads with exquisite warmth to the return of the first subject in the tonic. The beginning of this recapitulation is expanded and adorned by beautiful new counterpoints in the first violin. Otherwise the recapitulation is quite regular, an imperceptible change of harmony being all that is required for the transition. The coda is grafted on to the recapitulation by proceeding for a few bars as at the beginning of the development. This brings us to the subdominant, B flat, in which key the first theme bursts out forte, but is instantly checked and gives place to a delightful dance-like variation of the cadence-theme (Ex. 3) in smooth triplets. It moves round to the tonic and there again bursts out forte and is developed to a broad climax. From this a slow diminuendo leads to a terse and lively phrase built out of figure (*b*), a very different kind of treatment from that which it had in the development; and then a clarinet turns figure (*c*) into a brilliant dance. When this has died away, the first three bars of Ex. 1 float upwards into the air as lazily and as imperturbably as a cloud. Suddenly the movement rouses itself, for everything must have an end, even if the last chords are as soft as the opening.

I once said that the slow movement is one of the most powerful things in music, and the statement can be proved by merely drawing up the facts as to its form. The form is that of a fully developed first movement. To achieve this in a slow tempo always implies extraordinary concentration and terseness of design; for the slow tempo, which inexperienced composers are apt to regard as having no effect upon the number of notes that take place in a given time, is much more rightly conceived as large than as slow. Take a great slow movement, and write it out in such a notation as will make it correspond in real time-values to the notes of a great quick movement; and you will be surprised to find how much in actual time the mere first theme of the slow movement would cover of the whole exposition of the quick movement. Any slow movement in full sonata form is, then, a very big thing. But a slow movement in full sonata form which at every point asserts its deliberate intention to be lazy and to say whatever occurs to it twice in succession, and which in so doing never loses flow and never falls out of proportion, such a slow movement is as strong as an Atlantic liner that could bear taking out of water and supporting on its two ends. The brook goes on for ever; the importance of

that fact lies in its effect upon the poetic mind of the listener bask-
ing in the sun on its banks. The representation of its flow with the
aid of two muted solo violoncellos is a stroke of genius that will
always seem modern. The broken character of the first bars of the
overlying theme, settling down in the later bars to an enthusiastic
sustained melody—

is a perfect explanation of the poet's mood, as shown by the natural
way in which his thoughts and utterances gradually take shape.
The murmur of the brook becomes more continuous (in other
words the accompaniment is broken into semiquavers) throughout the rest of the movement; not because it has changed in itself,
but because the poet is no longer attending to it. The whole
first phrase is repeated, and there are bird-song trills above it.
Now comes a new theme in which, as with other themes in this
symphony, there is the tendency for various instruments to come
in one after another in the fashion of a round.

In its formal aspect this theme might be guessed to be the transition-theme; and if the highest ideal of form were that everything
should turn out exactly as one expects, it would be the duty of
this theme to effect the transition. By so doing it would achieve
a comparatively low kind of efficiency. But its higher duty is
to express the mood of the poet accurately. Transition-themes
belong to something a little nearer town. This theme is going to
close quietly in the tonic; and if we are going to move to any other
place on the banks of this brook, we will do so quite contentedly
without any theme in particular. The music gathers itself up in
quiet broken phrases and starts the first theme again. It follows
the course of the brook (which is never tired) into the dominant, and
there with all requisite deliberation and breadth prepares for the
second subject. This begins with a sort of tonic-and-dominant
theme not unlike that of the first movement (Ex. 2). Beethoven
intends no allusion, any more than he does in the similar case of
the second subject of the finale. These themes have come to be
of the same type, because the moods and situations are the same.
But in each case the theme takes a different course. Here its richly

melodious fourth bar drifts into a new phrase starting on a remote chord—

Ex. 6.

and repeating itself again and again as one instrument crowds in upon another. It comes to a massive cadence of which the final trill is dying away into dreamland; but it is so beautiful, and the sunlight has shifted through the trees to such new purpose, that we must look at the scene again. This time the cadence is still broader and the colouring is slightly grotesque, as if the poet were laughing at his own laziness, but it is all too beautiful not to be serious. Below the trill Ex. 5 re-enters and is answered by an increasing chorus of other voices. A fine account of the slow movement of the Pastoral Symphony has been written by the eminent composer Hans Pfitzner, in a pamphlet dealing with the whole theory of absolute music and programme music. I gratefully borrow from him the notion that this particular theme, with its constant recurrences at cardinal points of the structure, closely corresponds to the kind of mood in which one would say to oneself on a sleepy summer's day by Beethoven's brook, 'How beautiful!' The perpetual motion of the brook is now outlined in a short cadence subject which dies away gradually. And now comes the most subtle master-stroke of all; a feature far more abnormal than the passage in the coda representing the songs of the three birds. It is time for the development to begin, and of course it should begin by discussing one of the extant themes. But just as we saw that Ex. 5 was too deeply satisfied with the beauty of the moment to set about any such business as a transition-theme, so we find that here there is no hurry to begin the development. Having had the effrontery to give his second subject twice over, Beethoven has here the yet more sublime effrontery to start a new theme. It is another of these simple tonic-and-dominant affairs, the laziest of them all.

Ex. 7.

And Beethoven has no intention of following it up. It has the energy to move in its own stride into the brilliant key of G major, and now the development is ready to begin. The first theme (Ex. 4) comes out on the oboe with several new accessories in the accompaniment, including poor Schindler's giraffe-throated yellow-hammer, and a slow descending arpeggio in the violins. Weingartner advises that this last detail should not be brought out, as it makes the scoring too thick. I am unable to agree with him. It seems to me that the thing to keep in the background is the incessant rippling of the brook, which by this time cannot fail to be recognized, however slightly it is touched in; whereas this new detail is systematically elaborated throughout the development and recapitulation as an integral part of the scheme, and is by no means easy to hear. The continuation of the theme is quite new and moves broadly to a cadence with a trill. Below the trill comes Ex. 5 and moves ecstatically to E flat, the key of the subdominant and of shade. Here the whole process is repeated with new scoring and with the new accessory details still further enriched. The modulation which led from G to E flat is now begun in another direction, and leads from E flat to G flat. (Precisely the same plan, with the same inexact correspondence, but with keys of the opposite colour, was to be found in the development of the first movement.) The deep shadow of this remote key of G flat becomes still deeper as C flat, which, changing enharmonically to B natural, swoops round to our original key B flat. At the outset of this wonderful passage the theme was that of the first subject with the murmur of the brook becoming articulately melodious in the clarinet and the bassoon. At the moment when the melody gathers itself up into a sustained phrase and makes its enharmonic modulation, there comes a phenomenon full of deep meaning. From this point nothing is left of the melody but sustained notes and bird-song trills; the whole of the rest of the return to the main key is harmonic and rhythmic. In this as everywhere else the movement remains true to type, a perfect expression of happiness in relaxation.

In its own due proportions the passage brings back the recapitulation. This time the theme reaches its climax of rich scoring, the flute having the melody, the quick arpeggios of poor Schindler's yellow-hammer being multiplied by three instruments in three different parts of the bar, and the slow descending arpeggios being similarly distributed among horns, clarinets, and the second flute. Thus the air is full of tiny sounds which no one can tell to be less vast and distant than the stars of the Milky Way. Beethoven does not give the first subject a restatement now, but passes on in two bars to the second subject. This he preserves in full, repetitions and all. It has never been heard in the development, and to shorten it would be to violate the mood of the composition. And now after the cadence-theme comes the final consummation. There is a crescendo, but the melody is again drawn out into notes more sustained than any articulate phrase. Suddenly for a moment all is silent; we have no ears even for the untiring brook, and through the silence comes the voice of the nightingale, the quaint rhythmic pipe of the quail, and the syllabic yet impersonal signal of the cuckoo. This trio is answered by the motto of the whole movement, figure (*a*) from Ex. 4; and much nonsense might have been spared about this passage if the superior persons who regard it as violation of the absoluteness of music had taken the trouble to notice that the three birds make with this motto a perfectly normal four-bar phrase. Even if the whole passage were a new irregular theme, it would still be a closer structure than, say, the last bars of the slow movement of the D minor Pianoforte Sonata, op. 31, no. 2, or of the whole last pages of the slow movements of the Violin Sonatas in F major, op. 24, and in C minor, op. 30, no. 1. In fact it may safely be said that this coda is a perfect example of the form which Beethoven had only just contrived to suggest rather too broadly and with rather insufficient means in that page in the C minor Violin Sonata. Once more the three birds are heard and answered by the poet; and with his motto-theme a short dialogue of wind instruments brings this gigantic movement to its beautiful close.

The scherzo may claim to be programme music inasmuch as its programme implies all that is most typical of the strictest form of a Beethoven scherzo. Like its parent form the minuet, the scherzo originates aesthetically in the general notion of dance music, and in the specific notion of two dance melodies alternating with each other. And when out of the minuet, which had already in Haydn's hands utterly transcended its original limits, Beethoven developed his own gigantic type of scherzo, far from obliterating the typical dance character of the form, he emphasized it to the utmost. He did not in his most typical examples allow the themes to become so developed as to give the movement a character of dramatic progress; on the contrary he insisted that, however large his scherzo and his trio might be in themselves, the listener should thoroughly realize that they were two dances that were going to alternate not once but twice, and but for the intervention of some rather drastic closure even thrice. Since Beethoven's time, the doctrine has arisen that the purpose of music is to convey information; so that what has been said clearly once need not be repeated to listeners of ordinary intelligence. On the same principle we may as well demolish any part of a building which symmetrically repeats any other part. Experience soon convinced Beethoven of the necessity of writing out the repeats of his typical scherzos

in full, as performers will be more afraid to cut out whole written
pages than to disobey a mere repeat-mark. But this has not protected his scherzos from serious damage to their typical character;
and nowadays it is not preventing damage to much more dramatic
structures. The whole question depends upon whether architectural and formal motives or dramatic impulses and processes
preponderate. In discussing the C minor Symphony (which Beethoven produced at the same time as the Pastoral) I have pointed
out that there too the scherzo had originally been made to alternate twice with the trio; and that, in consequence of traces of
the long repeat-mark being left in the score and parts, commentators were for many years puzzled by two superfluous bars at the
return to the first theme. Beethoven had seen during the rehearsal
for the first performance that the dramatic power of the scherzo of
the C minor Symphony was far too intense for any such insistence
on its dance-form. But here in the Pastoral Symphony it would be
a crime not to let Beethoven's rustics have their dance out before
the thunderstorm intervenes. The whole movement is thoroughly
in character. It has Beethoven's full wealth of contrasted themes,
beginning with a couple in the brightly opposed keys of F and D
major.

Ex. 8.

The trio begins, not, as some commentators would have it, with
the change to 2/4 time (there is a double bar there simply because
the change of time demands it), but with the following delightful
theme:

Ex. 9.

Sir Henry Hadow has wittily commented upon the rustic bass
notes supplied by the second bassoon who is 'never quite sure how
many of them to put in'. I respectfully submit that the point is
rather that the bassoon knows this so well that he is a little too
proud of the fact. The realism is comic, but it is in keeping with
the dazzling brightness of the poet's holiday in the country, where
the commonest things are enjoyed as if they had never been seen

before. To say that the Pastoral Symphony is animated by the
spirit of folk-music is to show an enthusiasm for folk-music. But
any one who says that the three themes we have hitherto quoted
are actual folk-songs is talking obvious nonsense: those rhythms
and key relationships do not exist outside classical symphonies.
A real, or at least a possible folk-dance asserts itself boisterously
in 2/4 time as follows:

Ex. 10.

And now we have an instance of the clear characterization of every
instrument which Beethoven uses in this symphony. Nothing is
more familiar, or more often troublesome in the performance of
classical works, than the primitive set of glaring notes to which the
trumpets of classical days were confined. It is to be presumed that
good players and good conductors did not allow the trumpets to
run wild with their fragmentary signals and their frequent inability
to provide suitable notes for rapid changes of harmony. Modern
conductors and modern trumpet-players are constantly moderating
the force of the trumpets in a classical tutti; but to think this
moderation a purely modern refinement is to make rather hasty
assumptions as to the stupidity of musicians in Beethoven's
time. Now, however, at this point in the Pastoral Symphony,
the trumpet in its most primitive state enters for the first time.
In all the previous five symphonies trumpets and drums were
present from the outset, and were in no sense kept in reserve for
special effects. In this trio the trumpets are active in the dance;
they enter as personalities, and when they mark time on the notes
of the chord of C, they crown the festivity. Their last note dies
away romantically and leads back to the repetition of both scherzo
and trio. When the scherzo comes back for the third time it is
shortened, its conclusion being given presto; when suddenly there
is a murmur of distant thunder and large raindrops fall.

This is what Beethoven obviously tells us by the titles of his
movements. What he achieves is something much higher; it is
a physical shock of terror, which is far more thrilling when all
that is at stake is the prospect of getting one's clothes wet than
when there is any real human danger. Soon the thunderstorm
bursts; and the thunder is very simply and efficiently represented
by the entry of the drums, which are used in this symphony for no
other purpose. The rumbling passages of the 'cellos and double-
basses are generally cited as Beethoven's representation of thunder,
but they are only a part of it; they give, not the roll and the clap
of thunder, but a peculiar shuffling sound that pervades the air

during a thunderstorm, and is not accounted for by the rain. The modulations of this thunderstorm are musically superb. Current arrangements for pianoforte duet give a number of unauthorized indications as to what represents hail and what represents wind and all the other incidents of the thunderstorm. Some of these are fairly obvious, and none of them can affect the musical value of the piece. The storm moves in grand steps to its climax. This is marked by the entry of the trombones (only two of them instead of the normal group of three), and it would be best appreciated, both in its realism and in its ideal grandeur, by the listener who notices that the trombones fall into a slow articulate fragment of melody. Then the storm dies away, until with the last distant mutterings of the thunder the oboes give a long slow fragment of bright sustained melody on the dominant of F. This has been aptly compared with a rainbow. Sir George Grove has noted that in Beethoven's sketches this rainbow was itself derived by gradual transformation of the quaver figure of the raindrops with which the storm begins. The real moral of this is that Beethoven found it easy thus to arrive at this passage in a sketch, but did not imagine, as so many theorists nowadays would teach, that any such process constitutes 'logical development' when it comes to getting the real composition into shape.

And so we come to the 'Thanksgiving after the Storm'. It begins on the dominant with a kind of yodel on a pastoral pipe, which settles down into the following peaceful rondo theme:

Ex. 11.

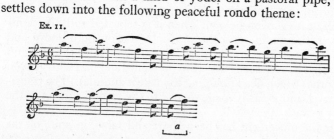

In accordance with the expression of utter leisure which dominates this symphony, the theme is given three times, the second time an octave lower, and the third time another octave lower on the full orchestra, the trumpets and trombones joining in with solemn glow. From the last two notes of this theme arises an important transition theme—

Ex. 12.

which leads to a short second subject of much the same type as that in the first movement. Like most of Beethoven's rondo second subjects, this comes to no definite end, but makes a point of leading back as quickly as possible to the rondo theme, drifting back through its yodelling introduction. The rondo theme with new details of scoring seems as if it was again going to be given more than once, but the repetition drifts towards the subdominant and leads to a middle episode, where a new theme comes with all the manner of being about to settle down to a broad cantabile.

Ex. 13.

But its very enthusiasm is too much for its strength. It modulates ruminatingly to the comparatively distant key of D flat, where it cannot resist the temptation of slipping back to C major as dominant of F, and anticipating a return to the rondo theme. A new semiquaver counterpoint here requires quotation.

Ex. 14.

This passage soon leads back to the tonic, and again the yodelling above the new semiquaver figure leads into the main theme. This is now given in a brilliant variation, a semiquaver version on the top, a pizzicato version below. Then it is repeated with the semiquavers in the middle and the pizzicato version both above and below at different parts of the bar. Then for the third time the full orchestra has it, with semiquavers in the 'cellos and pizzicato version in the horns (which need doubling to make it audible). The transition follows, and is easily made to lead to the second subject in the tonic.

So far the movement has been short and terse, in spite of the spacious effect of those repetitions of its main theme. But now comes one of Beethoven's broadest codas. In this the theme is worked out first in a somewhat round-like scheme with new counterpoints, leading to a grand solemn tutti, glorious as the fields refreshed by the rain. Suddenly this subsides into the passage which led to the round-like development of the main theme. Again we have this round-like development, but this time in the semiquaver variation; and now the tutti rises to a solemn height and descends slowly to a not less solemn but very quiet song of thanksgiving on the figure of the main theme. At last the movement is dying away on the continuation shown in Ex. 14, with the yodel figure on a muted horn, an effect employed nowhere else by Beethoven. This is abruptly cut short by the final chords.

VIII. SEVENTH SYMPHONY IN A MAJOR, OP. 92

1 *Poco sostenuto, leading to* 2 *Vivace.* 3 *Allegretto.* 4 *Presto.*
5 *Allegro con brio.*

Beethoven's Seventh and Eighth Symphonies, written in 1812, were, like his Fifth and Sixth some four years earlier, produced almost as twins. He was vaguely meditating a third companion of which he knew this much, that it was to be in D minor. After some ten years the Ninth Symphony did take shape in that key.

The Seventh Symphony has been called the romantic symphony; rightly in so far as romance is a term which, like humour, every self-respecting person claims to understand, while no two people understand it in the same way. There is no 'programme' to the Seventh Symphony, and no reason why we should not call it heroic (which is one aspect of romance) except that Beethoven himself has bespoken that title elsewhere. The symphony is so overwhelmingly convincing and so obviously untranslatable, that it has for many generations been treated quite reasonably as a piece of music, instead of as an excuse for discussing the French Revolution. Berlioz, it is true, talked sad nonsense about the vivace being a *Ronde des paysans*. But that was a long time ago; and though, as W. E. Henley pointed out, Berlioz is very good reading, we need not go to him for information about anything but his own state of mind as he would like us to conceive it. Nobody now sees anything 'rustic' in the main theme of the vivace, and though it would be quite easy and even profitable to devote a voluminous analysis to the subtleties and profundities of this one of Beethoven's greatest works, there is no popular heresy or pitfall for the listeners of to-day. Probably of all Beethoven's works the Fifth and Seventh symphonies are at present the best understood both in detail and as wholes. This does not make either of them the less exacting for orchestras and conductors; the scoring is exceedingly full of pitfalls, though the deaf composer's imagination never fails in the essentials of his miraculous inventions.

The introduction is in itself a movement of considerable development, containing two fully-formed themes. The first I quote in combination with its sequel and accessory, the scale figure here given in small notes.

Ex. 1.

The second alternates with it twice, in a pair of remote keys (C and

F). Here again I give with it in small notes the accessory rhythmic figure which eventually leads, in one of Beethoven's most famous (and, when it was new, most notorious) passages, to the vivace.

Ex. 2.

That famous passage gives rise to the dactylic rhythmic figure which pervades almost every bar of the vivace, much as the four taps of 'Destiny at the door' pervade the first movement of the Fifth Symphony.

Ex. 3.

The letters by which I mark the figures of the first subject may help any one curious in such matters to trace the many and various derived themes to their origin. But it must not be forgotten that the individual character of a derived theme is a fact of perhaps greater importance than its derivation, interesting and natural though that may be. Indeed, it is possible to hear too much about the way in which a whole work is based 'on the one idea embodied in its first four notes'; and some day an analyst may arise who will administer a drastic cure by persuading people to swallow the soul-stirring doctrine that every piece of music whatever is based on the one idea embodied in a figure of one single note.

The beginning of the second subject, like that in the Eroica Symphony, has often eluded the commentators, in spite of its containing one of the most important figures (d) in the movement. The only difficulty in finding it comes from the habit of searching for something that looks different on paper, instead of listening for the point at which harmony and phrasing settle firmly in the new key.

Ex. 4.

Most of the development is derived, often very surprisingly, from the figures of the first theme. One of its most original features is the kind of round with which it opens. I cannot resist the temptation of quoting the passage compendiously in the notation in which rounds and catches are usually written.

Ex. 5.

Soon afterwards the figure (*d*) from the second subject (Ex. 4) plays a considerable part. It also reappears in the final climax of the coda, after the mighty *crescendo* which arose from that grand sustained note which frightened young Weber into declaring that Beethoven was 'ripe for the madhouse'.

At its first performance the slow movement was an instant success, and was encored, a thing which slow movements very rarely experience. Its popularity grew at the expense not only of the rest of this symphony, but of other works; and concert-directors used at one time to insert it into the Eighth Symphony to make that brightest of comedies 'go down'!

A fairly good clue to the tempo of this most impressive and solemn of allegrettos is given by the fact that Beethoven afterwards thought he ought to have called it andante. This sometimes leads, like all corrections, to the opposite extreme; one must always hold the two facts of the published thought and the afterthought together. Beethoven could never have called it allegretto if he had not thought it a little too fast for an ordinary andante. Neither quotations nor descriptions seem necessary here.

For the scherzo I quote the principal theme, not as it occurs at the fiery outset, but as it slips in quietly half-way through the second part. I do this partly for the sake of the new counter-theme in the bassoons, which grows enormously; and partly to display the inversion of rhythm which makes this scherzo one of Beethoven's most incalculable movements. The subsequent crescendo seems a bar short, but really brings the theme back into step.

The trio will always remain as marvellous as ever, though we may not be able to remember a time when we did not know it by heart.

The finale is and remains unapproached in music as a triumph of Bacchic fury. I can attempt nothing here by way of description; and my quotations can do no more than show the first part of the first theme, with the figures duly lettered for those who will promise not to be too curious about their development—

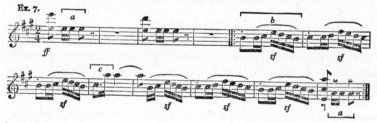

its second part, for the sake of an important figure (d) in the bass, which in the development is fiercely brandished on the surface—

the transition theme (e), which is rather difficult to catch at first, as the scoring is not favourable to it, but which is destined to make an immense climax in the coda—

Ex. 9.

and the beginning of the second subject, in an unusual key soon afterwards varied with romantic modulations in an exciting crescendo.

Ex. 10.

One of the profoundest characteristics in this symphony is the fact that when the time comes for recapitulating these romantic modulations, while the general framework of the passage remains unchanged, the modulations are quite different. Schubert alone of Beethoven's younger contemporaries understood what this means to the life of the classical forms. Brahms understood it also, and thus was able to make those forms live after nearly half a century of pseudo-classicism had driven most of the active-minded musicians into revolt. These points may be called technicalities; and they are, no doubt, symptoms rather than causes. But they have their meaning after the music is finished and the memory tries to recapture some of its vibrations.

IX. EIGHTH SYMPHONY IN F MAJOR, OP. 93

1 *Allegro con brio*. 2 *Allegretto*. 3 *Tempo di menuetto*. 4 *Allegro*.

When an artist is great enough to produce a number of works widely differing in character, there is nothing he enjoys so much as the strongest possible contrasts between two successive works. And nothing is more likely to annoy his contemporaries. When the hero of Mr. Arnold Bennett's *Great Adventure* burst on an astonished Royal Academy with a huge picture of a policeman, he ought, by all the etiquette of pictorial boom, to have painted policemen for the rest of his life. But he never painted a policeman again.

Beethoven's Seventh Symphony was too big for its time. But its slow movement was an instant and sensational success. To the indignation of the critics and the public the Eighth Symphony turned out too small. They had pestered Beethoven all his life with exhortations to learn from Mozart and Haydn, those unapproachable masters of true beauty and proportion. And now he was incapable of imitating Haydn and Mozart; but he was also no longer to be bound by any sense of the mere novelty or range of an idea or form apart from its intrinsic character. And so he produced in the allegretto of his Eighth Symphony a movement which would have earned from both Mozart and Haydn the hearty wish that they had written it themselves, so full is it of all that made them feel happy, and so free from anything that could disturb their artistic habits. And then the public did not like it! A demand grew up for performances of this rather trivial Eighth Symphony with the wonderful allegretto of the Seventh, released from its monstrous surroundings, and put where it could redeem an otherwise unworthy work from oblivion. This raises the question, what on earth Beethoven's contemporaries could after all have seen in their favourite allegretto of the Seventh Symphony; a question perhaps to be answered by the dismal person who at that time made a pot of money by turning it into a male-voice part-song entitled *Chorus of Monks*.

Beethoven took the matter with grim good-nature; and when told that the Eighth Symphony was less of a success than the Seventh, said, 'That's because it's so much better'. This is neither a matter-of-fact judgement nor wholly ironical; what it expresses is the unique sense of power which fires a man when he finds himself fit for a delicate task just after he has triumphed in a colossal one. In the finale of the Eighth Symphony this sense of power causes the work to stretch itself, with a glorious effect not unlike that which must have been produced by Lablache, when the sightseer knocked at his door instead of at General Tom Thumb's. Lablache's magnificent voice was all the grander for the colossal figure from which its tones proceeded; he was nearer seven than six foot high. But he answered to the name of the General, and drawing himself up majestically, explained, 'Voyons donc, monsieur! quand je suis chez moi je me mets à mon aise!'

The first movement, though by no means a dwarf, begins with a pocket-size theme. The first three phrases, with their opening in forte, their answer in piano, and their chorus-like forte confirmation of that answer, at once mark out the scale to be small and the action lively.

Ex. 1.

But the next theme promptly shows that, like Haydn, Beethoven does not depend on the mere scale of his work to give a sense of boundless freedom. The sky is always on the same scale, whatever the size of your garden.

Ex. 2.

The leisurely giant strides of this theme bring about the most
singular of all Beethoven's transitions to a second subject. There is
a pause after four insistent staccato chords on a harmony which,
though simple enough in itself, is of curiously doubtful import
here. I cannot recall any other passage in classical or modern music
in which, if the composer had abandoned his work at that point,
it would be so impossible to guess how to continue it.

The dubious harmony had indicated a sombre unrelated key on
the wrong side of the subdominant, as far as it indicated anything.
It now resolves, with a chuckle, into one of the brightest keys that
can be brought into relation with the tonic at all; and in this key the
second subject begins with an exquisitely graceful tune, which I do
not quote. A cloud comes over it at its sixth bar; and it finishes its
first sentence by explaining that it didn't mean to turn up in such
a gaudy key, and will, if you will kindly overlook that indiscretion,
continue in the orthodox dominant. It does so; blushes again over-
come it at the sixth bar; melodramatic mystification ensues; but if
any one has been pretending to be shocked, the incident is closed in
shouts of laughter. From the remaining group of themes I quote an
important pair, first a short fortissimo answered by a long cantabile—

Ex. 3.

of which figures (*d*) and (*e*) are destined to give great power and
breadth to the coda of the whole movement; and secondly the
blustering wind-up which leads, first back to the beginning, and
afterwards on to the development, where, in conjunction with
Ex. 1, it plays a great role.

Ex. 4.

The development storms along through broadly designed modulations in an unbroken course towards a grand climax, over which the
recapitulation sails with the first subject (Ex. 1) in the bass. It is
not easy to make out the tune with all the noontide glare beating
down over it; but Beethoven leaves us with no grievance on that
account, for the wood-wind restate it in the most good-natured
way in the world. Then the basses take it up again, crescendo, and
proceed with Ex. 2, which the violins imitate in an ingenious
variation. Here again the theme eventually rises to the surface; the
ambiguous modulation takes a different turn; and the second
subject, determined not to offend with remote keys again, now
enters in the too humble key of the subdominant. This is easily put
right, and the rest of the recapitulation is quite regular.

The coda, plunging into a soft remote key, begins by holding a
conspirator's discussion of figure (b) of Ex. 1, which soon flares up
into a triumphant insistence on the whole theme. At the first performance of the symphony this climax was immediately followed
by the comic quiet ending; but Beethoven speedily recognized
that, though that is the right ending, his coda was inadequate and
more suggestive of an imitation of Haydn and Mozart than of a
new classic bringing their spirits back to an emancipated world.
With complete success Beethoven inserted the new expansion of
the second phrase of Ex. 3, which gives his peroration its characteristic power and breadth.

For the allegretto I should need at least five quotations if the
listener demanded a correct account of its themes. This statement
of fact sufficiently indicates the concentration and variety that
go to the clear and unaffected presentation of this Marjorie
Fleming of symphonic movements. A man must possess wisdom,
a healing touch, and have been young for a very long time, before
he can describe children of this kind; which shows how much less
the sad distractions of the artists' biography can tell us of him
than almost any one of his works. Beethoven's life was a tragedy,
and he lived in constant and often undignified discomfort; but
the damper musical biographers ought to be shoo'd off the premises
by the allegretto of the Eighth Symphony. Its last bars would do
that very well; but perhaps they more nearly express Marjorie's
mature conclusion that 'the most Devilish thing is Five times
Seven'. (Four times Six and Six times Eight are Beethoven's
propositions.)

This was not the first time that one of Beethoven's slow movements had refused to be slow enough; consequently, as in the
Sonata in E flat, op. 31, no. 3, instead of a lively scherzo we
have a minuet in the old dignified slow tempo. It is a curious
instance of the complete ignorance shown by Beethoven's con-

temporaries concerning the very classics they professed to revere at Beethoven's expense, that till as late as Mendelssohn's last years and Wagner's manhood this minuet was taken like a German waltz, though the trio must have been a mere scramble at any such pace. Wagner accuses Mendelssohn of acquiescing in this tradition; but it is clear from his own account of what Mendelssohn said to him, that Mendelssohn was good-naturedly trying to keep two tiresome people's tempers for them; a routined conductor's, whom he had done his best to persuade, and Wagner's, who was waving his red flag and would recognize no improvement short of the mark.

I quote the theme of the minuet in order to call attention to the extremely close work developed from the short figures (*a*), (*b*), and (*c*), into which the flowing melody divides itself. No fugue of Bach is more complex than the treatment of these figures in what sounds like a smooth and old-world flow of gallant tune.

Ex. 5.

The trio I quote for the sake of an interesting point in which it is not difficult to carry out Beethoven's final intentions.

Ex. 6.

On the stave I give the rhythm of the third bar as Beethoven first wrote it, making it rhyme with the others. Below the stave I give the alteration which is now in the score. Beethoven regretted it, and called it 'that tiresome little witticism' (*das kleine pikante Zuviel*). So he wished to restore the original reading, which is difficult for us now to view as he did. Still, we would gladly obey him: but the brilliant violoncello accompaniment fits only the second reading; and so it must be altered, if it is not to make a bad pair of octaves with the other. Beethoven was no pedant in such matters, but here he would certainly draw the line.

The finale is one of Beethoven's most gigantic creations. Yet its peculiar form results, with perfect artistic fitness, from the fact that it begins by executing a complete sonata form on a scale no larger than that of the first movement. It has a witty rondo-like first subject with a stumbling-block in its last note.

Then follows a leisurely transition-theme. Elephants, says Kipling, move from place to place at various rates of speed; if you want an elephant to overtake an express train you cannot hurry him—but he will overtake the train.

This, as the quotation shows, leads to a serenely melodious second subject beginning in the dark remote key of A flat, but soon brightening, with a slow smile, into the orthodox dominant, with another theme to follow and lead to a climax. Then there is a rondo-like return to the first subject, swimming out at the eighth bar (see Ex. 7) into a short but vigorous development, based on figure (c) of the theme. This development, having reached a key that has not the remotest suggestion of tonic about it, effects the funniest return in all music, parent of all the bassoon jokes in the Sullivan operas, and poetic with the mystery of the drums.

Ex. 9.

Upon which the recapitulation sails in and follows a perfectly regular course (the A flat of the second subject now becoming D flat, and so leading to the tonic) until the point is reached where the first theme returned. This point is now the subdominant; and there is some hesitation, whereat the basses, with figure (*b*), show annoyance. What is to be done about it?

With all its originality and wealth, there has so far been no puzzling or abnormal feature in the movement, with one glaring exception. What on earth did that irrelevant roaring C sharp mean at the end of Ex. 7? Thereby hangs a tail, videlicet, a coda that is nearly as long as the whole body of the movement. My pun is not more violent than Beethoven's harmonic or enharmonic jokes on this point. The coda begins quietly on an obviously huge scale, with a new figure (unquoted) stealthily stalking in minims beneath figure (*a*), and rising in a slow crescendo to a climax, upon which the idea of Ex. 9 brings back the main theme. This reaches that C sharp; and now it suddenly appears that Beethoven has held that note in reserve, wherewith to batter at the door of some immensely distant key. Out bursts the theme, then, in F sharp minor. Can we ever find a way home again? Well, E sharp (or F natural) is the leading note of this new key, and upon E sharp the trumpets pounce, and hammer away at it until they have thoroughly convinced the orchestra that they mean it for the tonic. When this is settled, in sails the radiant second subject again. Now Ganymede is all very well; but the original cup-bearer of the gods is Hephaestus, who is lame, and grimy with his metallurgy in the bowels of the earth. However, he will not be ousted; and so the basses sing the theme too. Straightway unquenchable laughter arises among the blessed gods as they look at him bestirring himself about the house. The laughter has all the vaults of heaven wherein to disperse itself, and to gather again into the last long series of joyous shouts, which, after all its surprises, brings the symphony to its end as punctually as planets complete their orbits.

X. A PRÉCIS OF BEETHOVEN'S NINTH SYMPHONY, OP. 125

Supplementary to the larger Analytical Essay in Vol. II

The following analysis represents, without use of abbreviations and technicalities, the kind of précis-writing which I was taught by Sir Hubert Parry. As any diplomatic official on an interesting frontier knows, it is essential to good précis-writing that events should be narrated as they were known at the time by the persons concerned, and not as they appeared in the light of wider or later knowledge; human ignorance of the future and of the round-the-corner being an essential element in the shaping of the events. This is nowhere more true than in the case of music. Half the musical miseducation in the world comes from people who know that the Ninth Symphony begins on the dominant of D minor, when the fact is that its opening bare fifth may mean anything within D major, D minor, A major, A minor, E major, E minor, C sharp minor, G major, C major, and F major, until the bass descends to D and settles most (but not all) of the question. A true analysis takes the standpoint of a listener who knows nothing beforehand, but hears and remembers everything.

Whether this précis prove more, or less, unreadable than frontier official documents, a glance at it will show several useful points. For instance, it will make it evident that a full account of any exposition section enormously simplifies the task of analysing developments. The result almost seems as if the analysis grew more perfunctory as it continued. This is not so; though in the finale I have not thought fit to give that detailed phrase-analysis of the fugues and of the final prestissimo that I should require in a class-room. But on the whole the account of the whole choral finale is as complete as that of the first movement. You will find the same appearance of growing simplicity in the analysis of a Wagner opera or of a pure drama.

FIRST MOVEMENT

Allegro ma non troppo, un poco maestoso

Bars

1–16   Bare 5th on A sustained through 14 bars, and deepening to 5th on D at bars 15–16. Rhythmic fragments descend through it in gradually accelerating rhythm, foreshadowing and culminating in—

17–35   Main theme, beginning with figures (*a*) and (*b*) (the first two notes of (*a*) were the substance of the opening);

Ex. 1.

continued in long paragraph with several other figures; closing into tonic (with characteristic late-Beethoven overlapping of tonic chord upon dominant bass).

35–50   Counter-statement of bars 1–16 on tonic bare 5th, changing at 14th bar to B flat, and so leading to

Bars	
51–63	Counter-statement of main theme, Ex. 1 in B flat for 4 bars, upon which figure (*b*) is developed in rising sequence and tapering rhythm for 8 more bars, leading to new theme.

Ex. 2.

TRANSITION

| 64–73 | This, repeated in canon, leads in 3 extra bars to the dominant of B flat, where 6 bars of a new dialogue-theme by way of |
| 74–79 | dominant preparation— |

Ex. 3.

lead to the

SECOND GROUP (or 'Second Subject'), B flat major. Four-bar melody in dialogue—

Ex. 4.

| 80–92 | repeated with variation and continued in a paragraph ending with new figure— |

Ex. 5. *cres.*

| 92–101 | which is developed for 6 more bars, leading to another theme— |

Ex. 6.

| 102–119 | which modulates to the flat supertonic (C flat = B natural), from which it returns in a pianissimo rising sequence leading to |
| 120–137 | 12 bars of tonic and dominant dialogue in tapering rhythm, crescendo, with rhythm of Ex. 6 in drums. Further energetic |

Bars 138–149	rising sequences lead to a 12-bar paragraph of dialogue beginning thus—

150–158	and closing into a final outburst, in the main rhythm of Ex. 6, on the tonic chord for 8 bars.

DEVELOPMENT

158–161	Two more bars collapse from B flat to A, and so to the opening bare 5th on A.
162–179	Introduction resumed and extended without compressing the rhythm; moving to dominant of G minor, always pianissimo.
180–187	Ex. 1 (*a*), treated in dialogue (*pp*), for 8 bars.
188–191	Outburst of Ex. 8 on dominant chord leads, in 4 bars, to the
192–197	following treatment of (*b*)—

198–217	The process of these 28 bars is repeated, leading in 2 more
218–252	bars to a free triple fugue with (*b*) as its main subject. Starting in C minor, it proceeds for 34 bars through G minor and B flat, and thence drifts towards A minor, where
253–274	it subsides into cantabile dialogue on its first figure, piano.
275–296	After 22 bars of this quiet passage Ex. 4 appears, and, passing through F major, leads again to the cantabile dialogue in that key. Suddenly the dominant of D minor is suggested,
297–300	and in 4 more bars the development is violently ended with a plunge on to the D major 6th.

Bars	
301–314	The introduction is transformed to a fortissimo on a D major chord with the F sharp in the bass. This turns to the
315–338	minor in the 12th bar, and so to B flat: thence to Ex. 1, which, with its sequels, is expanded, each item being echoed by the wind in dialogue with the strings; all on a tonic pedal in the drums.
339–344	Suddenly Ex. 3 appears quietly in D major.

SECOND GROUP

345–426	Ex. 4 begins in D major, but 2 bars (351–352) added to its continuation transform the whole sequel into the minor mode, into which everything is accordingly translated. (See Ex. 4 to Ex. 8).

CODA

427–452	Following immediately upon Ex. 8, the coda begins with a quiet dialogue on Ex. 1. In a slow crescendo this culmi-
453–462	nates, after 25 bars, in 10 bars of Ex. 5, which lead to 6 bars
463–468	in the rhythm of Ex. 6.
469–494	Suddenly, through a sustained dominant 5 octaves deep, figure (b) is treated in D major for 8 bars by the horns and wood-wind; and then taken up in the minor (4 octaves deep) by the strings in the style of the fugato in the development (bars 218 foll.). This, with a crescendo and diminuendo, leads in 25 bars again to Ex. 5, which after 10 bars ends
495–512	with the close of Ex. 9, twice (making 8 bars). This closes
513–538	into the final tonic-and-dominant peroration, which is on a new theme, punctuated by rhythm (a) in trumpets and drums.

Ex. 10.

513

539–547	closing, after 26 bars, into Ex. 1 expanded into an 8-bar phrase ending with figure (b).

SCHERZO. (A) The Scherzo Proper.

FIRST SUBJECT

1–8	First figure (a) of main theme dispersed, through 8 bars, down the chord of D minor—

Ex. 11.

(a)

Bars   exposition of 5-part fugue on main theme—
9-32   Ex. 12.

33-56   continuation leading with a crescendo to
57-76   tutti restatement of theme modulating to dominant of C
                major (the flat 7th).
77-92   Passage of dominant preparation (8 bars, repeated).

SECOND SUBJECT. C major
93-108   8-bar theme (4+4) repeated with variation—

Ex. 13.

109-126   and followed by shorter phrases (on (a)+(b)) including one
                in 6-bar rhythm (2+4)—

Ex. 14.

127-142   an echo of the last 4 bars of which leads to a cadence-theme—

Ex. 15.

                the sequel of which closes into a passage of 8 bars (the
143-150   last three silent) in which chords of (a) descend in 3rds from
                C to D minor.
                Exposition repeated from Ex. 12 onwards.

DEVELOPMENT
151-174   Descent in 3rds continues, at first with the 3-bar pause,
                then steadily for fifteen steps round a wide circle of keys
                landing on A which is screwed up through A sharp to B
                natural, where there is a pause.
177-194   In 3-bar rhythm (a)+(b) is treated in dialogue between

Bars	
	bassoons and oboes; first for 9 bars in E minor, then for 9 in A minor.
195–233	The drums, in F, suddenly force the music into F major, where it develops, passing into D minor (the tonic). The 3-bar rhythm is retained steadily for 48 bars from the entry of the drums; when suddenly the music drops back into 4-bar rhythm as shown here—

Ex. 16.

234–240	(Figure (a) is present in every bar now till the recapitulation begins.) Quiet preparation ensues on the unexpected dominant of E flat (the flat supertonic) reached in 2 bars
241–271	through C minor, and held for 18 bars; then resolved into D minor, the chord of which is built up on figure (a) by drums and brass.

RECAPITULATION

FIRST SUBJECT

272–295	First theme (Ex. 12) tutti, with its second 4-bar phrase insisted on, passes from D minor through G minor to B flat where the passage of dominant preparation (bars 77–84)
296–329	appears. A pause of two extra bars on B flat brings it on to the dominant of D where it is repeated and expanded with a third repetition and new harmonies, leading to—

SECOND SUBJECT

330–387 (399)	This, mostly changed to the minor mode, is recapitulated in full, right down to the descending 3rds, which are here so placed as to lead, in the first instance, back to the beginning of the development. [This repeat is never observed in performance, and Beethoven at first erased it in the autograph. But he afterwards changed his mind and wrote over it 'bleibt Alles' or *stet*.]
388–413	In the second instance, it leads to a coda based on a new

Bars   imitative treatment of (a) (b) which, quickening in pace,
              arrives at a presto in duple time, thus—

Ex. 17.

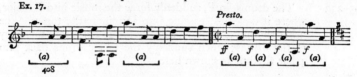

TRIO. D major, *Alla breve*

First strain—

414–421   Self-repeating melody in double counterpoint [note dis-
              tinctions drawn by the bass at the asterisks]—

Ex. 18.

Second and other strains—

421–436   New 8-bar melody, repeated with fresh counterpoint, and
437–452   closing into Ex. 18 with bass put into treble (i.e. inverted in
              double counterpoint)—without the distinctions marked by
              asterisks. This, given twice (or four times), with the counter-
              point in lower octaves, leads to a further development on the
453–473   dominant; the theme and its counterpoint leaving their
              primitive lines and rising in a crescendo, which suddenly
              subsiding and passing through F major (on a rising bass)
              leads back to Ex. 18 on the nearly full orchestra. This is
474–490   brought (in 16 bars) to a tonic close; and the second strain
              (with its sequels) is repeated.

490–529   A coda ensues, on the tonic, working up Ex. 18 by the full
              orchestra in a 16-bar crescendo, closing into its repetition
              (inverted in double counterpoint). Eight more bars of plagal
              cadence lead, with a diminuendo and a G minor chord at the
              last moment, to the da capo of the scherzo. This extends to
              the lead into the trio, and to 7 bars of the trio itself fully
              scored, broken off, and concluded with the last bars of
              Ex. 17.

ADAGIO.   Theme with Alternative and Variations.

FIRST THEME. B flat major

1–24   Two bars of introduction lead to a theme containing three
              phrases, punctuated by echoes and expanded by repetitions
              in the following way.

Ex. 19.

change of key

ALTERNATIVE THEME. D major

The foreign chord at the end leads to a second theme in D
major, the major mediant, and in another measure—

Ex. 20.

Bars	It is 8 bars long and is repeated with a counterpoint (given
25-42	in small notes in the quotation). Its last bar is then repeated
	with a turn back to B flat.

FIRST VARIATION

43-64   The violins vary the melody of Ex. 19; the winds preserve
the echoes and the last 6 bars unvaried. The foreign chord

Bars   now leads to G, the major submediant, where Ex. 20 re-
65–82   appears with fresh scoring. Its close now leads to E flat, in
            which key, the subdominant, there is an—

INTERLUDE

83–98   This interlude takes the first 2 bars of Ex. 19 as if to begin
            a variation or plain repetition of them, but drifts in dialogue
            into C flat (the flat supertonic) and, meditating there for
            a while, suddenly resolves into B flat and so into the second
            variation.

SECOND VARIATION

99–120   The violins, in 12/8 time, vary the melody, while the
            wood-wind give it unvaried, and reveal the unvaried echoes.
            When the last bar is reached, the foreign chord does not
            appear—

CODA

121–124   but the coda begins with an emphatic assertion of the sub-
            dominant, followed by imitations on the first 2 notes (a) of
            the theme.

Ex. 21.

125–130   This leads to a beginning of a new free variation of the
            first strain passing into the bass thus—

Ex. 22.

131–137   and leading again to the subdominant and to Ex. 21, the
            latter part of which is plunged into D flat (the flat mediant,

Bars   the dark key thus balancing the bright keys of the alternative
       theme)—with the following augmentation.

Ex. 23.

138–141   The first part of Ex. 22 returns and is continued, in
          echoing dialogue, with a new figure—

Ex. 24.
Cantabile.

142–158   leading to a similar cumulative development of strain II of
          Ex. 19, which leads, in another 16 bars, to the end.

FINALE

INTRODUCTION. *Presto* 3/4

1–29   Seven (8 including pause) bars of confused agitation in
        D minor lead to 8 bars of indignant recitative in the basses.
        The agitation, resumed on dominant of G minor, is again,
        after 8 bars, interrupted by the basses, who in 6 more bars
30–37   call up the ghost of the first movement, of which the first
        (introductory) 8 bars appear—with C sharp in bass.
38–47   The basses protest again, and lead in 10 bars to A minor,
48–55   where the ghost of the scherzo (8 bars on the fugato theme)
56–62   appears. Still more indignantly the basses reject this, lead-
63–64   ing in 7 bars to B flat. Two bars of the adagio (Ex. 19)
        greatly soften the anger of the basses, who modulate to a
65–76   distant key, but in the course of 11 bars break into despair.
        From their half-close in C sharp minor a modulation reaches
77–91   A as dominant of D major, where a new theme appears
        which they receive with acclamation.

Ex. 25.

INSTRUMENTAL EXPOSITION. *Allegro assai*

Bars 1–24   The theme.

Ex. 26.

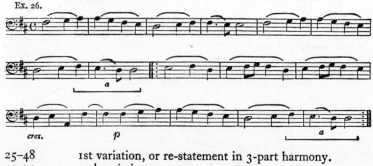

25–48   1st variation, or re-statement in 3-part harmony.
49–72   2nd variation, or 4-part statement.
73–96   3rd variation, or full orchestral statement.
97–111   From the last notes of this arises a codetta—

Ex. 27.

the last bar of which, instead of taking the shape here given,
leads through seven bars of rising sequence ending in A
major, the dominant; where a new figure—

Ex. 28.

poco ritenente.   *poco Adagio.*

112–116   asks a plaintive question with a vastly remote modulation,
which is cheerfully brushed aside in two more bars of A
major.

CHORAL EXPOSITION AND FINALE

1–9   But the chaotic storm of the introduction bursts out again.
        This time a human voice answers with the beginning and
10–29   end of the double-bass recitative—

(Literal translation.) Oh friends, not these sounds;
rather, let us attune our voices more acceptably and more
joyfully.

THE VOCAL VARIATIONS

1–4   Baritone solo and chorus basses having joined in the
5–28   introductory bars of Ex. 25, the first vocal statement (or

Bars   4th variation) is sung by the baritone to the following words
(Lady Macfarren's translation, revised version),[1] the chorus
(without sopranos) repeating the second strain—

Stanza I. Praise to Joy, the god-descended
Daughter of Elysium,
Ray of mirth and rapture blended,
Goddess, to thy shrine we come.
By thy magic is united
What stern[2] Custom parted wide:
All mankind are brothers plighted
Where thy gentle wings abide.

29–32   The orchestra gives the codetta as in Ex. 27, but in the
bass.

FIFTH VARIATION

Solo quartet; the second strain repeated by full chorus—

33–56 Stanza II. Ye to whom the boon is measur'd,
Friend to be of faithful friend,
Who a wife has won and treasur'd,
To our strain your voices lend.
Yea, if any hold in keeping
Only one heart all his own,
Let him join us,[3] or else weeping,
Steal from out our midst, unknown.

57–60   The orchestra gives the codetta as in Ex. 27.

SIXTH VARIATION

61–84   Solo quartet in florid ornamentation, the second strain
repeated by full chorus—

Stanza III. Draughts of joy, from cup o'erflowing
Bounteous Nature freely gives,
Grace to just and unjust showing,
Blessing ev'rything that lives.
Wine she gave to us and kisses,
Loyal friend on life's steep road;
E'en the worm can feel life's blisses,
And the Seraph dwells with God.

85–94   The codetta, given in due course by the wood-wind, is
accompanied by massive choral chords, repeating the words
'and the Seraph dwells with God'. In 7 extra bars the
music, passing on to A, plunges on to the dominant of B
flat (as events prove), and pauses there.

[1] Lady Macfarren's translation is published in revised version here by
permission of Novello & Co.
[2] Reading 'Was die Mode streng getheilt', as in the printed versions.
Beethoven's autograph reads, more Beethovenishly, *frech* getheilt', 'im-
pudently parted'.
[3] Should be 'He who cannot, let him weeping', &c.; i.e. if there be any
that could never make friends.

VARIATION 7 (*a*) and (*b*). *Alla Marcia, allegro assai*
Bars   *vivace*, B flat major (flat submediant) 6/8.

(1–12)   After 12 bars of rhythmic fragments building up the chord
13–44   of B flat (without the 5th) and arriving at a march-rhythm,
            the 7th variation treats the theme in a syncopated form.
            The second strain is not given twice, but the whole variation
            is restated with a tenor solo in stammering counterpoint to
            the following words—

45–92 Stanza IV.   Glad as suns His will sent plying
                   Through the vast abyss of space,
                   Brothers, run your joyous race,
                   Hero-like to conquest flying.

            (Here Beethoven has reversed the order of the third and
            fourth lines, in order to get a climax on 'Siegen'.)

            Now the second strain is repeated, the male-voice chorus
93–100   joining in and singing throughout the codetta, which follows
            in due course.

INTERLUDE

101–187   The orchestra breaks into a double fugue, in which a quaver
            derivative of the main theme is combined with another
            theme in the syncopated rhythm of the march, thus—

EX. 29.   (2)

            Six entries of this, with varying spaces between, and closer
            developments of the individual figures, pass through F,
            C minor, G minor, E flat, B flat minor, and G flat to B minor
            (= C flat), in which region there ensues much dominant
            preparation, until finally the fugue is abandoned and only
187–212   the syncopated rhythm is left, on F sharp, with a diminuendo
            back to D major, as follows—

EX. 30.

            (Note the fall of the bass from B to A.)

VARIATION 8

213–260   The chorus bursts out with Stanza I, with a running accom-
            paniment in the strings. As usual, it repeats the second

Bars

261–264   strain. Four bars of the codetta are given, and it is cut
short on the subdominant, with a silent pause.

NEW THEME. *Andante maestoso.* G major (subdominant), 3/2

Ex. 31.

O   ye   mil - lions   I . . .   em - brace   ye!

Here's   a   joy - ful   kiss   for   all!

Stanza V.

1–16   This theme, marked by the first entry of trombones since
the scherzo, is given out by the choral basses in unison, and
repeated in harmony by the full chorus.

17–32   The next lines—

> Brothers, o'er yon starry sphere
> Sure there dwells a loving Father

do not reveal their key (beyond the fact that it is south of
the subdominant) when given in unison by the basses; but
the full chorus harmonizes them boldly in F major. Having
thus obliterated the key of G major, they proceed in a kind
of Dorian mode to utter words of which I give a literal

33–52   translation, as the singing versions miss the point—

(*Adagio ma non troppo*). Ye fall prostrate, ye millions?
World, dost thou feel the Creator present? Seek Him beyond
the firmament of stars. Above the stars He surely dwells.

53–60   The climax on a chord of E flat is echoed on the dominant
of D.

DOUBLE FUGUE

The two themes (Ex. 26 and Ex. 31) are combined as

1–65   follows, each to their original text—

Ex. 32.

Bars
66–75
Five entries and several shorter developments of this 8-bar combination suffice to carry this fugue to its final climax where the sopranos hold a high A for 10 bars above the combination in the lower voices.

76–108
Then all themes vanish: there is an awestruck hush at the thought of falling prostrate; from which the thought of the loving Father beyond the stars brings calm, as the music passes in simple chords through the dominant to the sub-dominant, where there is a pause.

CODA. *Allegro ma non tanto.* Alla breve

1–20
The strings, with a diminution of the main figure of the Joy-theme, introduce a childlike new strain for the solo voices, which leads in 20 bars to the following free round, in
21–43
which the chorus gradually joins, to the words—

'By thy magic,' &c.

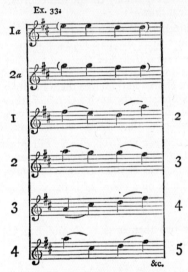

This culminates in the following outburst on—

'All mankind are brothers plighted.'

Bars
51–57
68–81

The expected Mozartean close is evaded and the round resumed. When it again reaches Ex. 34, the solo voices suddenly divert the poco adagio into B major (the major submediant), in which bright key they expand in a cadenza and finally vanish; the return to D being made by the drop in the bass that was already significant in Ex. 30.

Ex. 35.   *Poco allegro, stringendo.*

That drop from B to A is now taken up by the orchestra in 8 bars (*poco allegro, stringendo il tempo*) leading to the final stretto.

FINAL STRETTO. *Prestissimo*

Beginning with a diminution of Ex. 31, the chorus concludes with lines from the three main ideas of Schiller's poem—

'O ye millions I embrace ye!' 'Brothers, o'er yon starry sphere Sure there dwells a loving Father'—

and lastly—

'Praise to Joy, the God-descended.'

At the height of the climax the words

'Daughter of Elysium'

inspire the chorus to fall into a slow *maestoso* time in which they conclude—

Ex. 36.

leaving the orchestra to finish in due proportion with the diminished first figure in 20 bars of prestissimo, the very last five of which contain a new idea.

BRAHMS

XI. SYMPHONY, IN C MINOR, NO. 1, OP. 68

1 *Un poco sostenuto, leading to* 2 *Allegro.* 3 *Andante sostenuto.*
4 *Un poco Allegretto e grazioso.* 5 FINALE: *Adagio—Più
Andante.* 6 *Allegro non troppo, ma con brio.*

(These notes were written for the London concerts of the Meiningen
Orchestra, 1902.)

Though this is Brahms's first symphony, it is by no means his first
published orchestral work in symphonic form. His two early
Serenades, opp. 11 and 16, are, like the great orchestral serenades
of Mozart, symphonies in every sense of the word, differing from
those known by the more dignified name not so much in form and
length as in style. There is an exuberance of simple pleasure in
all representative works of the serenade type, that finds expression
in a larger number of movements than is usual in a symphony; so
that Brahms may be said to have had, so far as technical experience
goes, more than two symphonies behind him by the time that he
attacked that which is known as his first. We should also add the
great D minor Pianoforte Concerto, op. 15, bearing in mind that
the artistic problems of the concerto form are even more difficult
to solve in a truly classical spirit than those of the symphony.
When we finish the list with the extremely brilliant and highly
organized Variations on a theme of Haydn, op. 56 a, and take into
account the orchestral element in those wonderful choral works—
the *Deutsches Requiem*, the *Triumphlied*, *Rinaldo*, and the *Schick-
salslied*—we shall come to the conclusion that there is at least
as much experience of orchestral writing behind Brahms's first
symphony as there was behind Beethoven's third.

At the same time there is no doubt that Brahms moved with all
Beethoven's caution in the matter. He kept the first three movements by him for ten years before attacking the finale; and there
were probably many alterations meanwhile. Frau Schumann's
letters and diary show, for instance, that the first movement
originally had no introduction; so that its first phrase (Ex. 4) was
the most abruptly dramatic opening ever attempted. It may well
have taken ten years of a great man's experience to work out the
grand transition from the immense tragedy of the first movement
and the deep pathos of the andante, to the triumph of the finale.
That triumph, nevertheless, was inevitable, for in the first movement the tragedy was already completed and done with; and the
rest of the work is concerned with those larger issues which make
tragedies beautiful. It is the special privilege of the classical forms
of instrumental music that they can thus bring within the compass
of a single work something more than a tragedy; a work that ends

in triumph, not because the world has been stopped in its course in order to spare our feelings, but because our feelings are carried through and beyond the tragedy to something higher.

Among many striking parallels between Brahms and Beethoven may be mentioned the way in which their greatest orchestral works are grouped in pairs. Just as Beethoven's C minor Symphony appeared at the same time as the *Pastorale*, so Brahms's First and Second Symphonies appeared within a year of each other. Again, Beethoven's Seventh and Eighth Symphonies are a pair; the one 'important', though not tragic, and the other unquestionably comic. The parallel may even be pushed as far as to include the contrast between the works in each pair. Brahms's C minor Symphony is, like Beethoven's in the same key, a powerfully emotional work with an exceptionally dramatic transition to a triumphant finale. And his D major Symphony is, like Beethoven's *Pastorale*, full of happiness and sunshine, in every way sharply contrasted with its predecessor. Here, however, the analogy ends, for while Beethoven's Pastoral Symphony is decidedly of smaller range of feeling and in an intentionally lighter style than its companion, Brahms's D major Symphony is, if anything, on a larger scale than his C minor. It is, measured by the clock, the longest of his four symphonies, and its first movement is one of the few perfectly constructed examples than can be compared in length to that of Beethoven's Eroica.

INTRODUCTION

Brahms's tragedy has a solemn introduction, a very rare thing in his work. There are only two cases, with a possible third, in his earlier works, viz. the finale of the very early Sonata, op. 2, the finale of the Pianoforte Quintet, and possibly the short movement entitled *Rückblick*, in the Sonata, op. 5—though this might more appropriately be considered as just the reverse of an introduction.

The present introduction is a gigantic procession of cloudy figures, destined to take shape as the themes of the first movement.

Ex. 1.

Ex. 2.

Ex. 3.

ALLEGRO

The great clouds drift slowly away as the plaintive wailing of an oboe rises and falls, losing itself among the other instruments; and when the last anticipating chord has died down the allegro begins stormily. Its first four bars consist of figure (*a*) with a pendant (*d*).

Ex. 4.

after which the impassioned principal theme of the movement appears. This consists of a melody derived from Ex. 3, with Ex. 4 as bass, and containing an important new figure (*e*).

Ex. 5.

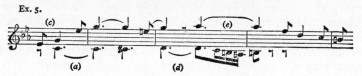

Then Ex. 2 appears in the following form—

Ex. 6.

and is continued stormily with very rich modulations till it settles down in the tonic. The main theme (Ex. 6) is now developed, with figures (*a, d*) in the bass inverted thus—

Ex. 7.

to the accompaniment of a very Beethovenish rhythm

Soon a climax is reached, and the key changes to the dominant of E flat (relative major, the usual key for the second subject in minor movements). Here follows a very beautiful passage of preparation for the second subject; a pathetic diminuendo, beginning angrily with figure (*e*) and softening (while passing quickly through very remote keys) to tones of profound tenderness and pity; till at last the second subject itself enters.

The beginning of this contrasts all the more vividly with the first subject by being constructed from the same figures. Here it is (*a*) that is in the treble, and (*c*) in the bass.

Ex. 8.

The pathetic continuation on the oboe gives rise to a new figure—

Ex. 9.

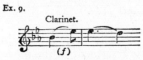

in dialogue with other wind instruments; and (after a lovely transition through C flat) the colouring darkens, and there are ominous gaps in the rhythm and minor harmonies. Then the storm breaks. A new theme in E flat minor bursts out from the broken phrases; its bass is in the inversion of the main theme and its rhythm is closely allied to the rhythmic figure heard before the transition began.

Ex. 10.

This is repeated with change of position, the new theme in the bass and the inverted first theme above; and then a stormy cadence theme, accompanied by figure (*f*) in the horns, brings the first part of the movement to a close. Figure (*c*), inverted as in Ex. 10 and divided between wind and strings, then leads, in the first instance to the usual repeat of the whole exposition from the beginning of the movement, and, after the repeat, to the development, with a plunge into the remote key of B major.

In this key the first theme appears in canon between basses and violins, in a grand fortissimo. This suddenly gives place to a mysterious pianissimo in which the theme is treated in long drawn notes ('augmentation') and divided between bassoon and basses thus—

Ex. 11.

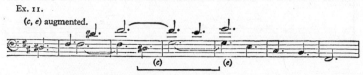

This modulates rapidly and mysteriously, till the dominant of F minor is reached and we hear the ominous broken phrases that led to the storm towards the end of the second subject. Then figure (g) from Ex. 10 appears in conjunction with a new figure that has no traceable connexion with the material of the first part.

Ex. 12.

This new figure, so casually introduced, throws into splendid relief the close thematic treatment of the movement. It is worked out by itself for several steps of a broad modulating sequence that leads to the dominant of C (our principal key) with bold major chords—a masterly example of that power of tragic irony which Brahms has grasped as no other composer since Beethoven. (Observe the grand effect of the deep notes of the contra-fagotto, the double-bass of the wind-band.) The episode, with (a) appearing in the bass, subsides into a long dominant pedal preparing for the return of the first subject. This passage of preparation is probably the longest and most intense that has ever been produced in this part of a first movement: at all events, it is a matter of five closely printed lines of music, breathlessly exciting from the moment of its quiet beginning in the clouds to its end, delayed at the last moment by the entry of the theme in an utterly unexpected and remote key. The whole passage is constructed from figure (a), with the rhythm (g) ♪♪♪ ♪ perpetually echoing between bass and drums.

From the reappearance of the first theme, quickly moving from the unexpected B minor into its right key, the recapitulation is perfectly regular. A single change of harmony brings the long transition passage into the tonic, and the second subject, with its pathetic beginning and its impassioned end, is not altered at all.

The coda grows naturally out of that stormy end, with a diminuendo; and the initial figure (*a*), turned into a song of sorrow by the wind instruments, closes the movement in almost the slow tempo of the introduction, while the drums and basses throb with the rhythm ♫ ♪—and at last figure (*c*) arises in a mighty sigh that tells that the tragedy is finished.

ANDANTE SOSTENUTO

The slow movement is in a very distant key, E major, like the slow movements of Beethoven's C minor Concerto, and Brahms's C minor Pianoforte Quartet. It is as close in its texture as the first movement, but does not need so many separate quotations, since the only themes that recur are all given out in the course of what appears to be a single melody. This melody begins with a beautiful four-bar phrase which one would expect to be continued in equally quiet and regular strains; but, as will be seen, the continuation is impassioned and expansive. Sir George Grove in his analysis of this symphony tells us that the passage which thus breaks into the quiet melody was an afterthought, added after the symphony had been performed in public. If so, the whole movement must have been different in design, for in its present form this passage plays a most important part in the structure of the last three pages.

The melody falls into two parts.

Ex. 13.

The passionate digression dies away in another important figure—

which is combined (in the bass) with (*b*). With hardly any break the second part follows.

Ex. 14.

When this has come to a close the strings introduce a series of
declamatory phrases, beginning thus—

Ex. 15.

&c.

and leading to C sharp minor, where the oboe has a plaintive florid
solo, which will attract attention without needing quotation here.
Experienced listeners will observe that its sighing syncopated accompaniment on the strings describes figure (*a*) in shadowy outline,
and that when the clarinet takes up the oboe's song this outline is
inverted. A moment later the song is taken up by the basses, and
figure (*b*) appears in the accompaniment quite distinctly. The episode now comes to a climax; but after a short outburst of passion the
music dies away in broken phrases, and a return to the original key
is effected by a singularly rich and terse rising sequence in dialogue
between strings and wind. The principal theme then reappears in
the wind instruments, with a gorgeous new accompaniment in the
strings, marked by the first entry of trumpets and drums. But a
surprise awaits us as soon as we reach the digression that follows
on the opening phrase. Instead of passing through the chord of
C, it goes straight to the dominant with a strangely bright effect,
and is much expanded before it falls to its close in that key. Then
the second part appears in its old position, but with fresh effect
after this new turn of harmony. Apart from that, it is given to a
solo violin in the octave above the wind instruments; and the
thrill of this new and yet familiar tone-colour crowns the pathos
of the whole.

A coda, bringing this second part into a tonic and subdominant
position, and giving somewhat more florid passages to the solo
violin, brings the movement to an end, with a gentle suggestion
of the passage that led to the central episode. The last phrase
of all is a touching utterance from the solo violin, founded on
figure (*c*).

UN POCO ALLEGRETTO

In the place of a scherzo we find one of those terse and highly
organized movements which are so short that contemporary
criticism frequently fails to see that they are on a symphonic scale
at all. With something like the familiarity that we should presumably have with the works of Beethoven, impressions change;
and we realize that five minutes, a small orchestra, and quiet
climaxes may suffice for a very large movement indeed. It is
always important to discount the first impression that such movements make of being small and fragmentary. The following line

gives us the whole first theme, its inversion (exact and complete), and part of the second theme in the dominant.

Ex. 16.

When the second theme has come to a close, both are repeated (listen to the delightful by-play of the clarinet); but the close in the dominant now leads to F minor, where the clarinet introduces a new and rather agitated melody, of which some is new while the rest is derived from (a). This soon returns to A flat and is merged into an accompaniment to the first theme, which, however, breaks off after its first phrase, leading with three notes (c) to the trio thus—

Ex. 17.

This trio, in B major, is a lively, well-developed complete section in the usual two parts, with the usual repeats, of which the first is varied by a change to a darker key. It makes a considerable crescendo towards the end, where its theme is given to the trumpets with brilliant effect. After the trio the first section, as usual, reappears; but this time it takes a different course, with important effect on the whole design. Not only has the first theme a delightful new continuation in place of the original inversion, but the second theme is brought into the tonic and expanded so as to lead to a short coda, up in the clouds, with the theme of the trio; thus rounding off the movement in short time while setting in balance far more themes and subordinate episodes than scherzos and trios usually have.

The finale is prefaced by the most dramatic introduction that has been heard since that to the finale of Beethoven's Ninth Symphony; and the allegro resembles Beethoven's finale in one of those enormously broad, square, and simple tunes that will always seem to form a family with striking resemblances. If the resemblance were confined to generalities, no sensible person would worry about it; but there is here a certain provocative element.

INTRODUCTION

Brahms's introduction to his finale brings all the future materials forth in a magnificent cloudy procession, as in the introduction to the first movement, but on a larger scale and with far more of human terror and expectation.

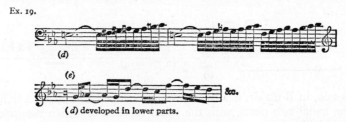

This first group of figures is repeated in different keys, giving place suddenly to a new group.

This quickly flares up to a climax; there is a moment's darkness and terror, and then day breaks. There is no more tragedy. The mode of the principal key changes to major for the last time in this symphony as the solemn trombones utter their first notes, and the horns give out a grand melody that peals through the tremolo of muted violins like deep bells among glowing clouds. (When this symphony was first performed at Cambridge, this passage excited special comment from its resemblance to Dr. Crotch's well-known clock-chimes. These chimes are, foolishly enough, alleged by Crotch himself to be derived from a figure in Handel's 'I know that my Redeemer liveth'.)

Ex. 20.

The melody is then repeated by the flute, and followed by a second part beginning with a wonderfully solemn phrase that should be

carefully noted, as it will be heard only once more, in a most
impressive context.

Ex. 21.

Example 20 is resumed in an intensified form, and brought to
a half-close with a pause.

FINALE

Then the finale begins with the famous melody that has been
compared with that in the Ninth Symphony, only because it is the
solitary one among hundreds of the same type that is great enough
to suggest the resemblance.

Ex. 22.

Allegro non troppo ma con brio.

Its first figure will be seen to be identical with (*b*) of the introduction. In the second part of the tune the resemblance to the
Ninth Symphony becomes obvious, but it is precisely at that point
that the essential meaning and harmony are most original. The
resemblance is, in fact, of the nature of a pointed allusion. And
this obviously gives some trouble to listeners who can notice it.
The melody is great enough to stand on its own merits; and our
attention is distracted if we notice that its most complex phrase
alludes to a simple figure in an older classic. So let us forget this
allusion. After the great tune has been fully stated, it is developed
animato, with diminution and new figures, leading to a transition
theme—

Ex. 23.

derived (with use of inversion) from Ex. 19, as subsequent developments show. This is brought to a climax, at the height of which
the bell-theme (Ex. 20) enters leading to the dominant.

The second subject begins, playfully at first, with a long theme on a basso ostinato consisting of the first bass notes (*a*) of the introduction.

Ex. 24.

Then follows a subsidiary in the minor, epigrammatic in style and treatment. This leads to E minor (note the bustling diminution), where we have the following version of Ex. 19 (*e*) from the introduction.

Ex. 25.

This is worked out with high spirits, and brings the second subject to a blustering close in the new key, E minor. The great tune of the first subject then reappears at once, as if the movement were, in spite of its elaboration, to be a rondo. Brahms, however, has a grander design, which shall give the tune its full repetition once for all in this place, while at the same time providing all the interest of more dignified forms. The tune leads to E flat, from whence it begins to modulate, alternating with (*c*) of Ex. 18 from the introduction (a dramatic surprise). Suddenly the animato transition that led to the second subject bursts in and leads to a grand development, treating the scale-figure (*d*) in rich counterpoint and broad sequences, with every variety of tone and colouring, in combination with a diminution of (*b*).

Ex. 26.

A tremendous climax is reached, and we are surprised at the following apparently new figure which staggers as if under a falling sky.

Ex. 27.

But we suddenly realize with a thrill that it is a transformation of the 'bell-theme', which returns in all its grandeur and leads quietly into the second subject in the tonic.

The recapitulation of the second subject is exact, except for the simple change of harmony needed to bring the high-spirited subsidiary themes into the same key as the playful opening.

The coda begins with a grand series of remote modulations with figure (*b*) looming large in the deep bass. The time quickens until we reach a *presto* with a new combination of the figures of the great first tune.

Ex. 28.

Suddenly, at the height of the jubilation, the most solemn note in the whole symphony is struck in the second and final appearance of that grand phrase from the introduction Ex. 21. A new version of Ex. 25 brings us to the end, with the repeated figure of Ex. 28.

XII. SECOND SYMPHONY, IN D MAJOR, NO. 2, OP. 73

1 *Allegro non troppo*. 2 *Adagio non troppo*. 3 *Allegretto grazioso (quasi Andantino)*. 4 *Allegro con spirito*.

Brahms's Second Symphony appeared so soon after his First, that the contrast between the two became a convenient topic for critics. Comedy will always tend to be more popular than tragedy; and critics will often exact too heavy a discount accordingly. On the whole Brahms's Second Symphony was well received. It was obviously on quite as large a scale as his first, and its brightness was a relief to a public that had no means of knowing that Brahms's symphonies were going to differ more from each other than Bruckner's. The slow movement was a stumbling-block; but probably, if it had been less difficult, Brahms would have encountered more opposition on the ground that his Second Symphony was less important than his First. Bruckner was far from anything like popular success; but he already represented the official Wagnerian view of symphonic art. According to that view it was vulgar to begin a symphony with anything so trivial as a tune; and in this matter Brahms's Second Symphony was a most dangerous indiscretion. I give, with some alterations, the analysis I wrote for the London Meiningen Concerts in 1902.

ALLEGRO NON TROPPO

It begins quietly with a broad theme for horns and wood-wind, punctuated by a very important figure in the basses.

Ex. I.

The continuation of this broadens out into a mysterious passage, in which the violins enter quietly and expand figure (*a*) into a strange sequence that falls slowly as the tone-colour darkens; till the solemn trombones enter with quiet minor chords and rolling drums, while a few instruments utter figure (*a*) like a plaintive question. The question is soon answered as the music closes in the major, and figure (*a*) becomes a new theme (*e*).

Ex. 2.

The solemn, quiet, pastoral character of the opening, with its mysteriously romantic continuation, thus gives place to a mood of daylight activity that speedily works to a climax. Figure (*a*), with (*b*) diminished (i.e. in shorter notes), is vigorously developed by the full orchestra (except the trombones, which for the rest of the exposition are reserved for a single crash). This short tutti leads to a diminished version of (*a*) which, in conjunction with (*b*) diminished, becomes a playful sequence—

Ex. 3.

and this, after modulating rapidly, leads through some sustained chromatic chords to the second subject. This begins with a large cantabile melody in F sharp minor (accompanied by (*b*) diminished).

Ex. 4.

Like all classical composers, Brahms here, as at the beginning, disturbs the complacency of his contemporaries by continuing his melody on an unexpectedly large scale. There are fully twenty bars of it before we reach a counter-statement, and the counter-statement pursues a different course, leading to the dominant, A major, the normal key for the second subject. To this key the whole remainder of the exposition is accordingly confined with a strictness that preserves the balance after the foreign key of No. 4 and the rich modulations that followed it. The group of short and independent themes that are now given in A major may be described without quotation, as they do not occur in other contexts. First there is an energetic theme in dotted quavers, repeating at cross accents its short phrases that leap over two octaves. Then follows a still more lively theme (partly derived from a new diminution of (*a*) in quavers and semiquavers), also very terse, and grouped in sequences across the rhythm of the bars.

This culminates in the single crash of trombones referred to above; and now follows a great expanse of impressive sequence in dialogue between basses and violins with an energetic syncopated rhythm in the inner parts—

Twenty bars of this lead through a stirring climax to a sudden *piano*; and Ex. 4 reappears in A major with a gay triplet accompaniment for the flute. After eight bars this is given in an expanded counter-statement with beautiful modulations and changed parts, the wind instruments having the melody and the violins a new triplet accompaniment. The close is expanded in a sequence that leads neatly in the first instance to the repeat of the exposition from the beginning, and in the second instance to the development, which begins in F major with Ex. 1. Figure (*c*) becomes expanded into—

Ex. 5.

This is treated in modulating sequences (the basses imitating the upper parts) until C minor is reached. Figure (*d*) (see last four bars of No. 1) is now treated in regular fugue, with several new figures for counter-subjects unnecessary to quote here. As the excitement grows and the steps become quicker, the trombones give a note of warning, and then enter with figure (*a*) in angry dialogue and harsh dissonance. The magnificent series of modulations that ensues leads (with the diminished version of (*a*) as in Ex. 3, but fortissimo) to a grand climax. Figure (*b*) is thundered out by the trombones,

H

giving place to Ex. 2 and another new sequence of (a), which seems to rise plaintively from the darkness as the harmony reaches a dominant pedal on A, anticipating the return to the principal key. The harmony brightens, and figure (b) crashes out once more on the full orchestra, gradually approaching the harmony of D major. Suddenly the trumpets have it in that harmony, quite softly, while figure (a) is heard augmented (in notes of double length) in the violins and basses. A few more bars lead us to the recapitulation of the first subject in the original key. Again the trombones have figure (a), greatly augmented.

Ex. 6.

(a) augmented

It will be seen that Ex. 1 is now combined with the transition theme Ex. 2, and that the alternate phrases ((d), with its answer in the next eight bars) are richly accompanied with a flow of quavers. The strange expansion, that followed in the exposition and led to that romantic passage with trombones and drums, now modulates in rising semitones and leads, with intense quiet and only a brief reference to its former sequel, almost directly to the second subject.

This is recapitulated bar for bar as in the exposition, but all the scoring and accompaniments of the quiet parts are entirely changed. The first great cantabile (now given in B minor) has a fresh accompaniment in dialogue between strings and wind. The continuation, leading to D, is exactly transcribed, and there is no alteration in the vigorous tutti themes that follow, except that the drums are able to aid the trombones in the crash that begins the grand broad expanse in the middle of this section. In the brilliant *piano* close where the cantabile (Ex. 4) reappears, the whole grouping of instruments is changed, the strings having the parts originally given to the wind, and vice versa. The close is diverted into the beginning of the coda. The wood-winds make a crescendo with figure (b), as at the climax of the development. Figure (c) is given in an expanded form by the trumpets, and is developed by the horn in a deeply expressive solo. Figure (e) may be heard floating through the accompaniment meanwhile. Then we settle down in a delightful

easy-going passage in which figures (*a*) and (*b*) are transformed into
the following tune:

Ex. 7.

This leads to an equally leisurely passage, in which the diminution
of (*a*) and (*b*), as in Ex. 3, is built into square eight-bar phrases with
other versions of (*a*). As this proceeds playfully the solemn bright
tones of high trumpets bring in figure (*b*) softly; and this wonderful
movement astonishes us, after its immense variety of material and
power of development, by ending with as quiet a glow as that with
which it began.

ADAGIO NON TROPPO

That solemnity which gave life and reality to the sunny pastoral
character of the quiet parts of the first movement, rises to the surface as the dominating characteristic in the slow movement. The
opening melody was considered very obscure by contemporary
critics, who saw nothing remarkable in the slow movement of
Mozart's G minor Quintet. They thought that what they did
not expect could not be right: but instead of listening to Mozart,
they assumed that he always wrote in eight-bar rhythm, and so
did not notice that he often deals with rhythms that expand as
irregularly as those of the slow movement of Brahms's Second
Symphony. It is never the complexity of Brahms that makes him
difficult for us; it is simply his originality. And this slow movement is intensely original. Its complexities are easily disposed of
by quoting its four principal themes.

Ex. 8.

This opening melody modulates to D major, and is then given by
the violins in a counter-statement, which however breaks off at the
fourth bar. Figure (c) is taken up by the horn as the subject of a
fugue, and answered by the oboes—

Ex. 9.

with austerely grotesque tone-colour, until the basses enter in the
subdominant. The modulations deepen, till, with the solemn
trombones to give warmth to the tone, figure (b) appears in the
dominant and rises to a climax. Then we fall into a lighter vein.
In the dominant, with a change to 12/8 time, appears a graceful
syncopated theme, contrasting with what went before, as a second
subject might contrast with a first.

Ex. 10.

This is built into a four-square structure, of which the end is left
open, so as to lead to another quiet and naïve theme—

Ex. 11.

which we naturally expect to remain in its key and round off this
section formally. A child may say the word which makes history;
and so this unpretending theme startles us by moving, with a rapid
crescendo, into distant keys, and blazing out in a stormy fugato
with a counter-subject in flowing semiquavers. A few rolls of
drums and some short trombone chords punctuate the stages of
this powerful development. Then, as Ex. 11 subsides into broken
phrases of three notes, while weird moans are heard in the brass
instruments, the strings come soaring above with the first phrase
of the first theme in G major ((a) of Ex. 8). This is interrupted
by a bar of agitated crescendo. Once more we hear that weird
moaning in the trombones, with the fragments of Ex. 11 in the
wood-wind. Again the first theme (a) appears, this time in the
oboe, in E major. Then, in three amazing chromatic steps,
the violins, clarinets, and flutes, in succession, bring the theme

round in one quiet bar and a half, through A minor and B flat,
into B major.

The whole first theme now returns varied in triplets.

Ex. 12.

(a)

(b)

The continuation, after the ninth bar, is put in a new (subdominant) position, and is, in compensation for this change, otherwise
unvaried, except in tone-colour. It leads to a reference to the
first fugato (Ex. 9), which makes a rapid crescendo. Then the full
orchestra with the stately tread of trombones and drums bursts out
in a grand florid sequence on figure (b).

Ex. 13.

&c.

Then we have Ex. 11 in the strings, imitated by the wood-wind and
accompanied by rolling drums. The music dies down; figure (a)
returns in the highest region of wood-wind, and the violins carry
it through falling sequences while the drums beat the triplet
rhythm of Ex. 11.

The clarinet dies away with the last low notes of the sequence,
and the grand song closes with a bright, soft chord for the whole
orchestra, except the trombones, which are always reserved for
dramatic effects.

ALLEGRETTO

The scherzo is one of Brahms's best-known movements. Like
many well-known things, it is not always remembered in its full
variety and range, or we should hear less of its being 'too small
for its place in a big symphony'. The answer is that in the first
place the symphony would be much less great if it did not contain
surprising contrasts of proportion and mood, and that in the
second place the scherzo is larger than it looks. It is scored for
small orchestra, without drums or any brass but three of the horns,

and begins with a simple melody on the oboe, with a luxurious
pizzicato accompaniment in the violoncellos.

Ex. 14.

Allegretto grazioso (quasi Andantino).

(a)   (b)   &c.

The second part of this tune grows out of the last two notes of
the first. The Beethoven-Schubert alternations between major
and minor as the theme draws to a close are the foundation of a
surprise at the end of the movement.

Suddenly the time changes to 2/4 with bars as short as the 3/4
beats. The theme changes also, but only in pretence.

Ex. 15.

Presto ma non assai ($\d = \d$).

(a)   (b)

Our delightful first melody cannot escape recognition so easily.
Perhaps when it springs up merrily in a freely inverted form it may
call itself a new theme—

Ex. 16.

f

but it soon returns to its other transformation (Ex. 15). However,
when we hear this rhythm | ♩· ╮ | ♩· ╮ | ⌐ | in the wood-wind,
recalling the original 3/4 slow time through the rapid tripping
quavers of the presto, we feel that we are returning to something
which has never been really out of sight; and so Brahms not only
harmonizes the original theme (Ex. 14) differently, but confines
himself to its first four bars and turns figure (a) into the following
basso ostinato—

Ex. 17.

which is repeated, crescendo, for eleven bars, while the wind instruments make loud comments in phrases of their own. This dies
away in an unexpectedly solemn little close in E major; and then,
with delicious effrontery, the strings run, with the triplet figure of
Ex. 17, to A major. This is the most unorthodox possible key for
an important point in the structure of a movement in G. Here
we have a new version of Ex. 16 in 3/8 time.

Ex. 18.

This soon leads to C major, where, allowing for the new rhythm, matters proceed as they did on the first appearance of Ex. 14. But the preparations for the return of the original theme are modified, and it calmly returns in the remote key of F sharp major, on the strings, who now retain it to the end. Its second clause (figure (*b*)) is given in B major, with a peculiarly happy turn that brings us easily into a position where the second part can follow in the original key. From this point there is no further change till we come to those alternations between major and minor at the close. Here a new figure appears in all the upper strings, giving rise to a beautiful bit of free inverted imitation in the wind—

Ex. 19.

thus adding an unexpected warmth of tone to the graceful movement, before the oboes and other wind instruments bring it to an end with its first figure, crowned by a quiet cadence in the strings.

FINALE

The finale, though it has an even greater number of richly developed themes, does not need as much illustration as the first and second movements, except for one subtle passage in the middle. The first theme is a flowing melody, of which the first figure (*a*) is used as an accompaniment in any number of different contexts, while the second (*b*) forms a basso ostinato to the rest of the theme, as the following extract indicates.

Ex. 20.

Allegro con spirito.

A subsidiary appears in the dominant.

Ex. 21.

The subsequent developments are quite easy to follow, though
Brahms maintains his inexhaustible variety of proportion and
his wealth of subsidiary figures. Among these we may note the
following version of Ex. 21, augmented by being broken up—

Ex. 22.

as it occurs some way on in the tutti that crashes with Haydnesque
high spirits into the ruminating continuation of the first theme.
Then comes a dramatic event. The clarinet suddenly swells out,
above the bustle of the orchestra, with the utmost vehemence
in an impassioned passage in F major. This is taken up by other
instruments and expanded more quietly in A major, the orthodox
dominant in which the second subject enters with the following
broad melody.

Ex. 23.

Accompanied by figure (b).

This also has a number of subsidiaries that need not be quoted.
The most important of these is a new derivative of (a), that leads to
some extremely brilliant scale passages for wind with pizzicato
strings, which I quote here for a reason that will appear later.

Ex. 24.

After some stirring syncopated chords, we have a short, lively,
snapping cadence-subject, that quickly calms down and leads playfully back to the first theme in the tonic. This finale is undoubtedly
the great-grandson of that of Haydn's last London Symphony
(no. 104), where we find in just the same part of the movement a
very similar series of whirling scales in terms of an earlier orchestral
language, followed by a snapping cadence-subject in terms nearly
as modern as Brahms's. Unlike Tennyson, Brahms, who to the last
years of his life used to puzzle the superior person by studying the
quartets of Haydn, was glad to acknowledge such ancestry, which

has no more to do with plagiarism than originality has to do with freedom from the restrictions of good sense and taste. When this symphony was plundered in its turn by a friend, Brahms met the composer's apologies with words to this effect: 'One of the stupidest topics of the noodles is plagiarism. Your theme is one of your freshest and most attractive ideas; the thing it resembles in my symphony is a mere accidental accessory.'

With the development of this finale we come to the most profound passage in the symphony. At first events are normal, though the treatment is very ingenious. The first theme, Ex. 20, leaves the tonic at the fourth bar, the last notes of which are taken up and passed through various keys in rapid dialogue, till the dominant of F sharp minor is reached. Then the theme (*a, b*) is freely inverted, the result being treated and diminished in quaint combinations.

Ex. 25.

The close, in C sharp minor, is followed by the bursting in of Ex. 21, forte, followed by its other version, Ex. 22, in B minor. This is worked to a climax, which is marked by the entry of the trombones for the first time since the slow movement. (In all Brahms's orchestral works the listener will find it interesting to watch the trombones or, where they are not used, the trumpets and drums, or other instruments useful in a climax. No composer, not even Beethoven himself, is more careful than Brahms to organize his resources with power in reserve.)

Now we come to the quintessence of Brahms. The main group (*a, b*) is transformed into an apparently new idea.

Ex. 26.

(Like all things that Brahms marks *tranquillo*, this passage has a peculiar atmosphere of tenderness and mystery, not unlike that which characterizes all passages marked *cantabile* in Beethoven.)

A change to B flat minor brings back Ex. 21 plaintively in the oboe; but we at once return to F sharp, and this new transformation, Ex. 22, modulates (*sempre più tranquillo*) through A and C, with increasing breadth and calm. Again Ex. 21 appears; but this time it is in solemn augmentation given out softly by the trombones, while the violins fall slowly with a legato tremolo. The original key is reached in darkness, and the cold unison of the first theme meets us like the grey daylight on a western cloud-bank opposite the sunrise.

The recapitulation is regular, except that Brahms with quiet humour inverts the subsidiary (Ex. 21) bodily, with all its accompaniments, and shortens the big tutti, varying its scoring and making it plunge straight into the second subject. This is given in the tonic with no alteration whatever; broad melody, subsidiaries, whirling scales, and Haydn's snapping cadence-figure which rushes immediately into the coda. This begins in the minor with a new version of the second subject on the trombones, which have rested since their solemn words in the development, but have now come to stay and sanction the glorious triumph that is to follow.

Ex. 27.

This transformation, beginning in darkness, becomes jubilant and bright, and gives way suddenly to an exciting combination of the figure of the second subject (Ex. 23) with that of the mysterious tranquillo development (Ex. 26).

Ex. 28.

Then the initial figures (*a*, *b*) are worked up in a tremendous dialogue between strings and trombones. The music broadens enormously, and at what appears to be the height of the climax we are startled by the appearance in the full orchestra of the whirling scale-figure (Ex. 24), punctuated by silent half-bars that take our breath away. Nor is this the crowning point of the movement. The main figure (*d*) of the second subject is turned into a flourish of trumpets on their highest notes. And perhaps the sustained blast of the trombones, during the penultimate staccato chords of the rest of the orchestra, is the most surprising effect of all in a coda which is among the most brilliant climaxes in symphonic music since Beethoven.

XIII. SYMPHONY IN F MAJOR, NO. 3, OP. 90

1 *Allegro con brio.* 2 *Poco Allegretto.* 3 *Andante.* 4 *Allegro.*

Of Brahms's four symphonies, the third is the shortest and, in externals, the most romantic and picturesque; yet it is, next to the Double Concerto and the D minor Pianoforte Concerto, perhaps the most neglected of his orchestral works. It is also technically by far the most difficult, the difficulties being mainly matters of rhythm, phrasing, and tone. These are unsuited to an age of hustle; but they are not to be dismissed as 'bad scoring'. It is much easier to practise works in which all the difficulty contributes rather to the production of special effects than to musical ideas. There is certainly no reason why the music, as music, should not be among the most popular that Brahms ever wrote: and this was certainly the impression which the work made upon me when I first heard it thirty years ago. I give here with slight alterations the analysis I wrote for the Meiningen Orchestra, when it played in London in 1902.

The symphony begins with three notes (*a*), which pervade the whole movement and even recur in the finale.

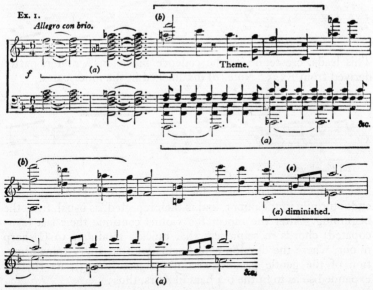

Ex. 1.

This closes in a quiet subsidiary, with bright and warm tone-colouring.

Ex. 2.

Figure (*a*) bursting out in the bass, answered by the violins, leads in a thrilling modulation to D flat, where Ex. 2 reappears. Precisely the same process leads, more gently but with yet more brilliant tone-colour, to A major, in which somewhat remote key, after a little quiet preparation, the second subject begins with a most graceful pastoral theme in 9/4 time.

Ex. 3.

This has a second part beginning thus:

Ex. 4.   (*e*)

The violins take up figure (*d*) freely inverted and, with a return to 6/4 time, figure (*a*) appears in a new form.

Ex. 5.

This leads, crescendo, to the cadence theme in A minor, partly derived from Ex. 5. Note (*a*) diminished in the inner parts.

Ex. 6.

8*ves* above and below.

(*a*) diminished.

The whole wind band takes this up fortissimo, and the exposition ends stormily in the minor, and is then repeated, as usual, from the beginning. After the repeat the violins continue their last (syncopated) chords in sequences that quickly modulate to C sharp minor, where the development begins with an angry transformation of the gentle pastoral second subject (Ex. 3), its rhythm expanded so as to fit the 6/4 bars in pairs, thus:

Ex. 7.

The second part of the tune (Ex. 4) is then worked up in inverted canon through various keys—

Ex. 8.

(e)

(e) inverted.

and the excitement calms down, till we are startled by an intensely
serious passage in E flat, of all keys the most remote both from the
tonic and from the other keys we have dwelt in. The horn gives
out figure (a) like the beginning of a sustained melody, while
the deep notes of the contra-fagotto make the tone-colour darker
than anything we have expected to hear. The passage ends,
più sostenuto, in profound night, while figure (b) appears in many
octaves, from the deepest possible notes of the contra-fagotto
to the violins descending from their upper register. From this
darkness and this distant key, E flat minor, we cannot conceive
any near prospect of returning to F; yet the three great opening
chords—(a) of Ex. 1—harmonized in a yet bolder way, burst forth
with all the sudden splendour of a tropical sunrise, and we find ourselves in the full swing of the recapitulation before we have re-
covered breath. The transition-theme (Ex. 2) is so turned as to
lead straight to D major, where the second subject (Ex. 3) appears
in ordinary course. The repetition of its first phrase is omitted, and
a slight change in its second part brings Ex. 5 into F major. So
far, this shifting of keys in the course of the subject is just what
Beethoven does in most cases where the second subject was in
a remote key in the exposition; but Brahms, for reasons which
appear in the coda, does not let his recapitulation remain in the
tonic, but shifts it once more back to D minor, before Ex. 6 appears.
The result is that, when Ex. 6 rises to a storm, as at the end of the
first part, it is able to lead back to the first subject at the beginning
of the coda with all the effect of another return to the tonic. The
first theme is now given with greater force than ever, and (a) in the
bass is in quite a new and surprising position (C, E flat, C) as a kind
of dominant pedal. Figure (c) and the remaining figures of the
theme are considerably developed; and the splendid outburst is
followed by the inevitable quiet glow of a sunset, as the two main
figures (a) and (b) rise and fall through the sustained final chords.

The slow movement, with its manner of pastoral plainness, is
really one of the most solemn things Brahms ever wrote. Its first
theme is a dialogue between clarinets and the lower strings, beginning thus:

Ex. 9.

(a)   (b)   (c)

The continuation will explain itself, but the end of the theme must
be quoted for future reference.

The sequel, in which the first figures (*a*, *b*) are varied in semiquavers and made to modulate to the dominant, crescendo, needs
no quotation. The mysterious passage in which figure (*b*) is treated
in dialogue between basses and violins should be noted; and the
wistful melody that follows in the dominant like a second subject,
is a thing to be taken more seriously than first impressions indicate.

In the lovely continuation the quiet quaver figure of the violins
and its equally naïve inversion must speak for themselves; but it
is necessary to quote the extraordinary series of harmonies that
bring this section to a close.

This is immediately followed by an ornamental development of the
first theme in the violoncellos, with triplets in the violins. I give
the gist of the variation here:

Passing through B major and other keys, with sequences of figure
(*b*) in its original form with the new accompaniments, this comes
to a climax as the bass reaches the tonic C and holds it as a pedal.
The trombones enter, for the first time in the movement, and hold
sustained chords, while figure (*a*) is passed from one wind instrument to another, and the strings keep up a flow of semiquavers
derived from the transition variation that followed the original
statement of the first theme. At last the theme itself returns
calmly with this flowing accompaniment and several delightful
details of ornament. It is given in full, and towards the end the
flow of the accompaniment slackens. The last notes—(*d*), Ex. 10
—give rise to a broad crescendo passage—

Ex. 14.

(*d*)   &c.

that dies away into the wonderful harmonies of Ex. 12, transposed
to the tonic. Then some quiet descending sequences on the first
theme over a tonic pedal, while the violoncellos and basses repeat
the rhythmic figure (*e*) of Ex. 12—

&c.

bring this movement to a quiet end, with chords that sound great
depths of solemn beauty. Humperdinck did not escape them at the
end of the prelude to *Hänsel und Gretel*.

The delightful poco allegretto is so easy to follow that I need
only quote the beginnings of the theme of its first section and the
two contrasted themes of its trio.

Ex. 15.

This melody, instead of being worked out in binary form like a
minuet, has a middle section in the tonic major (of all poetical and
surprising things) with a delightful return through A minor to the
first theme.

The trio is in A flat, and contains two themes—

Ex. 16.

&c.

and Ex. 17, which, though contrasted, is derived from the last
notes of its partner.

Ex. 17.

The da capo of the main section is complete and exact as to material,
but the scoring, which was astonishingly rich the first time, is
entirely changed, and new groups of the small orchestra come
forward with the melody. A single line, developed from the strange
chord that led to the trio, makes the coda of the movement.

The finale is very dramatic and terse; and it needs either a close
analysis or none at all. The listener will do well to be prepared
for short themes, violent changes of mood, and romantic depth
and power. Joachim, who fully agreed with Brahms in disliking
unauthorized literary interpretations of music, could not resist
the temptation of comparing this finale to the story of Hero and
Leander. Brahms said nothing, but did not snub him. The
opening theme is dark and quiet.

Ex. 18.

Allegro.

Figures (c) and (d) should not escape notice. A counter-statement
follows, shedding weird light on the theme by prolonging some of
its notes, and putting (c) in the bass with (d) above. Then the key
changes, and we have an exceedingly solemn theme of a strange
rhythmic character, with trombones and contra-fagotto.

Ex. 19.

To Sir Edward Elgar I owe the remark that this is the tragic outcome of the wistful theme in the middle of the slow movement
(Ex. 11).

Suddenly the first theme bursts out angrily in a transformed
version.

Ex. 20.
a, b, simplified.

This leads stormily to C minor, where a new figure appears.

Ex. 21.
(f)

The first notes of this (*f*) make a bass to the second subject, which begins victoriously in C major.

Ex. 22.

(*f*)   &c.

This, however, does not remain in triumph throughout. It leads to a climax in the minor, where several new themes and figures appear; among others a remarkable moment in the extreme distance of B minor, with figure (*a*) in the wind instruments. I quote the cadence-figure, which is necessary for future reference.

Ex. 23.
8ves.

Figure (*a*) in various strange positions (e.g. pizzicato, augmented in the stringed instruments) leads angrily back to the first theme in the tonic. This is not given quite as at the outset; figure (*c*) is augmented, and the counter-statement is expanded, not in the original way, but by a new development of the fourth bar of the theme. This leads to a mysterious passage, with (*d*) augmented in combination with a broken version of (*a, b*) in A flat minor.

Ex. 24.
(*d*)   (*d*)   (*d*)

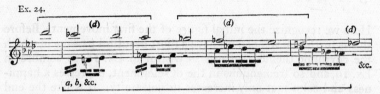

a, b, &c.   &c.

Suddenly this is taken up by the whole orchestra forte, except the trombones, which, however, soon thunder out the solemn rhythmic theme (Ex. 19) with a new accompaniment of whirling triplets.

I

This proceeds in sublime modulations till F major is reached, and
then we find ourselves in the midst of the recapitulation, for the
angry transformation of (*a*, *b*), Ex. 20, appears suddenly in F
minor. It gives place to new variants of the theme, and develops
figure (*c*) rapidly, leading to the transition-figure Ex. 21, and so to
the recapitulation of the second subject in the tonic with no alteration at all till we reach the cadence-figure, Ex. 23, which we are
now surprised to hear in combination with the first theme.

Ex. 25.

The short dialogue on (*a*), that led to the return from second subject to first, now leads to the extremely remote key of B minor,
where the coda begins mysteriously with a new version of the first
theme on muted violas.

Ex. 26.

This soon leads back to F minor, and the wood-wind give us the
original counter-statement, with its prolongations of notes here
and there, its rich harmony, and its semiquaver accompaniment of
violins, now muted. Suddenly the mode becomes major, and the
theme, augmented, becomes an eight-bar phrase.

Ex. 27.

Here we recognize the initial figure of the first movement. Before
this is further developed we have a most beautiful passage in which
the rhythmic theme, that was so wistful in Ex. 11, so sombre in
Ex. 19, and so tremendous in the development, expresses a happiness and calm that only increases its solemnity. It is like the end
of Brahms's First Violin Sonata with something tragic behind it.
Then the initial figure of the first movement reappears in combination with that of the finale; and the violins are heard floating

down with the melody—Ex. 1, figure (*b*)—with which the symphony began so vigorously, and which ends it with the romantic, quiet glow that we have now learnt to regard as its destined result.

Ex. 28.

&c.

XIV. SYMPHONY IN E MINOR, NO. 4, OP. 98

1 *Allegro non troppo.* 2 *Allegro giocoso.* 3 *Andante moderato.*
4 *Allegro energico e passionato.*

This symphony is one of the rarest things in classical music, a symphony which ends tragically. In drama a tragedy tells a story which a happy ending would weaken and falsify: in the music of the sonata forms this is not so. In so far as the first movement maintains a tragic note, it may be said to tell its tragic story from beginning to end, and the other movements are free to provide the most refreshing emotional reactions from it. Brahms, in his Fourth Symphony and a few other great sonata works (notably the Pianoforte Quintet and the Third Pianoforte Quartet), has done what Beethoven did only three times in all his works; he has given us a tragic finale. This finale is unique in form among all symphonic movements, and the form is by no means the scholastic display which contemporary criticism has imagined it to be, but a very powerful expression of a great dramatic truth. The first movement acts its tragedy with unsurpassable variety of expression and power of climax. The slow movement, heroic though in pastoral style and ballad measures, has also an eventful tale to tell. The third movement, functionally the scherzo, has all the features of such a blend of sonata form and rondo as is common in finales; yet with all its bacchanalian energy it is evidently no finale. It is not in the main key, and its extreme terseness, while increasing its energy, destroys what finality it might otherwise have had. After three movements so full of dramatic incident, what finale is possible? And how will the tragic note regain the domination after the triumph of the third movement?

The very reason why the finale of Brahms's Fourth Symphony was such a stumbling-block to contemporary critics is the answer to these questions. It is a passacaglia; that is to say, a set of variations in moderately slow triple time on a theme, or ground, consisting of a single 8-bar phrase. As this is one of the most ancient of musical forms and, as such, is taught to young students at school, popular criticism assumes that, like the Ablative Absolute, it must be something extremely learned and difficult. Common sense would rather indicate that an ancient form that can be taught in schools must be something simple enough for primitive artists to produce and clear enough for schoolboys to understand. Brahms chose the form of variations on a ground for this finale, because dramatic activity (always on the ebb in finales, alike in drama and music, no matter what surprises effect the dénouement) was fully exploited in the other three movements. He desired a finale that was free to express tragic emotion without being encumbered by the logical and chronological necessities of the more dramatic sonata forms. The climax of the first movement is as great as ten minutes of crowded drama could make it; but the full tide of emotion that it implies can be revealed only in a finale in which the attention is directed to little else but emotional contrasts and climaxes. All successful sonata finales, whether tragic or not, gain their emotional freedom by some simplification of this kind; and Brahms's ground-bass ranks with Beethoven's fugues as an extreme case of this law. It is the same law that makes rondo form preferable for finales, and that makes the phrasing of a sonata-form finale plainer than that of a first movement. (See, for example, the finales of Beethoven's Sonata Appassionata, and the Fourth, Fifth, and Seventh Symphonies.)

From the large procession of themes on which Brahms's first movement is organized I make three quotations, marking with letters and brackets those figures which are built up into fresh ideas in later developments.

No one experienced in great music could fail to see that the long, quiet opening sentence is the beginning of a great and tragic work.

Ex. 1.

Its close is overlapped by a counter-statement in which the first phrase is divided antiphonally between the violins, while the echo of the wood-wind is transferred to the basses (in another part of the scale), and the wood-wind weave a beautiful tissue of new polyphony. At the ninth bar of this counter-statement, with the entry of figure (*b*), the harmony takes a new direction and moves towards the dominant, B minor, where, after a climax, an impassioned transition theme appears. This I do not quote, except for the spirited triplet figure (*d*), which ends it, and, as will be seen, plunges into the broad violoncello melody that begins the second subject.

The sequel rises through heroism (figure (*d*)) to radiant happiness in a procession of themes which economy forbids me to quote. Then comes a cloud of mystery—

Ex. 3.

from which the triplet theme (*d*) emerges triumphant, and works up the exposition of this movement to an exultant climax, the final glory of which is its unexpected sweet and gentle close that leads back to E minor and the first theme (Ex. 1).

With this resumption of the first theme the development begins. As in the first counter-statement of Ex. 1, so here the ninth bar sees a change in the trend of the harmony, and we are moved to a more remote key. Figure (*b*) becomes more agitated, and forms the accompaniment to a new variation of the theme in G minor.

Again at the ninth bar the same change of harmony carries it to the extreme distance of B flat minor. From this point the theme, in its new variation, is carried through a passage of energetic action in which various orchestral groups answer each other, gaining and yielding ground in rapid sword-play, until a close is about to be reached in the very key in which the exposition had ended. Here, however, the theme of figure (d) (from Ex. 2) intervenes, no longer with its original bold spirit, but in hushed mystery. Then, through the solemn clouds of Ex. 3, figure (f), the wood-wind utter plaintive fragments of the first theme (a) and its variation, rising through distant keys in slow chromatic steps, till we reach the very threshold of our tonic. And here again the theme of figure (d) appears mysteriously. But it suddenly blazes into passion, and, plunging again into distant keys, leads to a solemnly heroic close in G sharp minor. This close, and the fierce passage that leads to it, will be heard again at the catastrophe of the tragedy.

Now follows a new and very rich variation of the first theme. As usual the ninth bar, with figure (b), brings a change of harmony, and the figure is passed from voice to voice in a series of wistful modulations, drifting steadily towards the tonic, E minor, in a long decrescendo. At last, in slow and solemn semibreves, we hear the first notes of Ex. 1. The great cloud-figure of Ex. 3 (f) separates the first two steps of the theme, with all the majesty of the Norns prophesying the twilight of the Gods. The rest of the theme is taken up from its fifth bar as if nothing had happened.

We are now in the full swing of a perfectly regular recapitulation. A slight change of harmony brings the impassioned transition theme (ending with Ex. 2) into the tonic, and the whole second subject with its radiant procession of themes follows in due course. Only when we approach the triumphant close there is a sudden catastrophic change of harmony, and we are confronted with a fiercer version of the sudden outburst of heroic passion which startled us in the middle of the mysterious part of the development. This time the climax is evidently going to be greater. Suddenly the cloud-figure (f) becomes a whirlwind, and the first theme bursts out fortissimo in the basses, answered by the violins. It is worked up in its entirety, together with the transition-theme (the unquoted part) and the whirlwind-figure, into a peroration which, from its inception to its final grim 'Amen', bears comparison with the greatest climaxes in classical music, not excluding Beethoven. And Brahms does not even use trombones for it.

With a heroic call from the horns in a unison, which suggests C major while emphasizing the tonic note, the andante lifts us from the world of our tragedy to some ancestral region of legend, the

unforgotten source of the hero's pride. The long and straight-
forward tune which begins with Ex. 4—

Ex. 4.

is scored with delicious varieties of the blending of sustained tone
with the pizzicato of strings. For all its ballad-like simplicity there
are signs of drama in its structure, and we are not surprised when
the strings take up the bow with the clear intention of breaking
away from rigid stanzas and leading into the larger flow of a developed sonata movement. Soon the dominant is reached; and an
energetic triplet figure prepares the way for the second subject
which, as Ex. 5 shows, builds its broad melody on an 'augmentation' of it.

Ex. 5.

The continuation seems as if it was going to lead to a crowd of
accessory themes, but it very soon shows signs of drifting back to
the tonic. The drift is slow, and its apparent indecision leads to one
of the most beautiful modulations Brahms or any man ever wrote.
By this modulation the main theme is brought back in the tonic,
with gorgeous new scoring. At the point where it showed signs of
dramatic freedom, there now arises an energetic passage of polyphonic development. This leads to a powerful climax with the
triplet figure of Ex. 5; which subsides quite suddenly, and then
the second subject sails grandly in, with sumptuous harmony
of divided strings. It is being repeated in soaring triumph, when
suddenly it melts into tenderness; a shadow comes over the harmony, and wistful questions from the clarinet and oboe bring
back the close of the first theme with an added sweetness. On its
last note the horns burst out with their opening call, and the conflict between the keys of C and E, implied at the outset, now
appears in full harmony as that solemn splendour which Palestrina
would have recognized as the Phrygian mode, used by him where
doubts and fears are given full expression in order to be convicted
of ignorance by the voice from the whirlwind (e.g. the Motet and
Mass *O magnum mysterium*).

Within six or seven minutes Brahms's third movement, perhaps
the greatest scherzo since Beethoven, accomplishes a form which
you may call either a sonata-rondo or a first movement, according

to the importance you give to the fact that the first six bars of its
theme—

Ex. 6.

return just between the short second subject—

Ex. 7.

and the quite fully organized and widely modulating development.
The shortness of the whole movement used to blind critics to its
bigness of design; and at one time people thought it clever to say
that the second subject (Ex. 7) was too slight, a criticism which
would have condemned nearly every second subject in Beethoven's biggest rondos and sonata-form finales, as, no doubt, in
Beethoven's day it did. A slender childish figure for a second
subject is of the very essence of this phase of Brahms's drama; and
nothing can be more quaintly original (or, in the sequel, more
powerful) than the way in which the counter-statement of this
innocent tune is reduced to a staccato outline, as indicated by the
small notes in Ex. 7.

What it throws into higher relief is the tiger-like energy and
spring of the whole movement. Some idea of the terseness and
swiftness of the action may be gained by noting that my first quotation (Ex. 6) contains three complete and sharply contrasted themes.
All three have important variations, one of which I have tried to
indicate by extra tails, while the others I have not space to quote.
The third (c), with its abrupt plunge into E flat, produces two
of the most powerful strokes in the movement; first by means of
the fact that the anxious, mysterious, questioning close of the
development is answered by it, and not by the first theme, as at the
beginning of the recapitulation; and secondly by its triumphant
outburst on the trumpets, for the first and only time in the tonic,
C major, at the end of the movement.

A piccolo, a contra-fagotto, and a triangle contribute with
grotesque poetic aptness to the bacchanalian fury of this movement. It is now thought correct to be shocked at Brahms's abuse
of the triangle in the only three movements in which he has admitted it to the orchestra. We are told that the triangle is an instrument of the highest poetic power when used for one single stroke
in a whole opera, as shown by the wonderful flash of sunlight at
the end of the second act of *Siegfried*, and the one note of the
triangle in the Vorspiel to *Meistersinger*. The statistics of these
miracles are not quite accurately given by the critics, who would
forbid Bacchants and processions the free use of triangles and
cymbals. After its first entry in the *Meistersinger* Vorspiel Wagner's
triangle is almost as shamelessly processional as Brahms's; and
there is no restraint on it when Siegfried is forging his sword.
Brahms was acutely sensitive to the effect of tones that arrest
attention by being on a different plane from that of the normal
orchestra. But he may see fit to arrest attention by such tones
without thereby becoming obliged to submit to the economics of
a music-drama in which the 'effects' have to be distributed over
several hours. In fact we know that Brahms occasionally preferred
that certain obvious effects should, if used at all, get over their
'effective' shock at once. Thus he projected, but never executed,
an orchestral and choral setting of the ballad *Edward*, and proposed
that the harps should be prominent at the very beginning 'so that
they don't go and make an effect' (*nicht etwa Effekt machen*).

So far, then, this symphony has shown us life and action. These
are what its heroism fights for; but the hero is not fighting for his
own happiness. He is to die fighting. After what I have said as to
the meaning of Brahms's choice of the passacaglia form, little
remains but to give the theme—

Ex. 8.

and to catalogue the variations. The listener need not worry as to
whether he can trace the theme in the variations. If and where he
can, that is well; but beauty is skin-deep, though it does need bones
to keep it in shape.

The theme, stated, with trombones, in harmonies too remarkable
to be intended to bear repetition, descends angrily with rolling
drums and pizzicato chords into the depths of the orchestra (Var. 1),
while plaintive melodies crowd above in the wood-wind (Var. 2),
rising to a bold reassertion of the theme (Var. 3). Then the violins
take up the bow with a striding declamatory melody (Var. 4, theme
in bass), which becomes more flowing and is agitated by a lively

cross-rhythm in the wood-wind (Vars. 5 and 6). A sharply
rhythmic variation follows (Var. 7), and leads to a pair of stormy
variations in semiquavers and triplet semiquavers (Vars. 8 and 9).
Plaintively the storm subsides into a pathetic dialogue of beautiful
sustained harmonies between the violas and the wood-wind (Var.
10). The same harmonies underlie the April sunshine of the next
variation (11), and then the time changes to 3/2, twice as slow—
which with triple time always produces a momentary sense of
cross-rhythm.

Now we have perhaps the most pathetic flute passage since
Gluck's wonderful adagio in the Elysian scene of *Orfeo* (Var. 12).
The theme, which had been in the bass since Var. 4, is now in the
outlines of the melody and the inner parts of the harmony. (I
mention this merely as a safeguard against the temptation some
listeners feel to hunt for it.) With the next variation (13) the major
mode quietly appears, in a pathetic dialogue between clarinet,
oboe, and flute. The cadence of this is reproduced in the two next
variations (14, 15), which bring the trombones forward with the
most pathetic and solemn passage in the whole symphony. When
this has died wistfully away on an inconclusive chord, the original
theme sternly reappears in the wind-band, to be fiercely cut across
by the indignant strings (Var. 16). Then there is a dramatically
agitated variation (17), followed by a sonorously determined one
(18), which leads to a pair of staccato variations increasing in
energy and movement (19, 20). The next (Var. 21) is the most
volcanic outburst of all. Suddenly it gives way to a panic-struck
and hushed staccato in which Var. 22 hurries by. With Var. 23
the staccato triplets recover courage and strength, working easily
up to a climax. This climax is of powerful and unexpected effect,
for it gives a sense of big design to the whole movement by
making the next two variations (24, 25) reproduce in a blazing
fortissimo the substance of the first two, while the 26th variation gives in an awe-struck *piano* what the third variation had
given boldly. Now two specially graceful variations (27, 28)
relieve the tension. Then in the next variation (29) we notice a
quiet series of falling thirds which may remind some listeners of the
theme of the first movement. I doubt, however, whether this was
Brahms's intention, and the doubt does not worry me. At all
events this sequence of thirds, taken up energetically in the 30th
and last regular variation, seems dramatically to set the ground-
bass reeling and staggering to its end, for the rhythm expands and
there is an ominous ritardando. Then the theme bursts out with
new harmonies in quicker time. Hesitating at the fifth bar, the
ground-theme suddenly finds that its second half (bars 5-8) is
capable of executing a grand series of modulations (very apposite

after all this confinement to one key), if the bass imitates the treble at two bars' distance a semitone higher. With this resource, a compressed version of the ground in crotchets, and a pathetic new derivative therefrom, one of the greatest orchestral works since Beethoven storms to its tragic close.

XV. SERENADE IN D MAJOR, FOR ORCHESTRA, OP. 11

1 *Allegro molto.* 2 SCHERZO *and* TRIO. *Allegro non troppo.* 3 *Adagio non troppo.* 4 MENUETTO *I and II.* 5 SCHERZO. *Allegro.* 6 RONDO. *Allegro.*

Brahms's First Serenade is an epoch-making work in a sense that is little realized. It sins against the first and most ephemeral canon of modern criticism, the canon which inculcates the artist's duty to assert his originality in terms so exclusively related to this week's news as to become unintelligible by the week after next. The Second Serenade, in A major, op. 16, is a much more acceptable work in an age where the nature and duty of originality are thus misconceived; but it could not have been written, or at all events could not have achieved its consistently subtle and intimate style, without the experience gained in the First Serenade. And the First Serenade is by no means the kind of school exercise that some critics have taken it to be. In any age when questions of musical style are understood like other questions of scholarship, Brahms will be admired for the wit of the homage he pays to Beethoven's Septet, Second Symphony, and F major Violin Sonata, in the second scherzo of this serenade. At present we have hardly yet emerged from the days when it could be supposed that Brahms did not know his classics too we l to be in doubt as to when and why he was alluding to them. We now, at all events, know enough of the musical history of the nineteenth century to realize that Brahms was effecting a renascence of classical principles. Such a renascence is no matter of putting new wine into old bottles; the forms are not imposed upon the material from outside, but they are principles of growth from within, just as they were in classical times. The modern environment reacts upon them because they are alive, and this reaction may be identified by critics as a mixture of styles. But the critic has not emerged far from the stage of the raw student if he mistakes the humours of Brahms's First Serenade for the primnesses of an academic exercise. The naïve listener is much more likely to see the point. It does not depend upon his being able to give chapter and verse for the influence of Beethoven's early scherzos; on the contrary, such a capacity is a mere hindrance to enjoyment, until it has become so ingrained as to produce no more than an automatic internal chuckle. The real point lies in the intrinsic quality of the ideas, and in the natural yet surprising effect of the juxtaposition of childlike themes with adventurous developments.

A very good game may be played between music lovers, if one person quotes the beginning of a piece and the others see how soon they can recognize it. With experienced musicians it is surprising how often the piece can be identified by its first chord, even when this seems quite commonplace. An advanced variety of this game is to ignore as far as possible previous knowledge, and to carry the quotation further, until it is possible to say that the music is of extraordinary quality. When the quality is of the highest order, it is possible to infer from it that the composer who has got thus far will not fail to carry out a great design. We cannot, of course, predict that his great design will have no inequalities; that Wotan's grievances will not put more of Schopenhauer into the second act of *Walküre* than the drama will bear; that Handel will always take the trouble to write his own works, or that, taking that trouble, he will not leave an unconscionably large margin for extemporization. But it is always interesting to fix the attention upon the way in which the quality of the music asserts itself; to see whether a beautiful opening is going to show something more than a gift for epigram; and (to come to the most interesting and difficult cases) to note the point after which a purely formal opening, having shown that its composer is a master in a good school, proceeds to prove that it is the shrine of the Olympian Zeus.

The opening of Brahms's First Serenade is an excellent exercise for beginners in this critical game. The drone-bass is one of the richer sounds of the classical orchestra, and already shows that Brahms was well advised in turning the serenade into an orchestral composition instead of leaving it in the state in which it was first performed as a nonet for strings and wind. Above this pastoral drone-bass a horn plays a pastoral theme.

Ex. 1.

(As with a similar theme in the finale, this is how Haydn would have used the horn in his last symphony if he could have trusted the horn-players of London in 1795. But as they were by no means the virtuoso horn-players of Esterhaz, they ventured upon their theme only under the shelter of a full orchestral tutti, leaving it to the violins in quieter passages.) Brahms shifts his drone-bass

to the dominant, and the theme is transferred to the clarinet. It
seems in no hurry; but suddenly the bass shifts to G. The transition is not beyond the bounds of classic wit, but it is abrupt
beyond the immediate expectation of the opening; and the next
step down to F sharp defines the scope of the wit, and shows that
the range of harmony and tonality is that of the later and not of
the earlier nineteenth century. The process reaches a climax which
shows that the work is to be on a large scale. How large we do
not yet know, but the proportions are already noble, and show a
freedom that ought to have convicted of error those critics who
explained Brahms as an imitator of Schumann. But they were pre-
occupied with the discovery that the opening theme, like most of
the themes in Mozart's Jupiter Symphony, was lacking in originality.

This climax is marked by a new theme on the dominant of B
minor.

Ex. 2.

Its continuation leads to a tutti counter-statement of Ex. 1,
glorified by Beethovenish high trumpets and modulating to the
dominant, from which the bass takes a new turn, passing through
F sharp minor and C sharp minor, to return from that remote
region abruptly to the tonic. Here Ex. 2 appears, and for the
moment we have an impression of a structure frequent in the first
works of Brahms's maturity, very large in its immediate impression,
but needing all Brahms's caution to prevent it from forming a completeness of its own that may prove destructive to the completeness
of the whole. Here that danger is averted, inasmuch as Ex. 2 now
proves to be not on the tonic at all, but to be running down the
dominant seventh of the key of A, thus presenting the old classical
feature known as 'dominant preparation' in a very drastic form.
Not less bold is the way in which the last two notes are turned
into the accompaniment to the main theme of the second group.
Theme and accompaniment are alike the quintessence of Brahms.

Ex. 3.

No one before Brahms had attempted musical sentences of such range; and Brahms alone developed a means of continuing them without stiffness or obscurity. Two short cadence-themes complete the exposition. The first is repeated with an expansion by echoes in a manner first invented by Brahms. The second—

Ex. 4.

is also repeated, and expanded by development. In its expanded counter-statement it is combined with a derivative of Ex. 3 in the bass. The exposition is repeated, and the repeat should be observed as an essential feature of the style. In spite of the great breadth of the design it is not inordinately long, and the tempo is exceptionally quick for Brahms.

The development begins by discussing Ex. 4, which leads to the remote key of C sharp minor. Here a new derivative of Ex. 1 appears. It is another kind of transformation invented by Brahms, and having the value of a spontaneous new idea.

Ex. 5.

Another novel transformation in double counterpoint bursts out hilariously in D flat (C sharp) major, and afterwards with reversed scoring in B flat—

Ex. 6.

alternating with another version combined with the figure of Ex. 3.

Then the untransformed first theme (as in Ex. 1) appears in the full orchestra in G, and is broadly developed, especially as to its second figure (*b*), modulating widely and quickly till it reaches a climax in D minor, a key which, being the home tonic, subsides on to the home dominant. On this, a long passage of preparation, punctuated by the rhythmic figure ♩ | ♩ ♩ | 𝅝 , slowly leads to the return of Ex. 1 in the tonic, with sunset glow from the subdominant. In this key the clarinet continues the recapitulation, which is easily brought into its normal course, comprising everything from Ex. 2 to Ex. 4 in the tonic. The coda is grafted into Ex. 4 without break. Beginning in triumph it dies away in one of the wittiest pianissimo exits since Haydn.

The first scherzo is an important movement with typically Brahmsish themes, of which the opening—

Ex. 7.

Sempre piano.

afterwards goes into close canon. It flows into another idea, as the quotation shows; and later on it gives rise to a more lyric phrase.

Ex. 8.

cres.

mf

The trio is a little quicker, and consists of a broad, symmetrical melody—

Ex. 9.

&c.

lounging in 8-bar periods over a bass that had been set swinging by the last two notes of the scherzo. The repeats of both parts are written out in full, the winds and strings having exchanged parts

In the slow movement Brahms writes in full sonata form with
second group, a big development, a full recapitulation, and a large
coda. He never did this again; in all his later slow movements, if
he approaches to sonata form in some features, he shortens it in
some others. Yet the present movement is not inordinately long:
the only question is whether *adagio* is not a misleading tempo-
mark for it, even with the qualification *non troppo*. Certainly there
is no part of it that would not be obviously ruined by dragging,
and the details are perfectly consistent with a flowing tempo
throughout. The listener, not taking the trouble to observe that
the conductor is beating quavers, will certainly think the first
theme very broad, with its shadowy turtle-dove crooning—

Ex. 10.

and its sequel not less broad, with its brighter colour and imitative dialogue.

Ex. 11.

Brahms alternates this pair in a miniature binary scheme which
saves itself from premature completeness by expanding and closing
into a new transition-theme.

Ex. 12.

Vibrating.

This owes much of its inspiration and quality of tone to the brook
in Beethoven's Pastoral Symphony; and it flows into a wide river,
passing through a remote key into a peaceful lake. Here, in the
dominant, reached through a remote key, we have the main theme
of a big second group.

Ex. 13.

This, also a paragraph of grand breadth, leads to another
big imitative theme in Brahms's most majestic and personal
style.

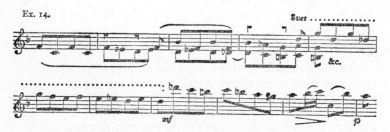

The exposition closes with a short cadence-group in counterpoint over the main figure of his theme. A spacious development
concerns itself first with Ex. 14; then with a peaceful rumination
on Ex. 13. This leads to the remote key of B major, really C flat.
And in this key the main theme, Ex. 10, enters in full, followed
after a moment's hesitation by Ex. 11. Before this reaches its first
close, it discovers that the home tonic is not so remote after all,
and so the counter-statement of both themes follows at home,
Ex. 11 being now richly varied. Its end gives rise to a debate which
eventually leads to the transition-theme Ex. 12, now flowing in
home channels. Ex. 13 sails upon it triumphantly, and the rest
of the recapitulation follows without further change. A quiet
coda alludes to the treatment of Ex. 14 towards the end of the
development.

The tiny pair of minuets (scored practically for the instruments
of the nonet which was the original form of this serenade) has
always been a popular orchestral trifle. In its rightful place it will
be still better appreciated. The second scherzo needs no quotation.
The more risky (*sittenverderblich*) features of the scherzo of Beethoven's Septet and Second Symphony have been bowdlerized in the
main body; and the trio of the scherzo of Beethoven's F major
Violin Sonata has been kept in order by Brahms's wind-band, led
by the horns.

The final rondo is on a grand scale, with a big rondo theme in
three strains of the usual A B A form for such members.

Ex. 16.

The epigrammatic twist in the 3rd and 4th bars of Ex. 16 is characteristic of many other simple-seeming utterances in this dangerous
work. Still more dangerous is the theme of the first episode or
second group. Its point is not that, like all possible horn-themes,
it reminds us of the first movement, but that where it seems to
repeat itself the repetition is at a different rhythmic place. This
makes a zeugma or syllepsis of the form typified by 'the lady left
in tears and a sedan chair'. Further, it consists of two themes in
double counterpoint.

Ex. 17.

The second episode develops the two themes of Ex. 17 indepen-
dently, beginning in an unexpected key thus—

Ex. 18.

A short circuit is made, eliminating a third entry of the rondo
theme and leading to a recapitulation of the first episode, in which
the themes of Ex. 17 are interchanged in position and the triplet
theme varied in semiquavers.

Ex. 19.

After this the expected return of the main theme is, for a few surprising bars, in the minor. But it soon brightens to major, and a magnificent coda broadens out in triumph, introducing several further transformations, and trailing clouds of glory to the end.

XVI. SERENADE IN A MAJOR FOR SMALL ORCHESTRA, OP. 16

1 *Allegro moderato.* 2 SCHERZO. *Vivace.* 3 *Adagio non troppo.* 4 *Quasi Menuetto.* 5 RONDO. *Allegro.*

Brahms wrote his first serenade in 1858, and his second, the present work, in 1859. The instrumental serenade of Mozart and Haydn is, at its largest, a symphony in cheerful style with a large number of movements, sometimes including a kind of intercalary concerto which counts as a separate work. Thus Mozart's Haffner Serenade has, besides a second minuet among its five symphonic movements, three large movements in concerto style with a solo violin; and his next largest serenade ('with the post-horn') has a concertante of two movements for a group of solo wind instruments. Not all serenades are so large; many contain no highly developed movements. A divertimento is supposed to be a serenade for a few solo instruments not constituting an orchestra; but the distinction is not clearly maintained. Mozart gives the name of serenade to his three largest works for wind instruments alone, though one of them is in perfectly regular form and was simply called a quintet when he arranged it as a string quintet. There is no accepted name for a piece for thirteen instruments; and perhaps Mozart had not heard of the word 'octet' as a current term, so this may account for his calling his C minor Octet a serenade.

Brahms's First Serenade, in D major, op. 11, was first written as a nonet, and accordingly called a divertimento. But it was immediately recast for 'grosses Orchester'. The term 'full orchestra' implies the use of trumpets and drums; trombones are not necessary for the title; but without trumpets and drums the orchestra ranks as 'small'. The D major Serenade contains much that is quintessentially Brahms, and also much that is ostentatiously reminiscent of early Beethoven—the Beethoven of the Septet. Every age has its own central criterion of art; and each later age sees how its predecessor's criterion was misleading. In the eighteenth century our central criterion was correctness. We are

emerging from an age in which the central criterion is originality,
a much less fruitful concept. Correctness may be wrongly defined
and wrongly valued; but it will always refer to ascertainable
things, and the mistakes in its use will be witnesses available for
cross-examination as to the truth. Originality is a concept which
everybody can apply without control, while nobody can judge of
it unless he knows every possible antecedent of the work he is
criticizing. After a century it becomes unrecognizable: unless the
power of extended composition is shown, there is not an expert
living who can tell Handel from Buononcini by ear; and the
contemporary poet was quite right in summing up the Handel-
Buononcini controversy in the lines—

> Strange that such difference there should be
> 'Twixt Tweedledum and Tweedledee.

Permanent values depend on more ascertainable things than
the question, who told the truth first. The artist's conviction of
the truth is not to be weakened by such a question; the poet can
call the sky blue, or even rhyme 'dove' with 'love', if these details
are the right things in the right place. The quality of the style
line by line, and the power to organize the work as a whole, these
things will remain, though 'tea' cease to rhyme with 'obey', and
though the embargo be removed that forbids the poet of to-day to
apply the epithet 'blooming' to his mistress's cheek. Meanwhile
it is extremely doubtful whether any valuable criticism, or any
artistic principle whatever, has been pronounced by people who
take originality for their criterion. They do not even make significant mistakes: they fail to touch permanent values at any point;
and their judgements will be merely unintelligible a generation
hence. But this useless criterion still dominates us to such an
extent that a performance of Brahms's First Serenade is a risky
undertaking for a conductor who cares for the fashion of to-day.
I have produced it; and shall produce it again if and when I dare.
But there is no danger in producing the Second Serenade. It ranks
high among Brahms's works for mellowness of style, and for the
number of peculiar features in whole and in detail. It was coldly
received in Germany, but had extraordinary success at its first
performances in England, which took place before Brahms's symphonies had come into existence. Since then it has dropped out
of the ordinary concert repertory, being quite as difficult as the
symphonies, and very quiet and intimate in style.

The 'small orchestra' has a full complement of wood-wind and two
horns, but no violins. At the beginning of the nineteenth century
Méhul wrote a rather beautiful opera, *Uthal*, on an Ossianic subject;
and, in order to obtain an atmosphere of Northern mystery and

fog, used no violins. Musical historians usually tell us that the
result was monotonous, and that Grétry cried 'Five francs for an E
string!' But they omit to mention that the opera was only in one act.
It is, in fact, not much longer than Brahms's Second Serenade.
Brahms is hardly likely, at the age of 26, to have read *Uthal*,
though Joachim produced it many years later in Berlin. If the
sound of violas as leaders came to Brahms from any source but
his own imagination, he may have heard it in the second act of
Tannhäuser, during the ascetic praises of love which exasperate
Tannhäuser into revealing his mortal sin. But Brahms's intention
in this Serenade differs from that of all previous examples of the
absence of violins. As in *Uthal*, the tone of the violas is dark and
veiled, and has its own value accordingly; but its main purpose
is to throw the wind into high relief. Thus the Serenade is a work
mainly for wind instruments, which are treated with the utmost
fullness and variety of tone, while they are at the same time relieved
from the burden of supplying their own background. Brahms took
great pains over this work and set great store by opportunities for
an adequate performance. Composed in 1859, it was twice revised,
first in 1860, to what extent I do not know, and again in 1875.
The revision of 1875 concerns only a few details of scoring.

The first movement, in normal sonata form, begins with a pair
of contrasted themes, of which the first—

Ex. 1.

establishes the tonic, and leads to the second—

Ex. 2.

which emphasizes the dominant chord with minor colouring. A
counter-statement shifts Ex. 1 into the subdominant, and brings
Ex. 2 on to the dominant of the dominant key, which key it establishes fully, leading to a second group containing two new themes.
The first of these, swaying indolently over a dance-rhythm—

Ex. 3.

is one of those long paragraphs in which Brahms, from his very
first works onwards, showed an inventiveness and mastery that
amounted to new resources in musical architecture. The second
is a quiet cadence-theme, still accompanied by the same dance-
rhythm.

Ex. 4.

The development, starting with the eight bars of Ex. 1, as if to
repeat the exposition, works Ex. 2 into an imbroglio which
modulates widely and comes to a climax in F. This dies down with
a sudden drop into D flat, where Ex. 1 is resumed and combined
in new ways with Ex. 2. The first two notes (a) of Ex. 1 become
accelerated into an oscillation, first in crotchets, then in triplets,
which settles down as a steady accompaniment. Again we have
covered a wide range of key, from which an oboe brings us back
with a long-drawn strain which lands us on a tonic pedal. This
pedal is on our home-tonic—though we may not at first be sure
of the fact. But it is a great moment when we first reach it as the
beginning of a dialogue—

Ex. 5.

that lasts for no less than twenty-six bars, and then, by drifting into
the recapitulation, reveals to us that we have been at home all this
time.

The recapitulation is quite regular. The coda begins with Ex. 1
in F major on the strings, with a beautiful new counterpoint on
the oboe. In the course of a very expressive dialogue the bass
drifts downwards. The climax of emotion brings us back to the
home tonic, and the bass thence descends in terms of Ex. 3,
while figure (a) makes slow cadences in dialogue until the movement
dies away.

A tiny little scherzo displays great energy with cross-rhythmed
epigrams in the key of C.

Ex. 6.

Its main rhythmic figure underlies the quieter but not less epigrammatic trio.

Ex. 7.

The slow movement, though not long, is one of the most
elaborate things Brahms ever wrote. Its main section moves on
a ground bass—

Ex. 8.

which, like those in some of Bach's slow movements, from time
to time changes its key. After eight rotations have brought us to a
full close in C major, an episode begins with dramatic modulations.

Ex. 9.

These modulations lead to the extremely remote key of A flat, on
the dominant of which a horn bursts out surprisingly with a
passionately triumphant urgency.

Ex. 10.

Two new themes follow in tonic positions. The first—

Ex. 11.

includes in its paragraph an inversion of the ground-bass figure.

The second I do not quote. It is given out by the clarinet and answered by the basses, and its close finishes the central episode.

The ground-bass reappears in C minor as a fugue-subject, answered in syncopated inversion and developed closely in modulating sequences. After a climax, the first of its original counterpoints (unquoted) appears in the horn, and is carried up through three steps of modulating sequence which bring us to the home tonic, where the original counterpoint is delivered in the manner of a return to the opening. At first, however, the ground-bass is 'diminished' to a quaver figure of accompaniment in the violas. But it soon resumes its original shape, and the movement is rounded off by the recurrence, in the home tonic with subdominant colour, of the counterpoint which had led to the close in C before the episode.

The *Quasi Menuetto*, in D major, brings the mellow mood of the whole serenade to its full ripeness.

The initial figure (*a*) of the main theme—

set at a different harmonic angle, underlies the whole of the mysterious and plaintive trio.

In the final rondo the mood changes to one of child-like high spirits. It is the childlike quality that keeps the rollicking details in touch with the thoughtfulness of the rest. The triplet figure (*c*) of the main theme—

Ex. 15.

is pure merry-go-round; but it is the merry-go-round as enjoyed
by the child, not as exposed by the realist. A transition-theme
in imitative dialogue—

Ex. 16.

leads to the main theme of the first episode, which is more reflective
in its Mendelssohnian way. (Brahms saw no reason to suppose
that Mendelssohn's idioms were inherently bad.)

Ex. 17.

It is elusive in its rhythm, sometimes, as here at the outset,
dating its period before its first note, and sometimes making its
first note an anacrusis to the rest, so that the first clause is three
bars instead of four. (A still more complex rhythmic quibble
characterizes the first episode of the finale of the D major Serenade,
in a theme which has often been accused of being quite unoriginal.)
A feature of the second episode is the augmentation of the
rollicking main theme into a quiet ruminating passage in D major.

A piccolo is added to the orchestra of this finale, and is used
with a recklessness about which Brahms does not seem to have
felt squeamish, since he left it in evidence after two careful revisions
at intervals of fifteen years. Presumably his standard of performance was high, and piccolos were not supposed to squeal without
restraint, even if their parts were marked like those of less demo-
cratic instruments.

XVII. HAYDN THE INACCESSIBLE

Handel and Haydn are, each in a different way, the most unknown of popular classics. What the public hears of Handel represents about one-fiftieth of his works, and that fiftieth is so disguised by modern 'traditions' and by ignorance of eighteenth-century technique that Handel would often have difficulty in recognizing it. But at all events his complete works are published, so that scholars can find out the truth.

Haydn is in better case in so far as it is etiquette to present his music in a fairly authentic way; but otherwise he is in worse case than any other classic, for not one tenth of his work is accessible in print at all. It is a thousand pities that Haydn was not included in the great series of soi-disant critical editions of musical classics which were produced in the 'seventies, and, with all their defects, have at least placed within reach of every respectable musical library a plain ungarbled text of the complete works of Bach, Beethoven, Mozart, Handel, Mendelssohn, Schubert, Schumann, Schütz, Palestrina, Victoria, and Sweelinck—to mention only those undertakings which have been completed. No doubt a critical edition of Haydn begun in 1875 would have been as badly begun and as imperfectly carried out as the rest of the series; but the later volumes would, as usual, have corrected and criticized the earlier, and our knowledge of the most interesting and important chapter in the whole history of music—the early history of the art which Beethoven consummated—would be incomparably clearer than it is at present. Moreover, hundreds of masterpieces would assuredly be brought to light which ought never to have been allowed to be buried. Mendelssohn and Schumann, whose copyrights have hardly yet expired, could well have waited; even Schütz was less important; and as for some of the 'historically interesting' composers whose works have since been produced with remorseless completeness, I confess that I sometimes wonder whether a cultivated interest in them is compatible with a cultivated interest in anything worth hearing.

Early in this century a complete edition of Haydn's works was begun. Unfortunately the great musical scholar to whom it was entrusted began his enormous task at the beginning, by publishing three volumes containing the first forty-one of Haydn's 104 symphonies. If the editor had been a dryasdust all would have been well. But his full powers as a scholar required mature and highly organized music to bring them out, music where textual problems are interesting and can be solved only by artistic insight and knowledge of style. Haydn's maturest style is far from precise: his early style is of a roughness that removes every vestige of interest from questions of detail. Pedants raised dull controversies over the first three volumes; the Great War intervened before the vast gap between Haydn's earliest and mature style was bridged; and Haydn still remains without the near prospect of an authoritative text of the works in which he formed his style.

We need hardly be surprised, then, if musical treatises prove to be rather at sea about most points in Haydn's art and style. He is rightly acknowledged to be 'the Father of the Symphony'. Accordingly the first edition of *Grove's Dictionary of Music and Musicians*, in the perky and up-to-date article on Instrumentation, quotes a passage from the *Surprise Symphony* (written somewhere about the time Mozart died) with patronizing approval as from an 'early work' of Haydn. He is rightly believed to be on a level with Mozart as a master of form: but his form is described as 'regular and symmetrical'. And when you come to look at it, you find not only that all the rules of form as observed by both Mozart and Beethoven are frequently violated by Haydn, but that they are so seldom observed that it would be quite impossible to infer them from his mature practice at all.

More recent writers have tried to show some recognition of this by saying that in Haydn's works we see the sonata forms 'in the making'. This only increases the confusion; for Haydn's most nearly regular works are his earlier ones, when he wrote on the lines of J. C. and C. P. E. Bach; whereas his freedom of form becomes manifest just about the time when he came to know Mozart. The mutual influence of Haydn and Mozart is one of the best-known wonders of musical history; and the paradox of it is that while its effect on Mozart was to concentrate his style and strengthen his symmetry, the effect on Haydn was to set him free, so that his large movements became as capricious in their extended course of events as his minuets had always been in the cast of their phrases. The orthodox theory of a sonata form with a first subject in the main key and a second subject in a 'complementary' key will do fairly well for Mozart and Beethoven as long as we understand by 'subject' no single theme but a large group of heterogeneous material. And it is fairly true for Mozart and Beethoven that, after the 'exposition' of these two groups, there will be a 'development' which develops whatever it chooses from these themes by grouping their fragments into changing combinations in various shifting keys; and that, with a return to the main key, there will be a 'recapitulation' which recapitulates the first and second subject, both in the tonic; while whatever then remains to be said, will be said as a 'coda'.

But with most of the mature works of Haydn this account simply will not do. Here follows a perfunctory analysis of eleven of

Haydn's last thirteen symphonies (Nos. 92–104). Précis-writing, such as I have given of Beethoven's Ninth Symphony, would, though unreadable except as a dictionary is readable with a Greek play, compel the student to see that no two such symphonies are alike. There is no such monotony in them as there is in my enforced reiterations that Haydn is not conforming to a scheme based on what Hummel, Spohr, and Clementi could make of him and Mozart in generalizations imitable by docile students. But, as I am only too thankful that there are any such students to write for, I must consider their needs and enforce my reiterations.

XVIII. SYMPHONY IN G MAJOR 'LETTER V'

CHRONOLOGICAL LIST, NO. 88

1 *Adagio, leading to Allegro*. 2 *Largo*. 3 MENUETTO. *Allegretto*. 4 FINALE. *Allegro con spirito*.

Haydn's own catalogue of his works numbers this as his 88th symphony, and so places its probable date as 1786, the year of the Paris Symphonies and five years before the first of the London Symphonies. The quality of Haydn's inventiveness is nowhere higher and its economy nowhere more remarkable than in this work. To judge a piece of music by its themes is never wise, and the habit of so judging rests on the mistakes of assuming that all musical ideas are expressed in that single category of musical articulation to which the word 'theme' belongs. A work of which the identifiable themes are conspicuously beautiful may be like this exquisite little symphony of Haydn's, or like Beethoven's great B flat Trio, or like any work whatever by Spohr. In Spohr's case the beauty of the themes is the reason why the works exist: their treatment is the same in all cases. But with Haydn, as with Beethoven, Mozart, Bach, and Handel, the themes are not really more separable from their treatment (or, in other words, are not more the sole repository of the ideas) when they are conspicuously beautiful than when they appear to consist only of tags. The themes of Mozart's G minor Symphony are for the most part highly original and pregnant in themselves. In the so-called Jupiter Symphony the only theme that is not common property is that of a little *aria buffa* ('Voi siete un po' tondo, mio caro Pompeo') borrowed for use and rich development in the first movement. But a critic who should say that Mozart's invention was drying up in the Jupiter Symphony, would be well advised to consult a doctor. Yet an eminent French critic (and all French critics are eminent) did notice this decadence in *Die Zauberflöte* and seriously pointed out that two bars of the theme of its overture (*not* including the sforzandos off the beat) were plagiarized from a sonata by Clementi.

There is a river in Monmouth and a river in Macedon; there is a B in both; there is in Haydn's 88th symphony a formal introduction that has no mysterious features, and there is the following opening figure of the allegro—

Ex. 1.

Very clever persons, who take in music by the eye, have pointed out the extraordinary resemblance between this theme and that of the finale of Beethoven's Eighth Symphony. The resemblance is equivalent to the scriptural warrant of the minister who, wishing to inveigh against a prevalent frivolity in head-gear, preached upon the text, 'Top-knot, come down!'—which he had found in Matt. xxiv. 17 ('Let him which is on the housetop not come down').

The Top-knot school of exegesis still flourishes in music. This theme of Haydn's is as pregnant as that in Beethoven's Eighth Symphony, but it means something totally different both in harmony and in rhythm; nor did Beethoven's theme, in all the transformations it went through in his sketch-books, resemble it more in the earliest stages than in its final form. But the strangest thing about Beethoven's originality was that he was quite capable of amusing himself by noting discoveries in the best Top-knot manner. There is a coincidence of no less than nine notes between the theme of the finale of Mozart's G minor Symphony and that of the scherzo of Beethoven's C minor Symphony, and he noted it in his sketch-book! The point of noting it is precisely the utter contrast and absence of any significance common to the two ideas.

A detailed analysis from phrase to phrase would be needed to show the originality of Haydn's treatment of Ex. 1, or indeed of any of his themes.

There is a second theme, besides counterpoints and bustling transitional matter; but the rhythmic figure (a) is never long absent.

Of the glorious theme of the slow movement—

Ex. 2.

I was told by John Farmer that he once heard Brahms play it with
wallowing enthusiasm, exclaiming, 'I want my ninth symphony to
to be like this!'

Here is a clear case of a movement that is to be measured by its
theme. From that theme Haydn himself tries in vain to stray. He
modulates to the dominant. That is treated as an incident in the
course of the melody, which promptly repeats itself in full. The
modulation is tried again with a new continuation. But the new
continuation wistfully returns in four bars through the minor mode.
Let us, then, have a variation. But not too varied; only a little
decoration in counterpoint to our melody. But perhaps the full
orchestra, with trumpets and drums, which were not used in the
first movement, can effect a diversion. What it does effect is that
a sequel shows enough energy to lead fully into the key of the
dominant, instead of merely on to its threshold, so that the whole
great tune now follows in that key.

The old sequel then returns to the tonic, and to the tune.
Another tutti introduces the minor mode, and leads to a key,
F major, related only to the tonic minor. This is definitely a remote
modulation, and in F major the tune enters, but has to exert itself
with new rhetoric before it can return to its own key. There we
hear it yet again, with a short coda in which Brahms's ninth
symphony retires into a heaven where Brahms, accompanied by
his faithful red hedgehog, can discuss it with Haydn, Beethoven,
and Schubert over a dinner cooked by Maître du Clavecin
Couperin, and washed down by the best Bach.

(*Der Rote Igel* was Brahms's favourite Vienna restaurant, and
when the manager told him, 'Sir, this is the Brahms of wines,'
he replied, 'Take it away and bring me some Bach'; scilicet:
brook, or water.)

The minuet is cheerful, with a quiet joke on the drums. The
trio is one of Haydn's finest pieces of rustic dance music, with
hurdy-gurdy drones which shift in disregard of the rule forbidding
consecutive fifths. The disregard is justified by the fact that the
essential objection to consecutive fifths is that they produce the
effect of shifting hurdy-gurdy drones.

Haydn never produced a more exquisitely bred kitten than the
main theme of the finale.

Ex. 3.

The first strain (8 bars) ends in B minor, the mediant, instead of the
usual dominant, which is prominent in the second strain. There
are bustling tutti themes, but the bulk of the movement arises from

the main theme. Its initial figure (*a*) is of two notes only, and is thus quite unconnected with the 3–note rhythmic figure (*a*) of Ex. 1. The movement is in rondo form, which is by no means so common as might be expected in Haydn's symphonies and larger quartets. Haydn has a way of beginning an important finale like a big rondo, and then, after one episode, running away into some sort of fugue that gives an impression of spacious development which suffices without further formal sections. The completeness of rondo form in the present finale thus rather reduces its scale in comparison with many finales that are actually shorter. This fact is a melodic quality, not a formal or dramatic defect.

XIX. SYMPHONY IN G ('OXFORD').

CHRONOLOGICAL LIST, NO. 92

1 *Adagio, leading to* 2 *Allegro spiritoso.* 3 *Adagio.* 4 *Menuetto, allegretto.* 5 *Presto.*

This typical product of Haydn's hilarious maturity was written for the occasion of his receiving the Doctorate of Music at Oxford. It proved too difficult for the available resources, and so an earlier work was substituted. It would be interesting to know exactly what it was that the players on that occasion found specially difficult. The work still has traps for the unwary, but I doubt whether we should find the one substituted for it much easier. Haydn's freedom and unconventionality will complicate the analysis of any of his mature works. Many of his eccentricities— including his difficult passages—show clear traces of his early practical experience, as distinguished from any theories of his own or of earlier times. For example, his love of long passages for wind-instruments alone has been ascribed (why, I cannot think) by some of our highest authorities to a survival of the groupings of instruments in the old concerto grosso. I am quite unable to remember any concerto grosso where passages like these of Haydn's occur; but they occur in operatic music both before Haydn's maturity and in later times, being an obvious means of effect. The early classical wood-wind group is, on the whole, feeble and shrill (especially when there are no clarinets), and makes a theatrical contrast of airy innocence against the bluster of the full orchestra with its rumbling basses and its kettledrums with their dignified thunder and rousing slam. All this is utterly foreign to the spirit of the concerto grosso; and, like other traits of Haydn's art which have been hastily described as primitive, it is far more characteristic of his later than of his earlier work. But he probably learnt its possibilities during his many years of daily practical experiment as court-composer at Esterhaz.

Another thing which might be deduced from the later works, even if the earlier works were not there to show it, is that the little orchestra at Esterhaz must, at various times and in various proportions, have contained some of the finest virtuoso players in Europe side by side with players whose tracks needed covering. In many of Haydn's later works there is something specially tricky for the horn, something of which a clever player can find the knack, but which practical composers do not write nowadays. In the Oxford Symphony the jumping figure of accompaniment to the theme of the finale (see Ex. 4, where, for convenience, it is given an octave higher) is a characteristic example. When we trace Haydn's art back to the Esterhaz period, we find that he was then in a position to write for a quartet of horns in a style compared with which Bach's horn-writing is almost easy. In the same way he treats his violoncellos with a confidence which you will not find in Beethoven, who never entrusts them with a melody unsupported by violas. Perhaps, however, there are two sides to this question, for I cannot recollect that Haydn ever gives the violas anything prominent; so that the question may be also whether Beethoven did not bring forward the viola, and support it by violoncellos.

On the other hand, one of the chief troubles in Haydn's maturest scoring comes from his unwillingness to let a wind instrument sing a tune above accompanying strings without making the first violins play it too. The publication of Haydn's early and middle works having been arrested by patriotic and pedantic jealousies, it is difficult to trace the course of this tendency; but I believe the explanation to lie in that obvious practical process which has dulled the colouring of many a later composer, by inciting him to make a dangerous passage safe by doubling it on a more trustworthy but less characteristic instrument. None of these things are at all primitive; and just as it is a misconception that refers them to survivals from older traditions, so is it a misconception which ignores their presence in modern music, in forms outwardly different, but easily recognizable by any one who understands their principles.

No one can listen to the Oxford Symphony without being struck by the varieties of orchestral colour that Haydn gets from his resources and habits. Often there is more in the score than any one performance is likely to bring out. In the small orchestra of Esterhaz every orchestral group was transparent to every other; and so Haydn never got rid of the notion that a single flute could make itself heard through a full orchestral forte without troubling to keep up to its highest octave. But I strongly suspect that Haydn asked for double wind in his later works whenever he found the string band at all strong; otherwise what is the origin of his custom of applying the word 'solo' to special passages for single

wind instruments ? It has now come to mean 'lead', irrespective
of the number of instruments in unison.

The forms of the Oxford Symphony are, with every appearance
of sonata style and symmetry, so free that adequate analysis
would involve describing almost every individual phrase. There is
hardly any long passage in the first movement that could be disposed of by a technical term, least of all by such terms as 'second
subject' and 'recapitulation'. The introduction was undoubtedly
in some former incarnation a saintly tabby cat whom Thoth or
Ra (or whatever deity is in charge of cats) has elevated to the
heavens of Haydn's imagination. My first quotation gives its
transition from the fireside to the outer world.

Ex. 1.

The allegro spiritoso, having thus begun as if butter would not
melt in its mouth, promptly goes off with a bang, and works up the
two principal figures (*a*) and (*b*) of its theme into a movement so
spacious and so full of surprises that it might well seem to be
among the longest Haydn ever wrote. As a matter of fact it is
among his shortest. But the so-called recapitulation is designed
exactly like one of Beethoven's biggest codas, while the so-called
second subject (which in the exposition differed in material from
the first only by introducing a single square little dance-tune) gives
rise to all manner of new features in this coda. Thus the prevailing
impression is one of perpetual expansion as regards themes and
phrases and developments, while the perfect balance of keys and
harmonies provides that sense of underlying symmetry which
makes the expansion so exhilarating.

From the slow movement I quote enough of the first melody
to show its breadth and its Haydnesque spirit of gravity and grace.

Ex. 2.

This theme is built up into a complete self-contained form, the repeats of its two sections being varied by fresh scoring. Upon its last bar the full orchestra bursts with a storm in the minor mode. The angry outbreak alternates with a quiet theme in F major.

Ex. 3.

The design of the whole movement is ostensibly the simple form describable as A B A, where A is the main theme and B the middle episode; but Haydn here lifts it altogether out of the sphere of such things as the minuet and trio (the obvious case of the form at its simplest) by reproducing Ex. 3 in D major, and developing it into a beautiful coda, mainly entrusted to the unaccompanied wood-wind.

The minuet and trio are splendid examples of Haydn's inventiveness and freedom of rhythm. The scoring of the trio is especially rich with its syncopated horns and pizzicato strings. I give no quotations. This movement cannot, like the minuets of Haydn's London Symphonies, be said to anticipate Beethoven's scherzos. It has its own business to mind, as a quick minuet such as Haydn was not yet tired of. He did not often write a slow one, except as a finale in rondo or variation form for small sonata-works; the minuet of the Military Symphony is almost the only minuet and trio of Haydn's (except one in the early Quartet, op. 9, no. 4) that belongs to the 'stately' type, which is, indeed, far less common in classical music than it is generally thought to be.

The finale begins with one of the most delightful of all Haydn's themes.

Ex. 4.

Presto.

Nobody can say quite how often this theme recurs; the orchestra itself gets into heated arguments as to how the tune really goes, and the doubts generally arise from the third bar onwards. A daddy-long-legs of a second subject sprawls affably into the discussion under pretence of satisfying orthodox theories.

Ex. 5.

It is impossible to describe Haydn's themes, when he is in his Oxford manner, without feeling irresponsible; but the life his themes live is one that has no room for meanness or triviality. This is great music; and nothing other than great music, whether tragic, majestic, or comic, can stand beside it.

XX. SYMPHONY IN G MAJOR: 'THE SURPRISE' (SALOMON, NO. 5; CHRONOLOGICAL LIST, NO. 94)

1 *Adagio, leading to* 2 *Vivace.* 3 *Andante.* 4 MENUETTO: *Allegro.* 5 FINALE: *Allegro.*

The 'surprise' in this symphony is the most unimportant feature in all Haydn's mature works; being merely a single loud chord in the course of an ostentatiously simple tune in the slow movement, at which, said Haydn, all the ladies would scream. There are many outbursts both louder and more sudden elsewhere in this and in all Haydn's symphonies; he was considered a noisy composer in his day; and if it is not noisy to make abrupt contrasts between the softest and the loudest values of an orchestra with trumpets and drums, we must reconsider our use of the term. At all events, no music expresses high spirits more efficiently than Haydn's. And his forms become the more subtle as his animal spirits rise. In this symphony the first movement and finale are among his most brilliant creations. The introduction begins with a broadly melodious dialogue between wind and strings, which might well be the theme of a developed movement. But romantic Haydnesque shadows pass over it, and it leads to the real first movement, which begins slyly, for a moment, outside the main key.

Ex. 1.

When a main theme begins thus on a foreign chord, two consequences are possible as to its return. The return may be prepared by a great emphasis on or towards the key of the foreign chord, in which case the arrival of the theme will be a surprise, inasmuch as the remote key did not at first remind us of home. This effect Haydn brings off on repeating his exposition. If, on the other hand, emphasis is directed to the dominant of our own tonic, the main theme, beginning there or thereabouts. will glide off in some quite new direction. Haydn is very well aware of all such possibilities; and he always uses the one you did not expect.

His 'second subject', more regular than usual with him, begins with as unrestrained an outbreak of dance-rhythm—

as can be found in symphonic music, and subsides into one of Haydn's inimitable pastoral tunes.

Ex. 2.

In the recapitulation Haydn interpolates (as usual) one of Beethoven's most brilliant codas between the waltz and this tune.

The theme of the slow movement, when taken as an andante according to Haydn's present instructions, has an anserine solemnity which undoubtedly enhances the indecorum of the famous *Paukenschlag*. Some years afterwards Haydn put it in a different light when in his *Seasons* he took it at a lively pace and gave it to a piccolo, to represent the whistling of the ploughman as he 'tunes his wonted lay'. But in the symphony it waddles through the poultry-yard in several variations, the first being in the minor and inclined to episodic developments. At the return to the major mode the oboe seems to have laid an egg. The subsequent variations show fine contrasts of colour; and the coda, as always in Haydn's mature slow movements, rises to poetry.

The minuet is lively and full-toned, while the trio, in the same key, gives one of Haydn's most original melodies to the first violin, doubled in various ways by solo wind instruments.

The finale works out a rondo-like melody—

Ex. 3.

into a highly developed sonata form with a well-contrasted 'second subject'.

Ex. 4.

The returns of these themes show the height of Haydn's power in the unexpected-inevitable.

XXI. SYMPHONY IN C MINOR (SALOMON, NO. 9; CHRONOLOGICAL LIST, NO. 95)

1 *Allegro moderato.* 2 *Andante.* 3 MENUETTO. 4 FINALE: *Vivace.*

The inexhaustible Haydn most nearly approaches to regularity in form when he is writing in a minor key. In quick movements (first movements or finales), the minor mode inspires him to a temper too blustering for tragedy, though solemnity is (as in his most comic moments) never far off. Unlike the cynics, he is literal-minded in his serious note, and it is his humour that is all in play. But he is no tragedian; and the minor mode impels him to become formal because formality is outwardly solemn. And then, as he once said, apropos of not wishing to be flattered by embarrassed portrait-painters, 'anybody can see that I'm a good-natured fellow'. He is too great to be compared with Dr. Johnson's friend Edwards, who found that philosophizing would not do because cheerfulness was always breaking in. But he could have put Mr. Edwards into a minuet or a mysterious introduction without waiting to collect the opinions of Bozzy's eminent friends that 'this was an exquisite trait of character'.

Of the twelve great London Symphonies written between 1791 and 1795, this is the only one without an introduction. An experienced musician will see at a glance that the pregnant opening figure is destined for polyphonic development; e.g. as the bass for all manner of modulating sequences: while all Haydn-lovers will know they may expect rhythmic expansion in the continuation.

Ex. 1.

The second subject, reached in a few masterly and masterful strokes, promptly shows that 'I'm a good-natured fellow'. I quote it with the scale-counterpoint which adorns it on repetition.

Ex. 2.

In most published scores this figure disappears in the recapitulation: but the new critical edition shows that Haydn (probably during a rehearsal) added it on a solo violin, a detail which enhances the heavenliness of Haydn's cheerful recapitulation.

The andante is an example of one of Haydn's variation-cum-rondo designs. It is no use offering a prize for guesses as to how Haydn will continue a given lyric melody—the Haydn kitten has more ways of jumping than the great god Whirligig himself (whom, as we learn in *The Water Babies*, mortals call Public Opinion).

Ex. 3.

The tune is followed by a normal variation (melody in the violoncellos). A second quasi-variation in the minor turns out to be an episode, shorter than the theme, but with rhetorical pauses and some feeling of action in its way of leading back. Then, after stating the first part of the theme unvaried, a complete variation (in demisemiquavers, forte) runs its course, and the movement ends with a peaceful coda on the first part.

The minuet is on a large scale, as always in Haydn's mature symphonies. Its main body is in C minor, and is not without agitation. The trio is a brilliant and difficult violoncello solo in C major, accompanied by pizzicato strings. All Haydn's scores are remarkable for the confidence he shows in at least the leader of orchestral violoncellos; a point in which Beethoven differs notably from him.

Heavenly as is the opening of the finale—

Ex. 4.

the second part of this tune transcends it. The first phrase is destined for polyphony, and is so treated with great brilliance, passages of close canon alternating with occasional dramatic storms and peaceful returns to the main tune, in a free rondo form. The total effect of the symphony is so spacious that you would never guess that it is one of Haydn's tersest works.

XXII. SYMPHONY IN B FLAT (SALOMON, NO. 8; CHRONO-LOGICAL LIST, NO. 98)

1 *Adagio, leading to* **2** *Allegro.* **3** *Adagio cantabile.* **4** MENUETTO: *Allegro.* **5** FINALE: *Presto, ending with Più moderato.*

The inexhaustible Haydn was no more an academic composer than Verdi, who once avowed 'I am not a learned composer, but I am a very experienced one'. So was Haydn; but he was also a very

learned composer, though our academic dogmas have taken this on
trust and have carefully avoided facing the facts of his technique
and form. His technique, by which I mean his handling of instruments and musical texture generally, shows deep traces of
two disturbing causes, often closely allied and much alike in some
of their results; the first, a long experience of disappointment
gradually turned to success in securing good, or at all events safe,
performances under bad conditions; and the second, a confirmed
habit of composing at the pianoforte. The orchestral works of
Haydn's middle period, the forty-odd symphonies written between
1771 and 1788, are not yet accessible in full score. Meanwhile there
is no means of tracing the presumably not abrupt change from
the orchestration of the Esterhaz symphonies (the first forty or
so), where a crudely primitive treatment of the band as a whole
contrasts with appalling displays of virtuoso technique for individual instruments, to the orchestration of the Paris and London
Symphonies, in which the general orchestral tone and style are
among the infinities of art where comparisons are irrelevant,
although painful precautions are taken to save solo passages from
disaster. Thus, the theme of the finale of his last symphony is
obviously typical of the horn; but Haydn will not risk it on that
instrument except once in a tutti. Yet at Esterhaz in 1765 he wrote
a symphony with a quartet of horns, all four of which were to
execute fireworks compared with which Bach's most elaborate
writing would be easy. And nowadays a trumpeter or horn-player
who wishes to play Bach must either have a special instrument constructed, or else develop his lip into a condition in which he can play
nothing else. What is certain about Haydn's work at Esterhaz is
that it was written for performance, that it was practised under
conditions which literally enabled Haydn to ring his sitting-room
bell for players to come and try experiments, and that it was satisfactorily performed. Such are the possibilities of an orchestra
endowed on a living-wage-and-retiring-pension basis, even at a
time when the art of orchestration was primitive.

At Esterhaz, then, Haydn learned the utmost capacities of
individual instruments, and made more rapid progress with them
than with the orchestra as such. Strange to say, the one orchestral
player in whom he never lost confidence in his later experiences
was the leader of the violoncellos, for whom, in the accessible
symphonies of all periods, Haydn writes important and often
difficult solos. It is not strange that he should have been interested
in the instrument, for it, and a kind of gamba called the baryton,
were the instruments of Prince Esterhazy; but Haydn's later
experience of orchestras in the cold, hard world must have been
different from Beethoven's, for Beethoven invariably doubles his

orchestral violoncello melodies by violas and uses the solo leader
only once in all his works, the early *Prometheus* ballet.

In saying that Haydn was not only an experienced but a learned
composer, I have specially in mind the style and forms of this symphony. The Haydnesque animal spirits are moderated though not
suppressed in the first movement by highly intellectual themes
developed in ways which, though not actually more thoughtful,
seem more learned than usual. Haydn never lost his love of
practical joking, from the day when he was expelled from the
church choir for cutting off the pig-tail of the boy in front of him
(during Divine Service) to the day when, in 1792, he 'made the
ladies scream' by an unladylike bang in the andante of the
'Surprise' Symphony (no. 94, the third of these London Symphonies). But in the present symphony all the surprises are in
matters of harmonic, melodic, and rhythmic interest; and not even
the Great Bassoon Joke has time to intrude. The first two phrases
of the severely solemn and dark introduction show at once the kind
of surprise we are now to have as a means of educating our sense
of what to expect in music. My quotation stops short of the
point. Listeners and score-readers are all the better for a chance
of guessing right or wrong in such matters.

Ex. 1.

Adagio.

A third phrase leads back to the dominant of our main key, on
which dominant the introduction, scored for strings alone, pauses
with gestures of imperious expectation.

The allegro turns out to be based on the same theme.

Ex. 2.

Allegro.

The sceptred pall of the introduction has gone sweeping by, and
solemn tragedy is now perhaps forgotten, in spite of the theme's
remaining the same. But the high spirits are occupied in things of
the mind; and Haydn does not even yield to his usual love of a
cantabile melody. Late in the course of the second subject the

vigorous tuttis are silenced for an exquisite appeal to finer
sensibilities—

Ex. 3.

the phrase taking a profound turn of harmony before it closes.

The slow movement is one of Haydn's broadest and gravest
utterances. It might almost be called his Requiem for Mozart, the
news of whose death had so deeply shocked him during his London
visit. Nowhere in the latest works of Haydn or the earlier works of
Beethoven can we find such accurate modelling of forms upon
Mozart, as distinguished from mere reminiscences of phrase and
style. Reminiscences are there also, and, as is usual with reminiscences, are looser in style than their originals—but only, in the
present case, to achieve a point of their own by way of compensation. The style is more severe than the kind of Mozart-music that
Haydn is thinking of. The main figure of the first theme is a
devout phrase which Haydn afterwards used in his last great work,
The Seasons, in the prayer 'Sei nur gnädig', which develops into
a positive quotation from Mozart's Requiem (see Vol. V, p. 152).

Ex. 4.

Adagio cantabile.

As for the second subject, the following comparison is emphati-
cally not the kind of thing Brahms meant when he said that
'plagiarism is one of the stupidest topics of the noodles'.

Ex. 5.

Haydn, 1792.

Mozart, 1788.

As I have already hinted, and as the divergence of bars 5–6 shows, Haydn's reminiscence of Mozart's last symphony (miscalled 'Jupiter') is a little looser in structure—at the moment. He has not caught the cross-rhythm which in Mozart compresses the chromatic sequence and leaves room for a broader expanse before the close. On the other hand, Mozart's more highly organized paragraph is intended to be capped by a formal cadence-theme, whereas Haydn's purpose is to plunge dramatically into a strenuous development. The contrast between the two masters is thus seen even where Haydn is most touchingly docile towards his spiritual son, who has left him alone in the world of earthly music with only the awkward and stubborn young Beethoven to fill the void.

With the minuet and finale, Haydn's high spirits return in spate. The minuet needs no quotation, but the finale has some unique features. Its main theme is of a type which Haydn first struck in a string quartet of his middle period (op. 33, no. 2, in E flat). He wagered that the ladies at court never could wait till a piece of music was finished; and he won his wager by making his finale a little rondo on a tune easily broken into two-bar phrases, so that towards the end he need only stretch out the 'pauses between the clauses' until conversation must inevitably intervene.

His present theme is more highly organized—

Ex. 6.

but it and the second subject—

Ex. 7.

lend themselves to a style of quizzical iteration with unexpected, or, more subtly, with flatly obvious conclusions—for example—

Ex. 8.

In spoken language I have seen the contemporary counterpart of this style in some published and more unpublished letters of Mozart; and the method is identifiable in English with the old joke about the piece of church music in which the choir's main occupation was 'to catch this flee, to catch this flee, to catch this fleeting breath'. Scholars of Musical Comedy and Revue tell me that this figure constitutes a well-established art-form in modern poetry, but I cannot remember its technical name. Of course, its crude origins were known in ancient Greece as the παρὰ προσδοκίαν of Aristophanic Comedy—e.g. the sleepless Strepsiades: 'I'm bitten through the bed-clothes by a b-b-b-b-bailiff.' But, like Haydn, we digress.

In the development a solo violin emerges with Ex. 8 in a remote key, and the range of modulation is wider than my widest digression. But the most special surprise in the whole symphony is the coda, where Haydn changes the tempo to più moderato. The main beats of the rhythm remain thus enlarged to the end; and of course all the energy has, for the moment, dropped out of the main theme, which becomes very demure when you can count its six quavers. But perhaps you forgot that they can now divide into semiquavers faster than anything yet heard in this symphony. And so the coda rushes away in a torrent—

Ex. 9.
Più moderato.

and when the main theme finally returns, a glorious afterthought, pencilled by Haydn into the completed score and fortunately accessible in the now slowly progressing critical edition of his works, maintains the new flow to the end. This afterthought incidentally reveals that even in these ripest works of the veteran 'Father of the Symphony' a harpsichord or pianoforte was still used, like Bach's and Handel's continuo, to 'fill out' what in fact was no longer capable of additional fillings. The conductor, indeed, sat (as the programmes used to say) 'At the Pianoforte', instead of using a baton. As to any genuine continuo playing, one can, with Haydn's or Mozart's mature orchestration, only compare the functions of a pianoforte to those of the Beaver in the *Hunting of the Snark*, who sat quietly in the bow making lace, and occasionally studied arithmetic under expert guidance, but who 'had often, the

Bellman said, saved them from wreck, though no one precisely knew how.'

The gentleman at the pianoforte must often have been strongly tempted to 'gag', especially when he was the composer; and on this occasion Haydn's gag becomes a vital part of the composition. I await with impatience the appearance of the rest of his middle and later works in the critical edition which alone throws such lights upon them.

XXIII. SYMPHONY IN E FLAT (SALOMON, NO. 10; CHRONOLOGICAL LIST, NO. 99)

1 *Adagio, leading to* 2 *Vivace assai.* 3 *Adagio.* 4 MENUETTO: *allegretto.* 5 *Vivace.*

This symphony conforms just closely enough to the orthodox scheme of sonata form to make that scheme a guide that can only divert our attention from its most important points. In the first movement (vivace—excluding the slow introduction) it is easy enough to call Ex. 1 the first subject and Ex. 2 the second.

Ex. 1.

Ex. 2.

&c.

And it is true that both are clearly and consecutively recapitulated after a long and varied development. But this way of describing them only blinds us to the meaning or the existence of such facts as that Ex. 2 enters a long time after the firm establishment of the complementary key, and that the so-called 'recapitulation' makes far more of it than it amounted to in the exposition. The fact is that Haydn knew nothing and cared less about first and second subjects and how to balance and distribute them. Balance of keys, balance of sentences, and balance of contrasts, animated by a sense of dramatic movement so powerful and rapid that he gave up opera-writing early in his career because the conditions of theatre-music paralysed him—these, and not the external signs of symmetry, are the principles of Haydn's form. And as to his 'recapitulations', why, the very use of the word has blinded historians to the fact that Haydn says in the place of his 'recapitulation' what Beethoven says in his codas. Again, it has often been noted that Haydn likes to make his 'second subject' out of the same theme as his first. A really clear contrast such as Ex. 2 shows is seldom to be found except at the tail-end of the exposition; and no doubt it is the extremely effective recurrence of such a tail-end as the last sentence of a whole movement (see the adagio of this symphony) which has made theorists talk of Haydn's neat symmetry. But could anybody seriously believe that, with a second subject mainly on the same theme as the first, anything like a regular recapitulation of both would be tolerated by a self-respecting artist?

No; Beethoven's coda was first invented by Haydn. Without spaciousness he could not breathe, and no prose-writer has shown more mastery of the long sentence. Ex. 1 is by no means an outstanding specimen of Haydn's inventiveness (none indeed of the themes in this symphony is that), but it shows at a glance that its inventor could no more help making his phrases and paragraphs lively and shapely than most composers can help making them halting and angular.

In saying that none of the themes in this symphony is a remarkable example of Haydn's inventiveness I am making no criticism, but merely observing that, like many of the greatest things in music, its originality does not come to the surface in the themes. Beethoven's so-called 'Harp' Quartet, op. 74, is perhaps the *locus classicus* for a work of extraordinary romantic power, in which just the most impressive passages are developed from 'tags' which no composer would look at twice. The inference is, neither that the great composer makes wonderful works out of insignificant material, nor that these themes are after all in some mysterious way 'distinguished', but that these themes do not by themselves convey so much of the dominating ideas of the composition as more 'distinguished' themes convey of the compositions to which they belong. The critic who regards 'distinction' as a *sine qua non* in the themes of classical music will be hard put to it to deny that on this showing Spohr was the greatest of the classics. He was undoubtedly the most fastidious in his social tone.

This symphony, on the other hand, is not a work in which the themes are deliberately reduced to formulas in order that the attention may be diverted from 'form' to 'colour', like Beethoven's 'Harp' Quartet and Mozart's greatest works for wind-instruments.

Haydn is simply making one of his greatest symphonies out of his ordinary vein of melody. In the introduction he is impressively romantic and serious; with one of his great surprises in the dramatic modulation to the remote key of E minor after the first pause, and with another fine stroke in the drift therefrom to a key which shows no sign of returning to the tonic at all, until the wood-wind introduces the right chord as an afterthought which leads straight to the vivace assai.

The vivace assai is, we have seen, a first movement in Haydn's own free form, with a 'recapitulation' which is really a typical Beethoven coda.

The adagio, one of Haydn's most majestic things, is also a first movement, in which what orthodoxy would call the 'second subject' comes only as the last eight bars of a very spacious exposition, which had long ago settled into its 'complementary key' with no other material than that of its first subject. If you turn to the end of the movement you will see that, with an interpolated climax that adds two bars, this same theme with its formal cadence-figure has the last word; but before you conclude that orthodoxy is for once right about Haydn's formality, please note that this is a second recapitulation of that theme; that it comes, with its gorgeous new scoring, after a coda which began by expanding the little cadence-figure into the biggest climax of the whole movement; and that the entire coda is actually longer than the very large development section. From the first note, which tells us that, like most of Haydn's later slow movements, this is in a key remote from that of the whole work, to the last note, which rounds the movement off with a touch that is epigrammatic rather than formal, this adagio is typical of that greatness in Haydn which moved Cherubini to tears, and of that freedom which taught Beethoven's inmost soul more than he, the uncouth pupil, could learn from Haydn the tired teacher.

It is well known that Haydn once, when bored by a musical grammarian, said, 'What nonsense this is!—I wish somebody would write a new minuet instead of bothering about pedantries.' Haydn did write many new minuets; and so did Beethoven. But Beethoven began to call his minuets 'scherzos' long before they were bigger or richer than such minuets as this one, with its characteristic capriciousness of rhythm, its freaks of instrumentation, and its trio in a remote key (C major).

The finale is a brilliant specimen of Haydn's comic vein; a sonata-rondo with some of Haydn's best fooling by way of 'second subject'. It has a brilliant fugued development in which the first theme is no more dignified by inversion than it was right-end-upwards; and it shows all that freedom of form that makes it necessary for us to anathematize our text-book knowledge before we can listen to Haydn with ears naïvely tuned to his note.

The scoring of the whole symphony is experimental and imaginative, as always in Haydn. Its eccentricities begin with the first note of the second clarinet, which is the sole support of the strings in the first phrase. This anticipates a famous passage in Weber's *Oberon* Overture, where low clarinets blend with the 'cellos in the introduction. Repeated chords for the wood-wind are usually supposed to have been 'invented' by Beethoven in the allegretto of his Eighth Symphony; but that is a comic passage; and Haydn has used them with glorious solemnity here at the end of his adagio. It would be easy on these lines to prove that Beethoven never 'invented' anything; but the truth is that such great artists always do invent everything, and that it does not in the least matter which of them invented anything first.

XXIV. SYMPHONY IN G MAJOR ('MILITARY'), (SALOMON, NO. 11; CHRONOLOGICAL LIST, NO. 100)

1 *Adagio, leading to* 2 *Allegro.* 3 *Allegretto.* 4 MENUETTO: *Moderato.* 5 FINALE: *Presto.*

The title 'Military' Symphony explains itself when, in the allegretto which does duty for the slow movement, the apparatus known in 1794 as Turkish music crashes in, with an import sometimes tragic, sometimes triumphant. Turkish music consists of the big drum, cymbals, and triangle. As used by Mozart and Haydn, the big drum is played with a big stick and a little stick together, the big stick marking the accents, while the little stick keeps up a trotting rhythm. The cymbals clash in time with the big stick, while the triangle rings an alarum, or trots with the little stick. The 'Turkish music' appears only in the slow movement and finale of the Military Symphony and in no way interrupts the development of Haydn's most characteristic forms. But recent criticism has discovered that Haydn's use of it is in Bad Taste. Turks will be Turks; Tasters will be Tasters; and it is neither in the primitive nor in the sophisticated, but in the mixture of the two that vulgarity lies.

Haydn's introduction begins with a melody which would be quite capable of developing into a complete slow movement. It is not so cat-like as the introduction to the Oxford Symphony, but it is a very exquisite and silky creature and develops a serious mood towards the end, the full orchestra entering in the minor and modulating to E flat; after which dramatic incident it is clear that this is no independent movement, but an introduction to something larger.

The allegro begins with a theme so typical of Haydn that we are apt to forget that in the whole range of classical music no other symphonic first theme has ever been scored in that way.

Ex. 1.

I cannot refrain from transcribing Gevaert's description of this passage: 'Couverts par un timbre velouté, les hautbois perdent leur aigreur, mais non pas leur finesse. Tout le petit édifice harmonique, s'appuyant uniquement sur la sonorité mince du 2ᵉ hautbois, est d'une sveltesse extrême.'

A blustering tutti leads to the dominant, in which key Haydn begins by throwing new lights on his first theme instead of proceeding to something new. But there is another personality to be reckoned with in this drama, and after the solemn formula of two bars of preliminary accompaniment, one of the gayest themes in the world enters and carries on the movement with an impetus remarkable even for Haydn.

Ex. 2.

The development starts in a remote key after an impressive pause, and is one of the richest and most dramatic in all Haydn's works. The recapitulation is, as always in Haydn's mature works, very free and more like Beethoven's larger codas than like any more formal procedure; but Ex. 2 is too strong a personality to be suppressed or cut short, and so the final effect of the movement is nearer to orthodox ideas than is usual with Haydn.

The slow movement (allegretto) needs no quotation. Its one theme is made of figures common to Haydn and Mozart, if not indeed to other contemporaries. There is a peculiar solemn brightness in the scoring and the simple phrase-rhythms, which comes from Mozart's *Zauberflöte*, and has the quality of some august ritual, masonic or military. The movement is in the simplest of forms, with one episode in the minor (introducing no new theme) and a dramatic coda. It is in the minor episode that the military instruments first appear. The coda dramatically introduces a

trumpet-signal. Research into the bugle-calls of Austria and
England at the end of the eighteenth century would doubtless
elicit some interesting anecdotage about the origin of the particular
fanfare used by Haydn; but for us the dramatic effect and its
immediate consequences in a powerful modulation will be quite
sufficient.

The minuet stands alone in Haydn's later symphonies and
quartets in that it does not anticipate the tempo and mood of
Beethoven's scherzos, but is a stately movement of the old type,
splendidly vigorous in its first part, with a graceful trio in admirable
contrast.

The finale begins with one of those themes which we are apt to
take for a kitten until Haydn shows that it is a promising young
tiger.

Ex. 3.

It sounds like a rondo theme, but the movement develops into full
sonata form. The second subject is introduced by the following
whimsical broken figure—

Ex. 4.

and is in itself purposely slight and perfunctory, like the themes
Beethoven puts in a similar position.

Ex. 5.

Its consequences are momentous enough in the coda, and it appears
in a remote key in the development. Beginning with Ex. 4, this
development is one of Haydn's most extraordinary passages,
modulating to extreme distances and building up Ex. 4 into the
most unexpected sequences, especially by inverting it.

The recapitulation represents Ex. 5 only in a rumbustious
fortissimo in which the military instruments suddenly reappear
in all their Turkishness. Even after this the first theme (Ex. 3)

M

is given leisure to return in peace and engage the flute, oboes, and horns (not forgetting the drums) in polyphonic discussion, before the full orchestra with its Turkish music brings this military symphony to a brilliant end.

XXV. SYMPHONY IN D MAJOR, 'THE CLOCK' (LONDON, NO. 11; CHRONOLOGICAL LIST, NO. 101)

1 *Adagio, leading to* 2 *Presto.* 3 *Andante.* 4 MENUETTO. 5 FINALE: *Vivace.*

Haydn's freedom of form is a topic illustrated differently by each of his mature works, but in this essay I will take the freedom of form for granted.

A solemn and quiet introduction in D minor lays stress on a slow but ominous rising scale. This, perhaps only accidentally, foreshadows the main theme of the Presto.

Ex. 1.

The five-bar rhythm of this lively theme is an indication that Haydn's ways of moving are going to be as unconventional as ever, in this obviously very experienced work. The tuttis romp in with all the vigour that gave Haydn the contemporary reputation of being a noisy composer; a reputation which is perfectly justified.

There is a definite new theme by way of second subject; a thing far from a matter of course in Haydn's later works.

Ex. 2.

It is full of coaxing and mockery, and leads to a more than usually boisterous climax. It would be a crime to omit repeating the exposition; the downward scale that leads back to Ex. 1 is among the most characteristic points in the movement.

The development is, as usual with Haydn, spacious, but has no great surprises. The recapitulation, on the other hand, is very free, and takes Ex. 2 a long new journey, working up to the biggest climax in the whole movement, and merging imperceptibly into a coda in which Ex. 1 returns to round off the form. (The fact is that Beethoven's codas are Haydn's recapitulations.)

The accompaniment to the exquisitely kittenish theme of the andante shows at once why this symphony is called 'The Clock'.

Ex. 3.

When the whole theme, with its two repeats, is over, its last bar
is trodden upon by a stormy episode in the minor, based on the
fourth bar of Ex. 3.

After this episode the main theme returns, scored with an
audacity and genius that produce something without any parallel
in earlier or later music. The theme is on the first violins, accompanied only by one flute and one bassoon ticking away at the clock-
figure at a distance of two octaves and a third. This scoring, with
a little help from an oboe, persists throughout the whole thirty-four
bars of the theme. Then there is a long pause. The ticking starts
again in the second violins, leading to E flat, from which point the
theme starts a crescendo leading back to G. By the way, whenever
Haydn is returning to the first bar of his theme, the introductory
bar is always present as an extra. Here it comes again, quite quietly,
and so by no means prepares us for a triumphant outburst of the
whole orchestra, turning the theme into a sonorous tutti. It is
given in full with this rich scoring, after which seven bars of quiet
pedal on the tonic bring the movement to an end.

The minuet is in Haydn's triumphant lively manner, mainly
with full orchestra. The trio requires quotation; for Haydn here
plays a practical joke which has, within my own experience,
caused critics (whom I do not blame) to accuse the orchestra of
'raggedness'.

Ex. 4.

1   2   3   4   5   6   7   8

The persistence of the tonic chord is not a misprint: in the autograph the bars are numbered, as is usual with repeated groups, to
prevent mistakes. Then the repeat is written out in full, and (here
is the strange thing) with a change of harmony at the question-
able bars. The joke is not inexplicable—but it needs pointing
out as a joke, which is unusual with Haydn. Perhaps it is a
bad one.

The finale is full of interesting features. A big ternary rondo
theme, 8 bars, plus 12+8—

Ex. 5.

is followed by a very spacious transition-passage leading to the dominant. In that key Haydn seems to be making a second subject out of the materials of his first, especially its first three notes; but just before returning to the tonic he gives us a new theme (slightly connected with the second part of his main theme, after Ex. 5).

Ex. 6.

Then, in true rondo style the main theme returns (with a forte repeat of its first eight bars and an ornamental variation of its last); and plunges into a stormy episode in the tonic minor. When this has blustered its way for about forty bars to a pause on the dominant, we expect another return to the main theme. Instead, Haydn runs away with a double fugue—

Ex. 7.

which eventually bursts into a grand tutti.

At last we are allowed to hear the first eight bars again. They have a lovely subdominant colour, like sunset light. The last two bars are reiterated and suddenly turned into a runaway wind-up.

XXVI. SYMPHONY IN B FLAT (SALOMON, NO. 12; CHRONO-LOGICAL LIST, NO. 102)

1 *Largo, leading to* 2 *Allegro vivace.* 3 MENUETTO: *Allegro.* 4 *Adagio.*
5 FINALE: *Presto.*

According to the autograph this is the ninth of what Haydn called the London Symphonies and posterity called the Salomon, after the impresario who arranged for their production in the years from 1791 to 1795. It is the 102nd of the 104 symphonies which the most recent musical scholarship has sifted out from the miscellaneous and doubtful works that have at various times passed as Haydn's symphonies.

Like every mature work of Haydn, it has a form of its own which constantly upsets the orthodoxies of text-books. If comparisons were any use in dealing with classics, I should be inclined to select as Haydn's three greatest instrumental works the String Quartet in F, op. 77, no. 2; the 104th and last Symphony, in D major, known as Salomon No. 2, and the present symphony. It has all Haydn's characteristic freedom of form, and more than Haydn's usual symmetry. He is a composer whose devices are singularly difficult to explain away by rules of symmetry; and there are works as large as this symphony where the orthodox methods of sonata analysis hopelessly break down. The main reason for this is that Haydn is a great master with an eminent love of spaciousness, working on a very small scale. In order to make the most of his small space he tends to write his largest movements on a single theme, and has a wonderful art of building that theme into paragraphs of all manner of shapes and sizes without ever falling into any confusion between the manner of formal exposition, where that is wanted, and a free discursive development elsewhere. But in such circumstances a regular recapitulation is out of the question; and what the orthodox text-books assume to be Haydn's recapitulation is neither more nor less than a true Beethoven coda of the ripest kind. Where then does the symmetry come in? It comes in at the end of the exposition, which Haydn always rounds off very neatly in a phrase quietly reproduced at the end of the movement, just where it is the last thing you would expect.

The possibility of asserting symmetry in greater volume depends for Haydn upon the scale of his work. This is generally so small that an extensive symmetry would run counter to the dramatic force of his style. The master from whom Haydn learned that a perfect maturity could be attained both in opera and instrumental music was, of course, Mozart. But the paradox ensued that Haydn failed conspicuously in opera because his style was too swiftly moving, in other words too dramatic, for the operatic forms at his disposal; whereas Mozart, the supreme master of comic opera, is the very composer whose instrumental music was on a large enough scale to emphasize formal symmetry. If, then, this symphony does show a recognizably orthodox scheme in its first movement and finale, with clearly marked second subjects and identifiable recapitulations, the reason is that Haydn feels that he is writing on a large enough scale to use a variety of contrasted themes such as will not waste his all-important space by being recapitulated. The only way to get the benefit of Haydn's or any great composer's sense of form is to listen naïvely to the music, with expectation directed mainly to its sense of movement. Nothing in Haydn is difficult to follow, but almost everything is unexpected if you listen closely and without preconceptions.

The introduction I leave without quotation. After a solemn initial note it begins, like most of Haydn's introductions, with a calm melody. This soon loses symmetry when the basses take up its main figure and carry it into rather remote keys; but the more the music broadens the more evident is its intention of leading to something quite different. It is developed just far enough to give a very definite feeling of breadth; and then after a pause the allegro sets in with the utmost energy.

The first subject begins with a symmetrical melody—

given out by the full orchestra and repeated by the flute, doubled, as almost always in Haydn's scoring, by the first violins. In this case the colour of the doubling has a definite intention which will appear later on. A rousing tutti on kindred material breaks in upon this repetition, and soon leads to the dominant (F major) where a very vigorous new theme enters, without ending or interrupting the flow of the passage.

It will be seen that the accompaniment of this connects it with the first theme. Before the passage has come to a close, there is something which a too clever analysis might connect with the introduction. As this appeals to the eye rather than to the ear, I have protected the listener from temptation by not quoting the introduction. Haydn is perfectly capable of having intended the allusion, and equally capable of laughing at anybody who taxes him with it. What really matters is the Beethovenish passage that follows the close of this tutti.

Its violent rhetorical pauses are impressive enough here; but what would not occur to a lesser composer is to make the passage take a slightly different course each time that it occurs, whether in the development or in the recapitulation. Haydn here concludes his exposition with a new version of Ex. 2, followed by a cadence formed from the third bar of Ex. 1.

The development is inexhaustible; it seems as if everything

happened here. All the above quotations are worked out into quite different themes. Ex. 3 becomes a romantic decrescendo, a cantabile, and a tutti. Ex. 2 becomes a grotesque three-part canon, which stamps its way through three different keys and finally disappears, one voice after another, on to the dominant of C. Here, after a pause, we have in C major (which is of all keys the most contradictory to our tonic) the first theme as a genuine flute solo. There is not the slightest prospect of getting home from here to B flat, but the full orchestra comes storming in with all Haydn's blustering masterfulness, and in its own good time works its way round in the right direction. The recapitulation, when it does arrive, is easily enough recognized in the rough, thanks to the variety of its material. But no doctrine prevents Haydn from combining it with a great deal of further development, such as one would find in a Beethoven coda.

The slow movement sums up an unappreciated chapter in musical history. It is considered correct to say that Carl Philipp Emanuel Bach effected the transition from the style of his father to that of Haydn and Mozart; and it is true that Haydn and Mozart regarded him and more than one other son of the great Sebastian as the elder masters who were contributing to the progress of music at the time. But when it is inferred from this that Haydn's and Mozart's types of form and development are in any way fore-shadowed by Philipp Emanuel Bach, the inference will not bear examination. We have in the slow movement of this symphony a splendid example of what that influence exactly was; and probably we have in it the very latest example. Philipp Emanuel Bach's tendency never was dramatic in the true sense of the word, and it became less and less so as he developed. (It was his more popular brother Johann Christian, the 'London Bach', whose works adumbrate certain dramatic details in the true sonata style; and it was the Bach and Abel Concerts which Salomon continued when he brought Haydn to London.)

Music can make an externally dramatic impression by means not in themselves musical—e.g. the most dramatic feature in Ex. 3 is the fortissimo unison followed by a bar's rest; in other words, a noise and a silence. And so Sir Henry Hadow is able to quote from one of Philipp Emanuel Bach's oratorios a musically very simple passage (dealing with the moment when Moses struck water from the rock) as sounding a new note in music, simply because there is really very little in it to interfere with certain obvious theatrical pro-cedures. But Philipp Emanuel Bach was very fond of music for music's sake, and his whole tendency, even in his oratorios, runs to luxurious lyric sentiment. And in his later sonatas he was so far from developing in the direction of Haydn's and Mozart's dramatic power, that his whole attention was concentrated on a question of ornamentation. Players and singers at that time were allowed great freedom in interpreting and adding to the ornamentation the composer indicated for his melodies; and it seemed to Philipp Emanuel Bach, especially as the art of ornamentation was falling into decadence and chaos, that the time had now come for writing sonatas in which the repetitions were written out in full with variations. These *Reprise-Sonaten*, then, were his latest contribution to the development of music; and it is impossible to conceive anything more calculated to confine music to lyrical and decorative expression and to slacken the sense of movement. The only composer of importance who has preserved this notion of Philipp Emanuel Bach's is Haydn, who in a number of early works showed that he recognized its value for a certain type of melodious slow movement. Unlike Philipp Emanuel Bach, he also saw that to repeat both parts would make the movement too long. He accordingly made a varied repetition only of the first part, and in the recapitulatory portion of the second part devised an ornamentation which would combine both versions. A slow movement of this kind need not be expected to occur in any work of Haydn's later than the date of his acquaintance with Mozart. Only once, in this ripest of symphonies, has he taken a favourite slow movement from a pianoforte trio,[1] an unusually beautiful specimen of Viennese musical rococo, transposed it from F sharp major to F, and written out a full repetition of the first part (which was not repeated in the original trio) in order to add, not fresh airs and graces, but perhaps the most wonderful orchestration to be found before Beethoven. It would be an educative puzzle to guess by ear alone how the last bars of this slow movement are scored. The orchestra happens to consist of one flute, two oboes, two bassoons, two horns, two muted trumpets, muffled drums, and strings. Even in this purely lyric movement there is a certain dramatic element besides the wonderful colouring, but it is notable that it occurs in the second part, which is not repeated.

Ex. 4.

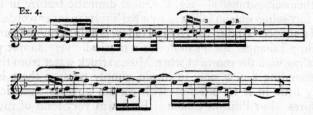

---

[1] The trio version is generally supposed to be arranged from the symphony; but the style of the first movement makes this very difficult to believe.

My quotation shows the first theme. If, instead of dismissing it as a familiar piece of Viennese rococo, we face the plain facts, we shall find that very few rhythms in modern music are as complex or as subtle as this. If you take its exceedingly slow main beats you will find of course that they will prove to be uniformly a simple matter of three divided by two; but the modern composer very rarely follows out so slow a uniform rhythm with so much variety of detail. It looks much more complicated to have no underlying uniformity and to change the time signature every two or three bars; and it also may look more subtle to have unusual groups such as 5, 7, or 13, whether uniformly or capriciously. But we may fairly question whether these are always real complexities or real subtleties. Some of the most imposing of them have been known to straighten themselves out into quite commonplace rhythms to the naïve listener who is deprived of the aspect of the printed page. On the other hand, the rhythm of Haydn's adagio is undoubtedly a combination of eighteen triplet semi-quavers in a bar alternating freely and combining with twelve semiquavers, though he uses the simplest possible notation to convey it. Moreover the very next note of the melody after my quotation fills a whole bar by itself. Modern studies in musical rhythm, such as the first movement of Ravel's Trio, closely re-semble metrical effects in poetry; and they have no room for such a phenomenon as a note or a syllable that is eighteen times the length of the prevalent rhythmic unit and yet does not check the flow.

The Minuet requires no quotations except for the rhythmic figure ♩ | ♩ ♩ which is treated in the second part with the humour which is often called Beethovenish when Beethoven is most like Haydn. The trio has a broader melody, over and under which various instruments from time to time make an acquiescing cadence of two notes. This, however, they put into different parts of the phrase, so that it never twice means quite the same thing.

The finale begins with one of Haydn's best themes of the kittenish type.

Ex. 5.

Young tigers are also very charming as kittens, and this finale has powerful muscles with which to make its spring. It has a well-defined second subject, almost as original as that in the first move-ment; beginning with a chromatic theme—

Ex. 6.

and ending with a rousing dance. The first subject, as might be expected from its character, returns in the tonic like a rondo theme, with some lively fresh touches in the scoring. Then it plunges angrily into the minor as if to start a blustering middle episode. This speedily turns itself into a lively development with some of that very efficient fugue-writing which is to be found in almost all Haydn's larger finales. It is tersely handled, and leads to a recognizable recapitulation of both the first and the second subjects in the tonic. But before the final dance-tune is allowed to conclude matters, Haydn's (*sc.* Beethoven's) coda intervenes. It does everything that even the coda of a Haydn finale can think of, beginning with the Great Bassoon Joke, and continuing with Haydn's characteristic insinuation that everybody in the orchestra has the theme on the tip of his tongue but cannot pronounce it. Then the rousing dance-tutti is allowed to conclude the matter, and even the drums assure us that they know the first figure of the theme, ♪ | ♩

XXVII. SYMPHONY IN E FLAT, 'WITH THE DRUM-ROLL' (SALOMON, NO. 1)

1 *Sostenuto; leading to* 2 *Allegro con spirito.* 3 *Andante.* 4 MENUETTO.
5 FINALE: *Allegro.*

In the autograph this symphony is entitled 'Londoner Symphonie No. 8'. No task could be more futile than the attempt to range Haydn's twelve London Symphonies in order of merit. Their differences grow upon us with their merits as we emancipate ourselves from the doctrine which regards them as pianoforte duets with smashed-china climaxes tempered by the inhibitions of two nice little school-girls with flaxen pigtails. As I have remarked in analysing other symphonies of Haydn, the orchestration of these works, though deeply scarred with evidences of primitive conditions in orchestral performance, is equally wonderful for its power and its subtlety. Haydn's contemporaries found him noisy; and to-day our more sensitive disciples of Rimsky-Korsakov blame Beethoven for a treatment of the trumpets which is demonstrably less violent than Haydn's. We also ascribe to Beethoven's deafness the fact that his scores are full of interesting detail which seldom, if ever, reaches the listener's ear. But in any mature symphony of Haydn you will find that more detail is thus lost than in Beethoven's Ninth Sympathy. And Haydn's detail is often lost beyond the recovering power of double wind and enthusiastic rehearsal; whereas to my own knowledge accident or design has at one time and another brought to my ears every detail that my eye has ever read in Beethoven's scores.

The fact is that neither Haydn nor Beethoven ever thought that aesthetic economy implies that everything in a symphony directly reaches the ear. Their view was in part that of the Greek sculptors, who, arguing that the gods see everywhere, finished the backs of statues which were placed where no mortal eye would see more than the front. But there was also a more human view. Mr. Crummles's leading tragedian could not put himself into Othello's skin until he had blacked himself all over. And the total experience of the players in a symphony is as that of the gods, who see everywhere. They play better all the time when their parts are more interesting than the listener realizes.

Although it is futile to compare the merits of Haydn's London Symphonies, it is permissible to compare their features. In this way we may venture to say that the Symphony with the Drum-roll is one of the most original of the twelve. Its forms are those most peculiar to Haydn and most unlike Mozart; and the opening drum-roll is merely the most obvious and the least remarkable of its unique features. The contemporaries of Beethoven must have forgotten the darkness of Haydn's introductory theme—

Ex. 1.

if they thought Beethoven's genius more eccentric than that shown in this opening. Perhaps, however, they had become accustomed to make too much allowance for Haydn's notorious humour when such awe-inspiring tones came to their ears. And indeed it is true that when this introduction has come to its deepest gloom cheerfulness arises out of its last notes, just as it always broke in upon the philosophy of Dr. Johnson's friend Edwards.

Ex. 2.

Butter does not remain long unmelted in the mouths of Haydn's kittenish themes; and the full orchestra immediately bursts in with a new idea, unquoted here. But Haydn is in no hurry to change his key as yet; nor, when he changes it, does he at once introduce contrasted material. At last, however, a waltz strikes up—

Ex. 3.

and is followed by the solemn theme of the introduction transformed to something livelier than anything Mr. Edwards ever imagined.

Ex. 4.

The exposition as a whole is terse; but the development is unusually rich even for Haydn, who is always ready to expand. A new version of Ex. 1 intervenes dramatically, in quick time but with something like the gloomy colour of the opening, and with chromatic wailings above it. The key is the tonic, but we do not realize that we are at home, and cheerfulness is more present to us when Ex. 3 intervenes in the quite irrelevant key of D flat. After these and other adventures the tonic is again established on really convincing terms, and a more or less regular recapitulation follows. By way of coda the introduction reappears in its original tempo and is dismissed with laughter.

The andante is a set of variations in Haydn's favourite form, with two alternating themes, one in C minor and the other in C major. The minor theme is bleak in its two-part harmony, but full of ironic wit. Note the three turns of meaning given to the figure marked (*a*).

Ex. 5.

The second theme, allied in melody to the first, bursts out in full sunshine.

Ex. 6.

Haydn usually finds room for two full-sized variations of the first theme and one of the second; but here, as in the wonderful pianoforte Andante in F minor, he has room for two of the second,

together with a very spacious coda. And so this movement ends
happily in the major.

The Scotch snap which is prominent in the theme (unquoted) of
the minuet indicates that into the courtly splendour of the famous
minuet of Mozart's E flat Symphony an element has been introduced with which the Hof-Marschall has not been accustomed to
deal. It is dealt with by the Great Bassoon Joke, aided by the
horns. But this gives rise to graver thoughts; and the modulation,
in the second part, to C flat and G flat is no joke. In the graceful
trio, Haydn and Mozart meet on the common ground of a raillery
in which the rustic is at no disadvantage with his urbane friend.

The finale begins romantically with the characteristic two-part
harmony of horns in a phrase which is destined to blaze gloriously
in the trumpets before the symphony is over. At present it serves
as accompaniment to a melody that has been found, like many
other of Haydn's themes, to be a Croatian folk-song—

Ex. 7.

(But perhaps too much has been made of Haydn's Croatian origins,
both racial and musical. Dr. Kuhac's famous book on the subject
was a by-product of one of the nineteen internecine national
propaganda which used to turn the nineteenth-century Austrian
Parliament into a bear garden).

Whether this theme has the honour to be Croatian or merely to
be Haydn's own, it pretends to be a brand-new second subject
when it appears later on in B flat with its phrase-accents turned
round—

Ex. 8.

There are other themes, besides inexhaustible other transformations of this one. The end is inspired by the enthusiasm with which
the trumpets take up the opening horn theme.

XXVIII. SYMPHONY IN D MAJOR (SALOMON, NO. 2; CHRONO-LOGICAL LIST, NO. 104)

1 *Adagio, leading to* 2 *Allegro.* 3 *Andante.* 4 MENUETTO: *Allegro.*
5 *Allegro spiritoso.*

In almost any edition of Haydn's works you may safely assume that the work called No. 1 or No. 2 is really the last. Modern research has sifted out 104 works as genuine symphonies from the innumerable crowd of symphonies, divertimenti, operatic overtures, and supposititious works that have passed as Haydn's: and this Symphony in D, arguably the greatest of Haydn's instrumental works (with the Quartet in F, op. 77, no. 2, as its compeer) is, of course, No. 104 in the chronological list of the symphonies now in course of publication in the long overdue edition of Haydn's complete works.

The solemn Introduction in D minor strikes one of those tragic notes of which Haydn knows the depth as well as or better than the gloomiest artists. But he generally prefers to use it as prelude to some such heavenly tune as this.

Ex. 1.

Students who believe that the text-book scheme of sonata form is anything like as close to classical precedent as a Dutch doll is to human anatomy, will get into difficulties if they try to prove that the mature style of Haydn follows the rules. This first theme does duty for the 'Second Subject' as well; and, of the two themes that are new in the second subject, the one—

Ex. 2.

is heard again in the course of something far more like a big Beethoven coda than a recapitulation, while the other I need not quote, as it never returns. The fact is that Beethoven derived his regular recapitulations from Mozart and his big codas from Haydn, and that his form differs from Haydn's and Mozart's mainly in combining the two procedures in the same work. The two figures labelled (*a*) and (*b*) in my quotations give rise to an unfailing variety of new phases and developments. The essential character of Haydn's form is dramatic surprise at the moment, with sym-

metry emerging as the final impression of a series of paragraphs,
no two of which are symmetrical to each other or in themselves.

After all the a-priorities have been accepted as to powdered
wigs and courtly formulas, will the a-priorists kindly predict what
modulation Haydn is going to make at the end of the sixth bar of
the following theme of the slow movement?

The peaceful codetta to this theme is another of Haydn's profundities—

which reveals its depth fully when, after perhaps the greatest of
all Haydn's ruminative digressions into the remotest of keys, it
returns at the very end of the movement and expands into a quiet
pastoral close.

The minuet and trio I leave without quotation. Both are full of
rhythmic and orchestral surprises. The inquiring first notes of the
trio are ambiguous until the harmony enters in the unexpected key
of B flat. The phrasing is irregular with more than the humour of
the dance in the third act of *Meistersinger*: and, like several of
Haydn's last minuets, the whole movement covers more ground
than any Beethoven scherzo before that of the Eroica Symphony.

I venture to think that Brahms would have thoroughly enjoyed
hearing this symphony at a concert that included his own Symphony in D. Haydn's finale is obviously the grandfather of Brahms's
in certain features to which I draw attention.

The first theme I quote as it occurs in its counter-statement, with
another melody below it.

This enables me to refer to derived themes by their 'figures' (*a*), (*b*), (*c*), (*d*).

In the course of the second subject (which begins with Ex. 5 turned inside-out with the lower melody on the top), the following whirlwind—

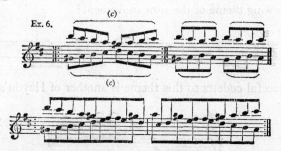

Ex. 6.

obviously inspired the brilliant passage in the corresponding position in Brahms's finale.

A more sustained figure—

Ex. 7.

is the only new theme in Haydn's second subject; for the following impudent prophetic plagiarism from Brahms's cadence-theme—

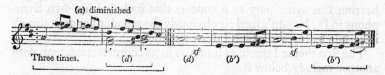

is, as indicated, an ingenious transformation, not to be outdone by Wagner or Liszt, of the figures of the main theme. There is not a line in the movement which could be guessed by rule; and one of the finest surprises is a sudden reversal of accent in the two notes marked (*d*) from which Haydn derives the last chords of the symphony.

MOZART

XXIX. SERENADE IN D MAJOR (KÖCHEL'S CATALOGUE, NO. 250), composed for the Wedding of Elisabeth Haffner, July 22, 1776

1 *Allegro maestoso: leading to Allegro molto.* 2 VIOLIN CONCERTO—*Andante*—MENUETTO—RONDO (*Allegro*). 3 MENUETTO *galante.* 4 *Andante.* 5 MENUETTO. 6 *Adagio: leading to Allegro assai.*

The Haffner Serenade is the largest of all symphonic serenades, and something more. Mozart understood by the term a symphonic work in a festive style, and with licence, or occasion, to extend itself to a greater number of movements than is usual in symphonies. The occasion for such a serenade was generally some such wedding as that of Mozart's friend Elisabeth Haffner to the excellent Herr Spath of Salzburg. Miss Haffner was the daughter of the mayor of Salzburg. For her Mozart wrote a serenade of dimensions suited to the wedding breakfast. This probably lasted from midday till nightfall; and the serenade concluded the proceedings by moonlight.

The Haffner Serenade resembles four other orchestral serenades by Mozart in the same key (D major, almost the official key for festive orchestral music) in containing a group of concerto-movements. In Mozart's own catalogue of his works these groups are mentioned separately as 'concerto in' such and such a serenade. The two greatest of these orchestral serenades, the Haffner and another work (Köchel 320), were for a long time accessible in full score only as symphonies, the concertante movements being omitted. It seems that Mozart himself used to produce these two serenades in this form. Even so, they would still amount to complete symphonies with an extra movement. But the scores published in this form have other defects which do not inspire confidence in their texts; and the complete original works are the more welcome since the concerted movements are not only very beautiful but are incomplete without the rest. The serenade may be a superabundant symphony without the concerto, but the serenade-concertos are manifestly incomplete. Nevertheless I have the strongest suspicion that a certain Concertante for flute, oboe, horn, and bassoon, written in Paris and supposed to have been lost, is really the Concertante for those instruments in the Serenade, Köchel 320. The Meiningen Orchestra toured Europe at the beginning of this century with a concertante for not quite the same group of instruments, which was supposed to be the lost work recently discovered. I had to write an analysis in the programme. Being thus retained as counsel for the defence, I could not say what I thought, viz. that no pupil of mine would be allowed to get

N

through the writing of two of those fifty-odd pages of blundering
form and inept scoring, to say nothing of ascribing them to Mozart.
It is my proud boast that a former Chancellor of the Exchequer,
on reading my carefully worded testimonial to the work, immediately asked me 'What's the matter with this?'

[No! That essay is not among my collected works. If I ever
deal with that concertante again, I shall not write in testimonialese.]

Authorities will differ about what constitutes a theme within the
meaning of the act. I have selected twelve items for illustrating
the Haffner Serenade. Those of the first andante (Exs. 3, 4, 5, 6)
fall, with the exception of the last, into a single complex paragraph,
being parts of a concerto-ritornello. If the whole serenade were
illustrated in the same way, the number of quotations would be at
least 32, and these would not include formulas and derivatives.

The opening allegro maestoso sounds like a first movement
until it proves to be only an introduction to a much livelier allegro
in alla breve time. This real first movement uses the second figure
(b) of the introduction as a transition-theme and makes much of the
first figure (a) as a feature in an otherwise mainly episodic development—

Ex. 1.

Figure (a) also forms the triumphant growl with which the movement ends. From the second group I quote one of Mozart's most
Rossinian themes.

Ex. 2.

The slow movement with violin solo is a worthy forerunner of
one of Mozart's sublimest adagios, that of the D major Quintet.
Its opening ritornello contains in an unbroken flow of melody the
following three figures:

Ex. 3.

Ex. 4.

Ex. 5.

Of these, Ex. 4 reappears in the D major Quintet, and reaches the highest circle of the musical paradise in the Kyrie of Beethoven's *Missa Solemnis*.

To these themes the solo violin adds a transition-theme—

Ex. 6.

and a new item (unquoted) to the second group.

A beautiful minuet in G minor follows. The trio, in G major, is scored for winds with the solo violin.

And now the solo violin is allowed to say a few words in rondo form. Few, if any, concertos have larger or livelier rondos. The solemnity of the occasion is well displayed in the main theme, scored with an exquisite bell-like figure in flutes and trumpets—

Ex. 7.

and the three well-contrasted episodes, in the dominant, the sub-mediant (E minor), and the subdominant, with a full recapitulation of the first episode in the tonic, are worthy of their august positions and responsibilities.

The concerto being now over, the full orchestra resumes its splendours, and the trumpets resound in a *Menuetto galante* in D major. The trio is in the minor, and is serious, as befits the majesty of a slow minuet. (In Mozart's later serenades we are almost as likely to find a serious note as anywhere in his works. The second movement of Köchel 320 is definitely tragic; and the only explanation of the title of serenade for so solemn a work as the wind octet in C minor that was afterwards arranged as a string quintet is that the term may have become generic for wind-music.)

Now comes an Encyclopaedia Mozartiana of rondo form. In the andante in A major we have the most luxurious rondo before that of Brahms's Sextet in B flat. Everything happens that can

happen in a rondo without disaster, and yet the movement is not
inordinately long. The amiable main theme—

Ex. 8.

goes through delightful variations and re-scorings, and good-
naturedly gives up its precedence to a more feline sister who always
turns up instead, and always makes quite sure that you have heard
what she has to say.

Ex. 9.

A third member of the family has a little the manner of an elder
person, being at once enthusiastic and conciliatory.

Ex. 10.

He, she, or it is the source of most of the episodes, and always has
the last word.

Another minuet follows. It is lively, and has two trios, the first
being in G major, with solo wind instruments, while the second
is in D, led by the winds with an undertone of military trumpet-
calls.

A solemn adagio begins as if to develop at leisure into another
meat-course of the wedding breakfastlunchteadinnersuppernight-
cap. But it knows its business and leads straight into the perfect
finale to this inexhaustible but accurately balanced work. The
main theme is one of those affairs that will combine with anything
whatever. Drive on, coachman!

Ex. 11.

The other themes work up into sonata form. Here is the beginning of the most serious one.

Ex. 12.

XXX. SYMPHONY IN C MAJOR (KÖCHEL'S CATALOGUE, NO. 338)

1 *Allegro vivace.* 2 *Andante di molto.* 3 FINALE: *Allegro vivace.*

Jahn believes this work to be the symphony of which Mozart writes
to his father that 'it went *magnifique*' with an orchestra of 40 violins,
12 double basses, 6 bassoons, and 'all the wind doubled'. Against
this identification is the fact that apart from the 6 bassoons the
symphony has no wind to double except the oboes and horns, for
nobody could suppose that the trumpets wanted doubling. Mozart
may have been writing of a revival of the Paris Symphony, which
has full wood-wind, including clarinets. It is surely not necessary
to suppose that every time his letters mention a symphony it was
a different work. The question of identity is not important: the
point is that already at the date of this C major Symphony, when
Mozart was 24, his orchestral style was inveterately grand and
suited for performance on a scale larger than that of the Bayreuth
orchestra. The substance of the first movement may have misled
Jahn to overlook the fact that the score contains neither flutes nor
clarinets to account for 'all the wind'. The themes of the first
movement certainly mark a new stage in Mozart's development.
Grandiose he had already been in the Paris Symphony; sometimes,
indeed, with his tongue in his cheek, as when he obeyed advice in
beginning it with a grand *coup d'archet*, and then, having satisfied
Parisian fashions, began his finale pianissimo. But in this C major
Symphony the grandiose note belongs to something deeper. Even
the piano echo and expansion after the fourth bar of the vigorous
opening formula—

Ex. 1.

is more like a serious dramatic question than any echoes in the
Paris Symphony. And the subsequent plunges into minor keys,
frequent throughout the movement, are wholly serious.

The 'second subject' (so called in our beautiful English terminology, because it may be anywhere about the middle of seven or eight
different themes) marks the epoch of Mozart's full maturity of
invention. Not of his full command of form; many subtleties were
to be added to that in his later works. Up to this moment he had

found out many musical tunes, and, especially in the early concertos, had shown himself bristling with epigram. But now he invents a melody, rich as the most brilliant epigram and broader than any he had ever put into instrumental or vocal music before. It attains the level on which comparisons become impossible. Different melodies may be invented, but not finer ones.

Ex. 2.

Following the custom prescribed for his Paris Symphony, Mozart does not repeat the exposition, but proceeds at once to the development. This is entirely episodic. Twelve impressively gloomy bars lead to the dark key of A flat, where a dramatic passage proceeds, in plaintive dialogue between strings and wind, to the dominant of C minor. There it remains in suspense just long enough to determine the right moment for the return of Ex. 1, with a regular recapitulation.

The slow movement is headed *andante molto*; which has led to mistakes as to its tempo, since we have come to consider andante as meaning 'slow'. But Mozart still has some recollection of its proper Italian sense of 'going'. His *andante molto* therefore does not mean 'very slow' but 'decidedly in motion' or 'ambling along'. *Andante assai con moto* would be tolerable musician's Italian for the purpose. In this light the movement is the richest slow movement Mozart had as yet produced, and he did not often surpass it in subtlety. It is eminently witty, and the attention is concentrated on its pure musical sense without any distractions of orchestral colour, for it is scored for strings alone, except for the bassoons, which however merely double the basses. The harmony gains a characteristic Mozartian richness from the constant division of the violas into two parts.

I give the first theme as it occurs in its counter-statement, where it is given to an inner part, with a counterpoint above.

Ex. 3.

Though the movement is short its effect is eminently spacious, the rhythm being expanded by echoes and interpolations with a mastery that anticipates the Mozart of ten years later.
There is a 'second subject'—

Ex. 4.

followed by plenty of accessories. After the exposition a link of four bars leads at once to a regular recapitulation. The link, which was derived from the first theme, is turned into a neatly epigrammatic end.

As in the Paris Symphony, there is no minuet. The finale is a lively dance in presto 6/8 time, like that of the opening of the ball-room scene in *Don Giovanni*. Imagine the Lancers becoming so fast that it would do for a Tarantella. Quotations are not necessary. The movement is thoroughly effective and appropriate; but this adds interest to the fact that in style and technique it is very like the finales of Mozart's earlier symphonies. It thus serves to measure the advance made by the rest of the work. Here it does not jar, yet you could put it on to an earlier symphony without damage. And if you transposed it into E flat few people would detect its substitution for the opening of the ball-room scene in *Don Giovanni*. But it would be unthinkable as a finale for the Linz Symphony; though it has its impressive minor passages and pianissimos.

XXXI. SYMPHONY IN C MAJOR, NO. 36 ('LINZ SYMPHONY') (KÖCHEL'S CATALOGUE, NO. 425)

1 *Adagio, leading to* 2 *Allegro spiritoso.* 3 *Poco Adagio.*
4 MENUETTO. 5 *Presto.*

The Linz Symphony, composed at that country town in November 1783, ranks with the supreme last triad of symphonies, the great concertos, and the great quartets and quintets, as one of Mozart's most perfect instrumental works. I cannot explain its neglect in recent years. I have only once heard it in my life; but it was evidently very well known in the 'forties, for extracts from it abound in the *Harmonicons* and *Musical Libraries* of that time. Later writers on Mozart trace in it the influence of Haydn. This would not have struck me, for I should expect that influence to enlarge the place of the development-sections in Mozart's sonata forms; whereas in this symphony the developments are even shorter and more episodic than is already usual with Mozart, while the recapitulations (where Haydn usually proceeds to digress) are typically full and regular. We might call the introduction a

Haydnesque feature, since an overwhelming majority of Haydn's later symphonies have it, while it is not easy to recall more than a dozen in all Mozart's works in sonata style. But it is of Mozart's dozen, and not of Haydn's majority, that the present example is typical. It is an architectural portico, not an avenue or a tunnel, like the openings—sometimes tuneful, sometimes mysterious—which make us wonder what Haydn is up to this time.

In the ripening of Mozart's symphonic style the Linz Symphony has much the same position as Beethoven's Fourth Symphony has in Beethoven's style. Both represent the supreme mastery and enjoyment of a sense of movement. Both also represent this as the composer had not so conspicuously or consciously represented it before. Few quotations are needed. The first theme of the allegro stimulates the sense of movement by its irregular phrasing.

Ex. 1.

answered by six bars.

This, and its free expansion, may point to the alleged special influence of Haydn on the Linz Symphony; and another Haydnesque technicality might be found in the difficulty of selecting a definite point at which we can say that the 'second subject' begins. But such technicalities are unimportant; and on the whole the Linz Symphony probably influenced Haydn much more than Haydn influenced it. Certainly it influenced brother Michael Haydn and Beethoven, both of whom copied Mozart's use of C trumpets and drums in an F major slow movement.

I quote the E minor outburst of the second subject—

Ex. 2.

in order to call attention to the spacing of a chord, of which the scoring for oboes, trumpets, horns, and bassoons is one of Mozart's miracles. There is a fine collection of rumbustious tutti themes after this, interrupted by an undoubtedly Haydnesque *piano* piece of quizzing. A running link-passage for the first violins leads back to the repeat of the exposition, and onwards to the short development, of which it forms the staple, also working up into an excellent short coda after the recapitulation. It is a fundamental error in criticism to regard the shortness of Mozart's developments as a defect. They carry enormous weight in his architecture.

The slow movement, in sonata form, is one of Mozart's most beautiful and characteristic inspirations. I have already mentioned how its solemn trumpets and drums impressed other composers. Here is the first theme.

Ex. 3.

The only other quotation I need give is the remarkable episodic link-figure which arises in the short development, and, with its changes of meaning on its penultimate chord, strikes the mysterious note of romance with a power that no remoteness of date can weaken. The penultimate B(*) is sometimes flat and sometimes natural.

Ex. 4.

The gallant little minuet, with its graceful trio, is on hardly a larger scale, though in freer rhythm, than those hundreds of orchestral dances which Mozart wrote for the public ball-rooms of Vienna.

The finale is a wonderful example of the art of spinning along like a tireless athlete, and *not* like a sleeping passenger in a motor-car. From its six distinct themes I quote four; the opening—

Ex. 5.

the transition-theme, which is worked out vigorously in the rather full development—

Ex. 6.

the opening of the second subject—

Ex. 7.

and the ensuing purposeful fugato theme—

Ex. 8.

without the spaciousness of which the remaining bustling and running themes would miss all that raises their glorious energy above the level of Rossini's volubility.

The Prague Symphony is, except for its finale, on a larger scale; but there is in all Mozart nothing greater than the Linz Symphony until we reach the last three symphonies and the great chamber-music.

NOTE

The three symphonies written in six consecutive weeks of the last years of Mozart's life express the healthiest of reactions on each other, and the very fact that they are all in Mozart's ripest style makes the full range of that style appear more vividly than in any other circumstances. Consequently, they make an ideal programme when played in their chronological order; and for such an occasion this prefatory note was written. The E flat Symphony has always been known as the *locus classicus* for euphony: the G minor accurately defines the range of passion comprehended in the terms of Mozart's art: and the C major ends his symphonic career with the youthful majesty of a Greek god. Within these three types each individual movement is no less distinctive, while, of course, the contrasts within the individual symphony are expressly designed for vividness and coherence. Even in the treatment of the orchestra, where Mozart's material resources would mean starvation to any but the most spiritual of modern composers, each symphony has its own special colouring: and that colouring is none the less vivid in that it is most easily defined by stating what instruments of the normal orchestra are absent.

Thus the E flat Symphony, being without oboes, is eminently the symphony with clarinets. Mozart was the first to appreciate the true importance of the clarinet both in chamber music and in the orchestra. He found it already released from its military duty of replacing the clarino or high trumpet of Bach and Handel; but he could not have found in Gluck's or even Haydn's earlier

clarinet-writing anything like his own sense of the value of every
part of the instrument's compass: the low 'chalumeau' notes,
hollow and ominous in sustained or legato passages, and deliciously
'nutty' in non-legato formulas of accompaniment as in the trio of
the minuet in this symphony: the glorious cantabile of the
soprano octave before it reaches the high military notes (in the
trio of the minuet the first clarinet has this to the low accompaniment of the second): and the four or five notes in the middle
register which, rather flabby and dull if brought into the foreground, are an invaluable background for any and every other
orchestral tone. It is this last modest use to which the orchestral
clarinet was devoted by Gluck, and, for the most part, by Haydn,
until Mozart taught him better: and it survives as late as Beethoven's tremendous *Overture for the Consecration of the House*,
where the fugue form requires a certain archaic severity of
orchestral tone.

In the E flat Symphony Mozart compels himself to use the
clarinets in all possible ways, because he does without oboes
throughout the work. In the G minor Symphony he at first did
without clarinets, and most editions of the score give only his
original version; but he afterwards rewrote the oboe-parts, giving
all their softer and less rustic utterances to the clarinets, and it is a
great mistake not to accept his revision. In the C major Symphony
there are no clarinets and no room for them in its scheme. The
whole orchestra is affected by these differences of scheme; and an
intimate knowledge of these three scores is the foundation of a fine
sensibility towards the possibilities of modern orchestration.

XXXII. SYMPHONY IN E FLAT (KÖCHEL'S CATALOGUE, NO. 543)

1 *Adagio, leading to* 2 *Allegro.* 3 *Andante con moto.* 4 MENUETTO:
Allegro. 5 FINALE: *Allegro.*

The E flat Symphony begins with a slow introduction, which, like
most of Mozart's other not very numerous examples, is in the
character of an impressive architectural feature. Haydn, whose
mature symphonies have slow introductions in at least nineteen
cases out of twenty, often makes the introduction mysterious, and
nearly always puts some element of dramatic surprise into it.
Mozart here aims only at the dramatic effect of formal impressive-
ness. Beethoven himself did not write a longer introduction
(though he wrote more directly dramatic ones) before his Seventh
Symphony; and Mozart in the last bars of his E flat introduction
has uttered one of those sublimities that are incomparable with
each other and with everything else, except as touchstones for
one's own sense of beauty.

Ex. 1.

Adagio.

Allegro.

&c.

The graceful theme of the allegro, thus introduced, is a distinguished example of a familiar Mozart type; but familiarity should
not blind us to the resourceful economy of its instrumentation,
and of its counter-statement in the bass, with new imitations and
figures equally rich and convincing in the treble. Then comes a
long and brilliant tutti, which, after stating several new themes,
brings about the transition. The bars that establish the dominant
key of the second subject contain a lively figure which I need not
quote, as its position makes it easily identified. We will call it the
transition-figure. Of the second subject I quote (with abbreviations) almost the whole of its first sentence. Familiarity is apt
to make us think this typical, not only of Mozart, but of his
period. As a matter of fact no other eighteenth-century composer
was capable of writing anything remotely like it; and Beethoven
himself, who attained the same freedom in his Fourth Symphony,
contented himself with handling simpler paragraphs in his Third
(the Eroica).

Ex. 2.

The violins finish this sentence by adding a gorgeous counterpoint to its last five-bar phrase, the fifth bar being obliterated by another outburst of the brilliant tutti, which now ends the exposition with the transition-figure in tonic position. The development is very short and formal, executing its few and simple processes by means of the transition-figure and the five-bar phrase at the end of Ex. 2. After another rousing tutti the wind-instruments lead in three quiet bars back to the recapitulation, which is perfectly complete and regular. There is no coda beyond an amplification, with plenty of trumpet and drum, of the close of the exposition. All this simplicity and symmetry are essential to the bigness of the scheme. The composer who can produce it is not the man who, having got safely through the exposition, turns with relief to the task of copying it out into the right keys for the recapitulation; but he is the man who conceives the exposition with a vivid idea of what effect it will produce in the recapitulation. This is why he can tell when to let it alone. Even here, in the most regular of all classical movements, you may notice a beautiful little enhancement of Ex. 2 at the repetition of its first phrase.

If the first movement combines free and varied phrases with a simple big design, the slow movement seems in its first theme to take its stand upon rigid form.

Ex. 3.

But this formal theme, which takes up a considerable time in building itself into a regular 'binary' structure, is the chief member of one of the most highly organized movements in all Mozart. Notice particularly a moment towards the close of the theme where it is clouded over by the minor mode. An obvious general feature is the surprising amount of development concentrated on the figures (a) and (b) of the theme, which pervade every instrument and almost every stage of the movement. The form of the whole is roughly that of a first movement with no repeats (I am not considering the small repeats of the two portions of the 'binary' first theme), and with no development section, but with a full recapitulation and a final return to the first theme by way of coda.

The transition to the second subject is made through a stormy tutti, beginning in F minor and subsiding into a broad passage of preparation on figures (*a*) and (*b*). This finally settles on a new theme in which instruments take each other up imitatively.

Ex. 4.

&c.

This is stated and counterstated with great breath, and then it leads back to the key of the opening. The recapitulation of the first theme seems to be going to make no changes except merely decorative additions to the scoring, borrowed from the quiet part of the transition; but just towards the close of the theme, where it is clouded over by the minor mode, it modulates to B natural (=C flat) minor, and in this very remote key the stormy transition theme bursts forth with enhanced vigour. It soon reaches the quieter preparations in the right key; and the passage which finally settles down into the recapitulation of Ex. 4 is so subtle and difficult that it has been selected in a volume of 'orchestral studies' for the violin, comprising the outstanding difficulties in Strauss and Wagner.[1] It is worth noting that throughout the movement Mozart's handling of the auxiliary notes in figure (*b*) of Ex. 3 boldly anticipates a feature in the harmonic style of Strauss that has shocked orthodoxy.

The colouring of the later stages of Ex. 4 in the recapitulation is particularly gorgeous and deep; and the crown of the movement is the new turn given to the final shortened summary of the first theme; a passage which looks forward to the close of the slow movement of Beethoven's C minor Symphony, though its beauty is complete in its own right.

I have already called attention to points of scoring in the trio of the most celebrated of all Mozart's minuets. Perhaps, if the minuet were less celebrated in bad pianoforte arrangements, there would be less widespread misconceptions as to its tempo. It is *not* a 'stately' and posturing dance: it is an allegretto, which in Mozart's and Haydn's minuets indicates something fully half-way to the tempo of a scherzo. When Mozart wants the minuet of *Don Giovanni*, he writes *menuetto galante*, or *moderato*.

The finale is in sonata form with repeats, like the first movement. All its themes, throughout the second subject, are derived

[1] The Leipzig edition of the band-parts has, as usual, ruined Mozart's beautiful phrasing, including the main point of his harmony, by editorial bowings. Every well-known orchestral composition of Mozart requires some eight hours' work with a blue pencil to remove the geological deposits of officious stupidity from the band-parts.

from figure (a) of its first subject—

Ex. 5.

(a) (b)

&c.

with the exception of the long and brilliant tutti which effects the transition.

The way in which the second subject pretends to make a new theme by the impudence of a flute and bassoon who cut figure (b) off from the rest, almost tempts one to think that Mozart had been reading the *Frogs* of Aristophanes: the manner is so exactly that of some one finishing an interrupted verse with a ridiculous tag. The truth is that Aristophanes (if he had been musical, as presumably he was) would have found himself very much at home in Vienna or even Salzburg ('the fatherland of clowns' says the librettist of Mozart's *Schauspieldirektor*) at the close of the eighteenth century.

One more quotation is desirable: the wonderful and by no means conspicuous passage for wood-wind at the end of the development, leading back to the recapitulation. It is, of course, the background for the all-pervading figure (a).

Ex. 6.

&c.

The recapitulation is regular, with a completeness that gives the utmost weight of finality to the abrupt end.

XXXIII. SYMPHONY IN G MINOR (KÖCHEL'S CATALOGUE, NO. 550)

1 *Allegro molto.* 2 *Andante.* 3 MENUETTO: *Allegretto.* 4 FINALE: *Allegro assai.*

The Symphony in G minor has been compared with all manner of tragedies; and if the motive of such comparisons be to induce us to take Mozart seriously, they have an excuse. It is quite impossible to exaggerate the depth and power of Mozart's thought; those enthusiasts who may seem to do so, have in fact merely mistranslated the language of music, or of poetry, or of both. The danger of such mistranslations is that they are as likely to misrepresent life as to misrepresent art. We can only belittle and vulgarize our ideas of Mozart by trying to construe him as a tragic artist; neither the literature with which he came into contact, nor the musical forms which he brought to such exquisite perfection could give him scope for any music which by legitimate metaphor could be called tragic. This does not imply that he could not have risen to an opportunity for tragedy; we have no means of knowing the limitations to his powers of expression. He died young, and he touched no problem without solving it to perfection. What is finished of his *Requiem* is of a world beyond tragedy; the *Dies Irae* is in one sense a catastrophe, but a universal catastrophe is not tragic if nobody (or everybody) survives it; for it is in 'the pity and terror' of the spectator that the tragic catastrophe does its purifying work. And in the true tragic sense the *Dies Irae* is not even a catastrophe, it is a universal ordeal that lies in the future; an ordeal for which Mozart prepares himself with solemn rites.

If we are to understand Mozart, we must rid our minds of the presumption that a tragic issue is intrinsically greater than any other. In music this is conspicuously untrue. There is no question that the most tragic of musicians is Beethoven; yet only three of his most powerful works have really tragic finales, while others, sounding fully as tragic a note in their first movements, end in triumph (the Fifth and Ninth Symphonies), or in some pathetic vision as of a happiness secured for the unborn (the F minor and A minor Quartets), or—let us face facts as Beethoven faces them— in a violent temper (the C minor Violin Sonata and E minor Quartet). If we can face the facts of Beethoven's tragic music, we can also face the fact that Mozart's whole musical language is, and remains throughout, the language of comic opera. He has even been blamed for using it in his *Requiem*; and the blame would be deserved if his language meant something he did not intend to say. But the blame should fall on the critic who allows the accidental associations of an artist's idioms to blind him to their true meaning. The word 'awful' does not mean in a modern drawing-room all that it means in Miltonic poetry; but need that prevent a modern poet from using it in a Miltonic way? or from using it properly in a drawing-room?

This is an extreme case for which there is hardly a parallel in Mozart; but the opening of the G minor Symphony, taken together with some of the comments that have been made on it, gives us as delicate a touchstone for the whole question as could well be devised. Sir George Grove in his analysis of this symphony very pertinently remarked that it is difficult to see, in the repeated notes at the end of each step in the theme, those depths of agony ascribed to the opening by some critics. Just so: it is not only difficult to see depths of agony in the rhythms and idioms of comedy, but it is not very intelligent to attempt to see them. Comedy uses the language of real life; and people in real life often find the language of comedy the only dignified expression for their deepest feelings. They do not want the sympathy of sentimentalists who would be hard put to it to tell tragedy from burlesque; and the misconceptions of people who would imagine their situation and language to be merely funny are altogether below their horizon. They rise to the height of human dignity by treating the ordinary language of their fellow mortals as if it were good enough for their troubles; and Mozart and Molière are not fundamentally at variance with Sophocles and Wagner in the different ways in which they immortalize this meaning of the word 'reserve'.

We need not, then, be shocked to find that the language of the opening of the G minor Symphony is much the same as that of the overture Rossini used for the *Barbiere* after writing it for some other purpose. Rossini's overture fits the *Barbiere* admirably; for its feebly shrill and bickering opening can hardly fail to suggest something like the state of mind of poor little Rosina ready for any adventure that may bring escape from her grumpy old guardian. Now, even to those of us who are most fond of the *Barbiere*, this sort of thing hardly bears mentioning in relation to the G minor Symphony. The language, we admit, is common to both: where does the gulf lie?

In the 'forties Liszt published, or at all events played in public, arrangements of Beethoven's nine symphonies, introducing them with a declaration to the effect that it was possible to produce on the pianoforte all the essentials of an orchestral score, except those of sheer mass and varieties of timbre. The arrangements are still in print, and prove conclusively (to any one who can read the originals without their aid) that Liszt was by far the most wonderful interpreter of orchestral scores on the pianoforte that the world is ever likely to see. Yet when Mendelssohn heard of Liszt's declaration, he instantly said, 'Well, if he can play the beginning of Mozart's G minor Symphony as it sounds in the band, I will believe him'. With his usual acumen, Mendelssohn hit upon a passage *scored for strings alone*, which for sheer impossibility of translation to the pianoforte surpasses anything that can be found in Beethoven, or perhaps in any later writer. Yet it is hardly possible to say that its mysterious agitated accompaniment of divided violas makes it much more complicated than the *Barbiere* opening with its coarse little accompaniment in repeated chords.

These two elements of utter simplicity and utter impossibility of translation are among the most obvious signs of the highest poetic power. We do not often find such a bundle of anecdotes and illustrations to demonstrate their presence as we have been able to find for this particular opening, concerning which still more might be said, as the autograph gives some interesting changes of detail, the first bar being an afterthought which changes the rhythmic ictus. But these qualities are equally present in every line and every aspect of the whole.

As has been mentioned above, Mozart first wrote the symphony without clarinets, but availed himself of them at the first opportunity. The Eulenburg score and the Edition Peters give only the original version; but no conductor with a feeling for Mozart's style (and a knowledge of how he sighed for clarinets where they were not forthcoming) would dream of neglecting Mozart's careful revision. The Philharmonia score gives the revised version.

As the Gesammtausgabe is the only one that fully displays both versions, it may be of interest to students of such matters to try and find out during actual performance what the changes are, if only such an exercise is not carried to a point where it rivets instead of stimulating attention to the music. Generally speaking, Mozart has substituted the mellow tone of the clarinets for the acid tone of the oboes everywhere, except in a few places (chiefly sustained discords) where the acid tone has a definitely pathetic effect, and in the trio of the minuet where the use of oboes and horns is in a definitely pastoral style. Where the oboes are not suppressed, they are extensively rewritten, to make room for the fuller harmony the clarinets can help to provide.

Another point in the study of the small orchestra is the ingenious use Mozart makes in this symphony of two horns pitched in two different keys, both of them high; by which means he anticipates Berlioz in a device which doubles the normal number of notes possible in his time on the limited scale of the horn. Much of the surprising fullness of tone in the first movement and finale of this symphony comes from the fact that the horns are able to contribute to the harmony, when in normal circumstances they would have to be silent.

Perhaps the most luminous thing ever said about Mozart was the remark of Edward Fitzgerald, that 'People will not believe that Mozart can be powerful, because he is so beautiful'. If these general observations can help to show his power, they will have proved more useful than any detailed analysis of the symphony from point to point. The contrasts between the four movements will then speak accurately for themselves without my attempting to characterize each with an 'appropriate', and therefore stifling,

epithet. We can learn to know them as we know friends whose
deepest feelings are not hidden from us because we tacitly agree
not to press on them with heavy words.

XXXIV. SYMPHONY IN C MAJOR (KÖCHEL'S CATALOGUE, NO. 551)

1 *Allegro vivace.* 2 *Andante cantabile.* 3 MENUETTO: *Allegretto.*
4 FINALE: *Allegro molto.*

Much may be forgiven to those who, like all sensible people, find
'C major Köchel, No. 551' a not very suggestive name by which to
distinguish Mozart's last symphony from the cheerful little work
in the same key (Köchel, No. three-hundred-and-something) or
the exquisite 'Linz' Symphony in C (Köchel, No. four-hundred-
and-something), which ought never to have been allowed to drop
out of the concert repertory; to say nothing of more than one
interesting juvenile symphony in C among the first three hundreds
of Köchel's Catalogue. Nor does symphony 'No. 41' prove much
more helpful; especially when the miniature score misprints it 49
on the inside, and calls it No. 5 on the outside.

At the same time, the title 'Jupiter' takes rank with the titles
'Emperor Concerto' and 'Moonlight Sonata' as among the silliest
injuries ever inflicted on great works of art. Mozart's musical
culture may have been Italian, but his artistic nature was neither
Roman nor Graeco-Roman. He was as Greek as Keats. He might
have written a Zeus symphony. He never did; and this one is
hardly nearer to Zeus than it is to Jupiter. It has pomp—but so
has the Messenger of the Gods. Hermes might do for it; he is
young enough, and Praxiteles made him reflective enough for
Mozart's slow movement. But, after all, nothing is satisfactorily
like the music but itself; and even the diverting light which another
piece of music sheds on an important theme in the second subject
of the first movement would mislead us, if we forgot that the origin
of the theme outside the symphony is as unlike its effect inside the
symphony as the moon by daylight is unlike moonlight.

One of the most significant differences between Mozart's last
three symphonies concerns the character of their themes. In the
E flat Symphony the themes are evenly poised between formulas
on the one hand and attractive melodies on the other, with euphony
always paramount. In the G minor Symphony almost every theme
is highly individual and, even when formal in phrasing, quite
unexpected in its course. In the last symphony we reach what is
really the final subtlety of an immensely experienced artist, such
as the god-beloved Mozart of the *Magic Flute* or the octogenarian
Verdi of *Falstaff*. Most of the themes are not only formal, but are

actual formulas. There are people who mistake this for a failure to achieve originality. They, as Mark Twain pointed out, whistle or hum the melodies during operatic performances, to show their culture, 'and their funerals do not occur often enough'.

Here is the opening theme, a formula typical of Mozart, and in common use before him: energetic gestures (*a*), alternating with gentle pleadings (*b*). The small notes show the radiant new accessories which adorn the quiet counter-statement which follows the majestic pageantry of the opening.

Ex. 1.

Analysts and historians make a plausible but unfortunate mistake when they prove Mozart a 'formalist' by the fact that in old scores the printer takes advantage of the exactness with which the first twenty-three bars are reproduced after the development, and simply makes a da capo sign. (Pages 19 and 20 of the Eulenburg miniature score.) Similar economies could be practised in the printing of the most modern music; and if Mozart uses formulas that are incapable of variation, it is always in alternation with passages of perfect freedom; indeed his use of the formulas is a part of his freedom. The recapitulation of the quiet counter-statement will be found to be a very different story. The second subject is almost as varied and voluminous as that of the first movement of Beethoven's Eroica Symphony. Besides its opening new theme, it produces several novel results from its treatment of figure (*b*) of Ex. 1, with the same touch of Straussian harmonic freedom that we may notice in the treatment of a similar figure in the andante of the E flat Symphony. Quite late in its course we have the following new theme. I give the text to which Mozart first wrote the tune in a little air inserted in some one else's opera a year before this symphony was composed.

Ex. 2.

Voi sie - te un po' ton - do, mio ca - ro Pom-pe - o, le usan - ze del
mon - do an - da - te a stu - diar, an - date, an - da - te, an - da - te a stu - diar

Perhaps it is Mr. Charles Surface (Lamb's appreciation of Joseph

takes us too far from the humble regions of *opera buffa*)—anyhow
it is some such perfect knight in the Utopia of Gallantry saying
to a young Sir Peter, or some such harmless, necessary husband,
'You are—may I say—a square-toes, my dear Pompeo; go and
study the way of the world'. The art of Sir George Henschel
would raise the naughty little aria to the poetic level it attains in
the symphony.

The slow movement, a very finely developed example of first-
movement form, can be thoroughly enjoyed without musical
illustrations; but listeners need not be deprived of a share in the
pleasure Mendelssohn felt when he found that the lovely reappearance of the first theme just before the final cadence-formula
(bottom line of p. 43 and top line of p. 44 in the Eulenburg score)
was an afterthought added in the autograph on an extra leaf.

Then comes the bright little minuet with its flowing lines, and
its trio which so gracefully agrees to everything so long as it gets
its own way.

Here is the whole thematic material of the famous finale, except
the various continuations by which these ancient 'tags' of counterpoint are turned into sonata-form tunes.

Ex. 3.

The aesthetic discovery that these themes are on the one hand
mere 'tags', and on the other hand suggestive of anything rather
than the sonata form into which Mozart works them—this discovery marks an epoch in the history of criticism second only to
that marked by Jeremy Collier's discovery that Shakespeare's 'genius
was chiefly jocular, but when disposed he could be very serious'.

Of these five themes, No. I first appears as the first subject with
a tune-like continuation. No. II follows it as pageantry, eventually
to round off the whole finale. It is sometimes inverted (i.e. beginning at the bottom of the scale and curling up to the top). No. III

brings about the transition to the second subject. Nos. IV and V appear in combination as the beginning of the second subject, No. IV being worked up into very close 'stretto', i.e. answering voices pressing on each other afresh at every note. The tune-like continuation of No. I then works up to a climax.

The development sheds new light on No. I in dialogue with No. II. After the recapitulation a large space is devoted to the exhilarating coda which has, in Germany, earned for this symphony the sub-title 'with the Final Fugue'. In a kind of fugal round all the five themes are combined. At last No. I breaks into its original tune-like continuation, and No. II brings Mozart's last symphony to an end with a flourish of trumpets.

XXXV. SONATA IN F MAJOR FOR PIANOFORTE FOR FOUR HANDS (KÖCHEL'S CATALOGUE, NO. 452)

The art problem of the pianoforte duet is one of those rare and interesting things in music which can be readily expressed in words. As usual, such musical problems are seldom rightly solved, and often radically misconceived by popular composers and popular criticism. Thus the pianoforte duet as an original composition has hardly been distinguished in popular parlance from the favourite type of pianoforte arrangements of orchestral music: and if you ask the casual music-lover to name some standard four-hand works, the answer will probably be, 'Oh, well, Haydn's Symphonies'. And if you buy an indiscriminate collection of four-hand music the chances are that very little of it will be genuine.

It is worth while to realize what are the actual classics of this form. There is, to begin with, a small volume of Mozart containing one of his greatest instrumental works, namely the present sonata, another large sonata in C, two amusing little sonatas (D and B flat), an unfinished sonata in G (finished by the original publisher), and a very beautiful set of variations said to have been originally written for a musical clock. Two really sublime fantasias for a musical clock are also arranged for four hands, probably by Mozart himself: the arrangement is certainly contemporary, and as obviously beyond praise as most early arrangements are beneath criticism.

Of Beethoven there is a small sonata (op. 6), three very characteristic marches, and two sets of variations.

Of Schubert there is more duet music than solos. Much of it is orchestral in conception, and would well repay the trouble of suitable orchestration; but this is generally rather because the fullness of duet-writing suggests the orchestra than because the music is not charateristic of the pianoforte. Only in the case of the Grand Duo in C and a few of the marches is it evident that Schubert is really thinking of an orchestra which can do well what the pianoforte can only do badly.

Schumann produced a delightful volume, containing several sets of his most characteristic lyrics, for pianoforte duet.

Lastly, we have one of Brahms's greatest and most poetic sets of variations, also his waltzes, and (what is not commonly realized) his original versions of the Hungarian Dances. It was as pianoforte duets that he set these, and the violin versions were based on them afterwards by Joachim.

The aesthetic problem of the pianoforte duet is twofold: the texture of the music must be characteristic of the pianoforte, though the two players command the full range of the orchestra; and the music must be evidently a duet, though the left-hand player is always playing in the bass and has not the advantage of playing on a different instrument. For Mozart the problem was both aggravated and simplified by the narrowness of his five-octave keyboard, at which there was only just room for the two players. However, the bass was nearly as deep as it is now: all that Mozart missed was the upper octave-and-a-half, which tempts later composers to give the right-hand player elbow-room for cut-glass brilliancies and smashed-china fortissimos.

This Sonata in F is a superb piece of chamber-music in no way inferior to the great string quartets and quintets of its period in Mozart's career (it was written soon after *Figaro*). I have often been tempted to arrange it as a string-quintet in G with two violoncellos. There are many difficulties, but the duet dialogue coincides remarkably with Mozart's fondness for the viola, which would produce a scoring remarkably like that of the andante of the C major Quintet. The adagio introduction is as impressive as any before Beethoven, and if you wish to see how a piece of music can show itself to be by nature a four-hand duet, and nothing else in the world, my quotation of the first theme of the allegro goes just far enough to show the point.

Ex. 1.

I refrain from quoting the delightful transition-theme. The second subject to which it leads is given over the page:—

Ex. 2.

The development contains a new episode delightfully characteristic of what I may call Mozart's Masonic style. He was an
enthusiastic Freemason, as the *Magic Flute* shows; and the rhythm
of this episode is full of the mysterious quiet energy and humanity
of Sarastro and his Priests of Isis in their close-tiled lodge.

Ex. 3.

The slow movement is also in full sonata form, and is one of
Mozart's broadest and most polyphonic designs. The spacious
melody of the first subject contains in its second clause a figure
(*a*) which is to form the text of the development and the coda.

Ex. 4.

The whimsical second subject, first stated in two-part imitation—

Ex. 5.

afterwards becomes an orgy in four parts in the recapitulation.
Four Chinese dragons might achieve its august poise and agility;
but it is also human and occidental.   The crowning stroke of genius
in the movement is the cadence-theme which gives Mozart's most
inimitable sense of physical well-being in the poetry of motion.

Ex. 6.

The finale is a rondo on fully the same symphonic scale as the
rest of the work. Its first theme may take rank with the phrase in
the finale of his C minor Concerto which impelled Beethoven to
exclaim to a friend: 'Oh, my dear Ries, things like that will never
occur to the likes of us.'

Ex. 7.

Of the many remaining themes the most important is the transition-theme—

Ex. 8.

which leads to the second subject (for which no quotation is needed). The middle episode develops Ex. 8 extensively in alternation with a new figure.

Ex. 9.

It returns, not to the first subject, but to the second, in the tonic: and the final glorification of the first subject is reserved for the broad and rich coda, where the transition-theme (Ex. 8) also plays an exquisite part.

XXXVI. SCHUBERT

The tragedy of Beethoven's deafness needs no comment; but the history of the arts is full of tragedies not less pathetic and far less inspiring to the imagination. If Beethoven had died as young as Schubert, he would still have been a very experienced master of the orchestra who had produced a large number of works easily the most important of their day, all of which were performed under his direction without serious hindrance from his as yet incipient deafness. But Schubert, who was not deaf, never heard his own mature orchestral music at all; except for one unfortunate experience in the rehearsal of an opera, which he indignantly withdrew on being asked to make alterations and cuts.

There are surprisingly few discoverable traces of this privation in Schubert's scoring. It shows certain typical habits that usually vanish with practical experience; and where Schubert miscalculates, he does not do so, like Beethoven, in pursuit of a definite new orchestral idea. There is no foundation in fact for the widespread notion that Schubert's orchestration is more 'modern' than Beethoven's: its experimental features, though interesting, are neither numerous nor various; and several things that appear to be experimental,

or even successful, are quite possibly due to misconceptions. This
is certainly the case with some of the trombone passages, where
a careful study of the harmony and structure demonstrates that
Schubert thought that trombones would balance nicely with horns.
And so they will, if you can guess where that is the composer's
intention, and if you explain it to the artists concerned. With
this and a few similar precautions, Schubert's orchestration is a
very powerful means of expression, and possesses all the essential orchestral qualities in typical simplicity. Brahms noted this
as a pronounced tendency even in Schubert's earliest chamber-
music; and it goes far to make his pianoforte-writing unplayable.
Perhaps the clearest symptom of distress at lack of opportunity
for hearing his own orchestral music is the magnificent quality
and enormous quantity of his four-hand pianoforte works, one
of which, the Grand Duo in C, proved, when orchestrated by
Joachim, to be essentially one of the most important symphonies
in the classical repertoire.

Few of Schubert's large instrumental works are free from
obvious redundancies and inequalities. But musical criticism is
apt to lose its sense of proportion, in consequence of the unusual
standard of perfection in design and execution set by the great
masters of classical music, and by the perfect preservation of most
of their works. Critics of literature and the fine arts are better
trained to recognize in imperfect examples the qualities which will
produce perfection under special conditions: thus they do not
so constantly make the mistake of assuming that work which shows
the highest qualities can be outweighed by work which does not.
Such a mistake is obviously made (*pace* Matthew Arnold) when we
say Shakespeare was 'no artist' because he very often neglected his
art; and such a mistake is made, less obviously, but more grossly,
when we say that Schubert is no master of form because any fool
can see where Schubert fails. Brahms at any rate made no such
mistake; the ancestry of his forms is pretty evenly divided between
Bach, Haydn, Beethoven, and Schubert. The influence of Mozart
is probably too subtle to be distinguished in Brahms's work from
the overpowering impress of Beethoven's huge forms; but the
traces of Schubert amount to an integral part of Brahms's personal
style.

I confess to seeing no reason for considering Schubert a less
great master of large forms than Shakespeare up to the time of, let
us say, *Richard II*. And it is a sure mark of a good judgement of
musical style when Schubert is regarded, on the strength of his
important works, as a definitely *sublime* composer. It does not
matter when, where, and how he lapses therefrom: the quality is
there, and nothing in its neighbourhood can make it ridiculous.

XXXVII. SYMPHONY IN B FLAT, NO. 5

1 *Allegro.* 2 *Andante con moto.* 3 MENUETTO. 4 *Allegro vivace.*

By the time Schubert was eighteen he had written five symphonies, of which the fifth, in B flat, is a pearl of great price. His First Mass, in F, and the charming one-act opera, *Der vierjährige Posten* (revived by Fritz Busch a few years ago, with a new libretto and additions from other operas), belong to the same period, and have, in common with this symphony, a style quite distinct from that of the later Schubert, and completely capable of justifying its own existence.

In his later and larger instrumental works, Schubert notoriously fails to achieve concentration and terseness. But no theory holds less water than that which imputes his later defects to his lack of sound early education. The criticism which accepts that view cannot, in the first place, tell defects from qualities; and there are unorthodoxies in Schubert which are the signs of new forms of music, and not mere failures to achieve old forms. Every work Schubert left us is an early work; and his gigantic latest works in big forms are in a condition little more diffuse than Mozart's *Entführung* (known in England as *The Seraglio*). As for his earliest successful works, no student of any academic institution has ever produced better models of form. At all events, no academic criticism has yet been framed that can pick holes in this little symphony in B flat. The only possible cavil is that Schubert does not seem fond of long developments, and that he so relishes the prospect of having nothing to do but recapitulate as to make his first subject return in the subdominant, in order that the second subject may come automatically into the tonic without needing an altered transition-passage. In other words, Schubert's early forms are stiff. And as the upholders of musical ortholoxy were in the 'eighties (and are still) painfully puzzled by any forms that were not stiff, they were in no position to criticize Schubert's early education or its early and later results.

Of the first movement of the B flat Symphony I quote the openings of the first subject, omitting the four delicious bars of introduction—

Ex. 1.

and of the second subject—

Ex. 2.

The whole movement is full of Schubert's peculiar delicacy; and its form escapes stiffness like a delightful child overawed into perfect behaviour, not by fear or priggishness but by sheer delight in giving pleasure.

The slow movement reaches a depth of beauty that goes a long way towards the style of the later Schubert; especially in the modulating episodes that follow the main theme. The main theme itself, however, is a Schubertized Mozart, as the following comparison will show.

Ex. 3.

But the rondo of Mozart's Violin Sonata in F (Köchel's Catalogue, No. 377) is a young lady whose delicious simplicity may get more fun out of prigs than they are aware of; while Schubert's theme never thought of making fun of anybody or anything. It is seriously beautiful, and the first change of key—

Ex. 4.

is unmistakably romantic, like those in Schubert's grandest works.

Any minuet for small orchestra in G minor, loud and vigorous, with a quiet trio in G major, must remind us of the minuet of Mozart's G minor Symphony. But Schubert's is much simpler. Its rhythms, though free enough, are square, just where Mozart's are conspicuously irregular; and where the only rustic feeling in Mozart's trio is that given by the tone of the oboes, Schubert's trio is a regular rustic dance with more than a suspicion of a drone-bass.

The finale is in first-movement form, with a binary-form theme on Mozart's models. I quote the two main themes: the first subject—

Ex. 5.

and the second.

Ex. 6.

It runs along merrily, and retains to its last note the early-Schubert flavour of this very perfect little work.

XXXVIII. SYMPHONY IN C MAJOR, NO. 7 *9*

1 *Andante, leading to* 2 *Allegro ma non troppo.* 3 *Andante con moto.*
4 SCHERZO: *Allegro vivace.* 5 FINALE: *Allegro vivace.*

The C major Symphony begins with an introduction which consists of a broad and leisurely working out of the following tune, given out at first in unaccompanied unison by two horns.

Ex. 1.

The figure marked (*a*) becomes the basis of many important themes in the ensuing allegro, which starts as follows, after the opening tune of the introduction has been stated in its fourth version and worked up to a great climax.

Ex. 2.

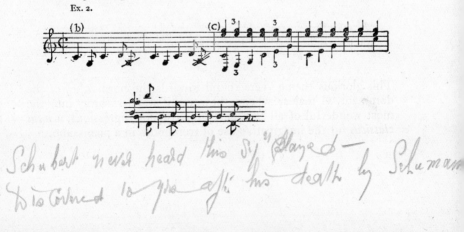

Schubert never heard this Sy "played —
discovered 10 yrs afte his death by Schuman

My quotation presents the theme as it stands in the autograph,
except that for obvious reasons I substitute cross-strokes for the
traces of Schubert's penknife. It is an impressive (though not
yet the most impressive) sign of the white heat at which this
huge work was written, that the whole first movement was fully
scored before Schubert noticed that he really must put more
meaning into the all-pervading figure (*b*) that constitutes the first
two bars of his main theme. The substitution of D for G at the
end of each bar does not spoil the natural way in which the figure
arises from the last bass notes of the introduction, and it suffices
to make the theme important in itself. But Schubert had to alter
this note, or substitute a rest, everywhere from beginning to end
of the movement. The figure is ubiquitous, and the alteration is
neatly made with a penknife literally hundreds of times.

This opening theme immediately closes into another, which I
quote in connexion with the close of Ex. 1, in order to call attention
to a figure (*d*¹ and *d*²) which becomes prominent near the end of the
movement.

The second subject, reached, as usual in Schubert, by a very
simple *coup de théâtre*, starts in a minor key in which it is not going
to settle.

This glorious theme veers round towards the normal key of the
dominant, G major; whence however it wanders away into the
most wonderful of all Schubert's unorthodox digressions, a *locus
classicus* for the imaginative use of trombones in a pianissimo.

Ex. 5.

This passage, which, as the quotation shows, is derived from (*a*) of the introduction, and leads to a triumphant climax in G major, is so masterly in design as well as in poetic power that it is far more like a new art-form than a failure to execute an old one. Many of Schubert's outwardly similar digressions are weaknesses, but every case must be taken on its individual merits; and nothing will induce me to believe that Beethoven would have tolerated a word against this passage in its present position if he had lived to see it.

The rest of the movement explains itself with all Schubert's fluency, and, long though it necessarily is, with more than Schubert's usual concentration. The development is conspicuously free from redundancy or digression, and the recapitulation, which keeps most of the first subject (Exs. 1 and 2) in an alert pianissimo, shows Schubert's characteristic vitality of form in changing the relations of the keys in the second subject.

The coda is in quicker tempo, and has the energy to make a splendid climax; a marked contrast to most of Schubert's codas, which are apt to collapse with a frank gesture of exhaustion. Here the movement ends with an apotheosis of the introduction (Ex. 1). The scoring, as Schubert finally left it, is notoriously miscalculated; but there is a better remedy for it than the horrible marine-parade custom of giving the tune to the trumpet. All that need be done (beyond the usual precautions with the trombones) is to restore Schubert's first version of the string parts, which happened to be perfectly transparent until he altered them, though not one listener in a hundred could tell the difference in sound or sense, except for the all-important fact that in the first version the theme in the wood-wind can be heard, and in the second it cannot.

The slow movement, in A minor, after establishing its in-
domitable march-rhythm in a few wintry bars of introduction,
sets out bravely with the following heart-breaking show of spirit
in adversity.

The burden of the song goes, with Schubert's characteristic half-
Italian pathos, into the major mode.

There is an energetic sequel, marching along in the same rhythm
and with the same brave figures (*a*) and (*b*); and again and again
the procession of themes comes round until at length there is a
change to another key.

The second subject is a broad working-out of a serene melody
of consolation, in F major.

The return from this to A minor is famous as one of the simplest
and most romantic passages ever written for horns. They toll like
a bell haunted by a human soul; and when the first subject returns
there is a new trumpet-part that enlivens and deepens the pathos.
The energetic continuation is worked up to a great climax, from
which the reaction, after a dramatic pause, is intensely tragic; and
then the second subject enters in A major, with radiant new colours
and a flowing accompaniment which continues even through the
returning passage, where clarinets now replace the horns. Then
fragments of the first subject are built up into a mournful coda, even
the burden of the song (Ex. 7) being now in the minor mode.

The scherzo has a far greater number of themes than can be
quoted here; and it yields to nothing in music as regards the
perfection and freedom of their treatment. Like the scherzo of
Beethoven's Ninth Symphony, the main body of the movement
is in miniature but highly organized sonata form. I quote the
beginnings of the first subject.

Ex. 9.

of the second subject—

Ex. 10.

accompanied by (a)   &c.

and of an important episode in the development which recurs very happily at the end of the movement—

Ex. 11.

&c.

leaving unquoted Schubert's afterthought, the wonderful new cantabile which, shortly after Ex. 11, breaks through all these activities and adds 'the gleam, the light that never was, on sea or land'; leaving also unquoted several other accessory phrases, mostly derived from figure (b) of Ex. 10. The variety of rhythm throughout is inexhaustible.

As for the trio, it is a huge single melody (in 'binary' form with repeats, as usual)—one of the greatest and most exhilarating melodies in the world: and it needs no quotation. Unfortunately the scoring, though full of interesting points, does not easily realize Schubert's evident intentions: and until we can afford a double wind-band we are compelled (as in many passages in Beethoven's later works) to damp the accompaniment down till it seriously loses in energy of character. A very eminent conductor once made one of the leading London orchestras play the string-parts pizzicato: a brilliant but thoroughly debased remedy, of which he afterwards had the good grace to be ashamed. Anyhow, the melody must be heard. Towards the end there is one remarkable effect produced by a solitary trombone in the middle of the harmony. This is usually damped down with extreme caution; but I have always had the impression that Schubert was here definitely exerting his imagination, and that the strange red-hot tone should be allowed to show itself. At all events none of these problems can be measured by degree-examination criteria.

The truest lover of Schubert confesses that he would not wish the Unfinished Symphony to have a typical Schubert finale. But Schubert wrote two finales which are typical Schubert without

being his typical finales. These two are the finale of the String
Quintet and the finale of this symphony. Possibly we might add a
third, also in C major—the finale of the Grand Duo that ought to
have been a symphony. And of course there are other finales that
have magnificent themes and passages, notably in the three great
String Quartets. But the two supreme finales are such that nobody
can accuse them of being weaker than the rest of the works. The
finale of the C major Symphony is in fact an example of grotesque
power fully as sublime as the griffin which Ruskin described so
splendidly in *Modern Painters*, part iv, chapter viii.

The two themes of its first subject—

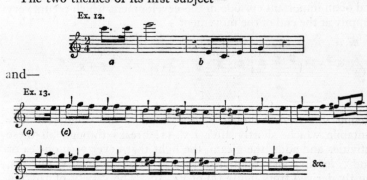

and—

set up a very energetic spin which, like all Schubert's openings,
promises well, but which does not, to people who know their
Schubert, offer any security that it will maintain its energy in the
tropical ease of its composer's mood after he has got through the
three other movements so triumphantly. And indeed Schubert had
a narrow escape here! If ever a powerful piece of music had a
backbone to it, that backbone is the sublimely grotesque main
theme of the second subject, arising so inevitably and so astonishingly out of the four premonitory repeated notes of the horn, and
stretching itself *ad infinitum* while the violins madly turn somer-
saults with the persistent figure (*b*) of Ex. 12. This was the passage
which, when Mendelssohn rehearsed it with the Philharmonic in
London, caused the players to giggle and behave so badly that he had
to withdraw the work; and even within living memory it roused the
pedagogue and blinded the humorist in that great musician Hans
von Bülow. Well, it is to be hoped that we know better now. But
here is what happened in Schubert's autograph.

accompanied by (b) inverted

He had got as far as the four premonitory notes of the horns; and then he dashed off into a schoolmasterly little fugue, from which the only possible reaction would have been a schoolboy's practical jokes. By good luck almost unique in Schubert's short career, he lost interest in this project before he had written nine bars of it—or perhaps the real gigantic inspiration came before he could develop interest in the frivolity he had started. Whatever the mental process was, it cannot have taken three-quarters of a minute; the dingy little fugue-subject was struck out before the answer had well begun; the danger was past, and instead of a weak facility, we have the momentum of a planet in its orbit.

From this weird new inspiration arises a vast variety of ideas. The figure marked (e) produces remote faëry music in the development; and throughout the movement the four repeated notes (d) are as powerful and terrible as anything in Beethoven or Michelangelo. The coda is one of the greatest in all symphonic music. A clever critic, somewhat obsessed with the notion that the only interesting art is morbid, once asserted that this coda expresses Schubert's terror of death. There is nothing to be ashamed of in feeling terror at things which overwhelm us by revealing their vastness; and Schubert can rouse this feeling as one who knows it. But he was not afraid.

XXXIX. UNFINISHED SYMPHONY IN B MINOR

1 *Allegro moderato.* 2 *Andante con moto.*

This, the most perfect of Schubert's large instrumental works, was written in 1826, and was left unfinished, like the scarcely less great Sonata in C major, simply because the remainder did not drive Schubert to the labour of writing it down. Perhaps it is a pity that Schubert did not finish the scherzo; its theme (of which nine bars were scored) is magnificent, and the sketches for it very promising. But we may be almost certain that the finale would have been like many another of Schubert's—there is a Rondeau Brillante in B minor for pianoforte and violin which would perfectly answer the digressive purposes of the typical Schubert finale. And we should much have enjoyed hearing Noll running on. However, the mood which inspired Schubert in the first two movements here, for once, dominated him like Dr. Johnson, and would not let him enjoy hearing himself run on.

Ex. 1.

The sublime depth and pathos of the opening is not without parallel in Schubert's larger works; indeed it is thoroughly characteristic of them. But it is maintained throughout the two complete movements as Schubert has never even attempted to maintain it elsewhere except in movements purely lyric in form. No doubt there are several themes and long passages which, taken out of their context, show no obvious difference from other picturesque and pretty things in Schubert's more unequal works; and there have been musicians who see the resemblance between Schubert's second subject (Ex. 2) and Viennese bourgeois types of beauty, just as there have been art connoisseurs who see the resemblance between a Madonna and a *contadina*. And if that is all they see, let them continue to enjoy music as a by-product of dancing, and art as a by-product of artists' models. Schubert's Unfinished Symphony is an excellent test for freedom from critical bad habits—a test such as the extraordinary perfection and integrity of classical music seldom offers.

The form of the Unfinished Symphony is on the same high level as the style. This will seem almost a wilful paradox to those who have throughout their lives imbibed the ordinary doctrines of musical form, according to which Schubert had no mastery at all. Though lack of space compels me to dogmatize here, I feel amply justified in saying that the real dogmatism is entirely with the ordinary doctrines. These are supported only by a dead weight of uniform 'masterpieces' which the world is politely letting die, whereas the record of the immortal classics presents a variety of forms which can yield their principles only to an attention concentrated on each individual case. The work stands or falls by itself. What may be irrelevant or crude in ninety-nine works, may be a crowning perfection in the hundredth.

For instance, the transition from first to second subject is always
a difficult piece of musical draughtsmanship; and in the rare cases
where Schubert accomplishes it with smoothness, the effort ex-
hausts him to the verge of dullness (as in the slow movement of the
otherwise great A minor Quartet). Hence, in his most inspired
works the transition is accomplished by an abrupt *coup de théâtre*;
and of all such *coups*, no doubt the crudest is that in the Unfinished
Symphony (Ex. 2). Very well then; here is a new thing in the
history of the symphony, not more new, nor more simple than the
new things which turned up in each of Beethoven's nine. Never
mind its historic origin; take it on its merits. Is it not a most impressive moment?

Ex. 2.

Take, again, the continuation of the second subject, generally
a weak point with Schubert, who did not grasp that the time for
exposition of themes is not the time for discursive development of
them. In this symphony Schubert seems indeed to stray into his
usual by-paths, inasmuch as the main theme of the second subject
contains figures that are used in two different derivatives before
the close of the exposition. But if we forget that Schubert wrote
other works, and confine our attention to the matter in hand, we
shall find that these derivatives are masterly in their terseness,
variety, and breadth; and even if we take the risk of comparing
what Schubert has done here with what Mozart and Beethoven
would do, we shall see every reason to believe that they would have
done exactly the same. The exposition is, in short, masterly; and
it in no way undermines the strength of the development. The
development is powerfully dramatic, and Sir George Grove never
made a better point than when he called attention to its pathetic use
of the syncopated accompaniment of Ex. 2 *without the melody*.
The recapitulation shows every quality of freedom and life which
only the greatest masterpieces can show. In choice of key, method
of return to the tonic, et cetera, every technicality is individual and
true. The short coda, beginning like the development, and blazing
up only to die of exhaustion, is very typical of Schubert; but the
exhaustion is here a realized poetic fact, not a mere convenience
to the composer.

The loose structure of the slow movement[1] is, again, a thing not to be confused with the mere digressiveness of Schubert's weaker examples: the weaker examples themselves should rather be taken as tending towards the definite and convincing breadth of design accomplished here. Nor should the pastoral and picturesque types of theme and style blind us to 'the gleam, the light that never was, on sea or land'. Two quotations are necessary, one for the first theme—

Ex. 3.
Andante con moto.

and the other, not so much for the wonderful clarinet theme with its answers in oboe and flute, as for the long notes that lead to it.

Ex. 4.

These four notes (*a*) are turned to such account in the coda that they produce as subtle a stroke of genius as can be found anywhere in music.

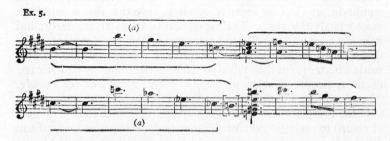

Ex. 5.

[1] It is a mystery why a movement marked *andante con moto* should be traditionally played *adagio sostenuto* by the very people who are severest in their criticism of Schubert's loose length. I remain unrepentant after stern rebuke for assuming that *andante con moto* means what it says.

Every one who knows a good theme when he sees it will be pleased and tantalized by the following. It is the beginning of the scherzo.

Ex. 6.

XL. SYMPHONY IN C MAJOR, ORCHESTRATED BY JOACHIM
FROM THE GRAND DUO, OP. 140.

1 *Allegro moderato.* 2 *Andante.* 3 SCHERZO (*Presto*). 4 *Allegro ma non troppo.* (*Allegro vivace, according to Schubert.*)

The Grand Duo is unique among Schubert's four-hand works in the disconcerting nature of its orchestral style. Not even the Funeral March for the Czar is so full of the kind of orchestral things the pianoforte obviously cannot do, or so deficient in the things, pianistic or orchestral, that it can do with enjoyment. Schubert is known to have written, or is firmly believed by Grove to have written, a symphony at Gastein at about the period of this duet; and the Gastein symphony has disappeared without trace. The autograph of the duet, in the possession of the late Mr. Edward Speyer, is one of the most flawless fair copies Schubert ever wrote; and it is impossible to imagine that it represents the process of composition. Nevertheless, the special authorities on Schubert are very unwilling to entertain the suggestion that the Grand Duo may be the lost Gastein symphony; though they do not seem to have very conclusive arguments against the idea. Be this as it may, the public owes to Joachim its only chance of hearing this specimen of Schubert's grandest symphonic style. I can answer for it that, even where four-hand music is played in public at all, Schubert's Grand Duo is a work that will seldom, if ever, be risked. An arrangement of Beethoven's C minor Symphony would hardly make the players feel more as if they were trying to play cricket with ping-pong bats. From beginning to end there is not a trace of pianoforte style in the work. On the other hand, Joachim's orchestration is exactly right, and differs from what Schubert would have written only in so far as Joachim had become, at an early age, one of the most experienced living masters of the orchestra, so that he avoids, almost instinctively, many a difficulty that arises from Schubert's idiosyncrasies.

The first movement begins with a quiet theme—

Ex. 1.

that soon develops in a crescendo interrupted by a bright pianissimo modulation. Then comes a fortissimo counter-statement in the basses. Here Schubert would certainly have given the theme to the trombones, and that is what Joachim at first did. But Brahms thought that the trombones would have a much finer first entry a little later on, where the music solemnly moves to the vastly remote key of C sharp minor. Accordingly, in a manuscript copy given to me by Joachim in 1904, the trombones are struck out, with the footnote, 'Von Johannes geändert.'

The main theme of the 'second subject'—

Ex. 2.

is in the same rhythm as the first. The dark key of A flat in which it begins, after some delay yields, as usual with Schubert, to the orthodox dominant.

The development is spacious but not inordinately long, though it manages to find room for features that recur in the usual Schubertian way. This is notably the case with a grandiose outburst of the full orchestra on the omnipresent rhythm of Ex. 1. The recapitulation may sound regular; but, in fact, the earlier part of the second subject is totally reharmonized, being mostly in the tonic minor. In the codas of his first movements Schubert often becomes abrupt and perfunctory, as if from exhaustion. Not so here; the coda is broad and impressive, making, before its quiet end, a noble climax to a movement which must rank with the first movement of the unfinished Sonata in C as one of Schubert's most perfect and subtle achievements in form on a large scale.

After so original a movement it is touching to find Schubert quite naïvely carried away by the slow movement of Beethoven's Second Symphony. The opening is pure enough Schubert—

Ex. 3.

&c.

and so is the ensuing first modulation to the distant key of E, with the energetic theme associated with it—

Ex. 4.

though Beethoven would hardly seem an intruder wherever Schubert is most like himself. But when the orthodox dominant emerges from these remoter keys Schubert's surrender is delightfully complete.

Ex. 5.

The Scherzo is one of Schubert's grandest grotesques.

Ex. 6.

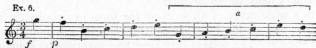

The theme is in the bass—

Ex. 7.

and its fluttering prelude (Ex. 6) becomes the subject of lively dialogue before the end. The irregularities of rhythm are unpredictable, and they keep up the sense of movement with Beethovenish power.

The trio is another inspiration of unique originality, consisting of a melody in F minor, in whole-bar notes as uniform as any *canto fermo* for a counterpoint exercise. The bass moves note against note below, and a syncopated throbbing middle part completes the harmony with the least possible deviation from monotony.

Much comment is excited by Joachim's change of the tempo of the finale to *Allegro ma non troppo* instead of Schubert's *Allegro vivace*. There is an obvious reason and an occult reason for the change. The obvious reason is that there is some danger in taking the movement very fast; it has delicate details, and it must have room to get faster at the end. The occult reason is that Brahms was about to write his intensely Schubertian Quintet in F minor; and Joachim may possibly have 'sensed' in the psychic atmosphere Schubert's proleptic plagiarism of Brahms's finale, which is in a moderate tempo.

Ex. 8.

The device of beginning the theme of a finale in a foreign key is
Beethoven's. It leads to various pretty consequences when the
theme returns. Schubert's finale, though full of poetry and of grand
climaxes, is inveterately comic, as its cheeky 'second subject' shows.

Ex. 9.

It is a remarkable sign of its inherent grandeur that it should have
inspired Brahms, as it undoubtedly did, in so tragic a movement as
the finale of his F minor Quintet.

With a wide range of modulation the form of Schubert's finale
is regular and under a sterner control than its garrulous manner
would suggest. The coda is very large and surprises by containing
a quiet passage in slower time, feeling its way from the ends of the
harmonic world. But the music flares up again, and ends in a
faster tempo than the opening. One more quotation will sum up
in three notes all that the pianoforte can *not* do by way of rendering
the typical sledge-hammer power of the orchestra.

Ex. 10.

MENDELSSOHN

XLI. ITALIAN SYMPHONY, IN A MAJOR, OP. 90.

1 *Allegro vivace.* 2 *Andante con moto.*
3 *Con moto moderato.* 4 SALTARELLO. *Presto.*

Although the Italian Symphony is one of Mendelssohn's most
perfect works, it was withheld from publication during the composer's lifetime. Before he had finished it, in 1831, he was com-
plaining that it cost him some of the bitterest moments in his life;
and in 1847 he died without having accomplished his purpose of
revising the finale. As Parry remarks, there are no signs of bitter
moments in the work as we know it. Nor can we see where the
finale could be improved. But the work may be perfect though
Mendelssohn was disappointed in it; and an instinct deeper than his
conscious self-criticism may have prevented him from altering it.

The Italian Symphony is the work of a young man with an
energy matched only by his technical facility. In relation to
Mendelssohn's musical experience, it stands where Mozart's Paris
Symphony stands in Mozart's career. Now, how would Mozart
have felt towards his Paris Symphony if, instead of being able
simply to enjoy his own sense of power and progress, he had become conscious of the existence of a much greater music that had
already dealt with similar problems? The only great music before
Mozart dealt with matters so entirely different from his symphonic,
operatic, and sonata-style affairs that it could inspire him without
interfering with his pleasure in new ideas. At first sight, and indeed
all the more on further acquaintance, the Italian Symphony seems
too unlike any other classical work to give us or its composer cause
to fear comparisons. But to Mendelssohn such originality was
not enough. The excitement of composing such energetic music
was tremendous, and was enhanced by the unique pleasure of
scoring it with an orchestration that remains to this day unsur-
passed for beauty and accuracy. This being so, the young composer might surely hope that when he had not only finished but
perfected his masterpiece, it would continue to excite in him the
feelings with which he composed it. While he was composing it
he must have felt like a personification of Beethoven's Seventh
Symphony. That classic is one of the things which Mendelssohn
knew so well that he was in no danger of plagiarizing from it. The
Italian Symphony was not meant to resemble it, and does not
resemble it in any indiscreet way. But the very idea of an energetic
symphony in A major must call up the memory of Beethoven's
Seventh. And the last consolation that would satisfy Mendelssohn
would be the plain fact that at the age of twenty-two a composer
cannot be expected to show the power of movement of a composer
of twice his age. It is not a question of technique. Neither
Mendelssohn nor Mozart is a good example of slow and late
development. The Italian Symphony, published as Mendelssohn's
fourth, must really be his sixteenth, since his first published
symphony was preceded by twelve unpublished ones; and Mozart
was overwhelming the Milanese with operas at the age of fifteen.
But there is a kind of easy-going spaciousness which suits a young
composer, and no longer satisfies an older one. Worse advice cannot be given than that which would have a composer pretend to
be past fifty when he is only just past twenty-one. The Paris
Symphony and the Italian Symphony are both—at least in their
main movements—young, loose-limbed works. Luckily for Mozart,
the devil was not able to produce the Jupiter Symphony before its
time in order to wet-blanket the young composer by showing him
how he ought to compose when he had become a considerably

different person. Mendelssohn had no such luck. He was docile, and had been carefully brought up to think his gifts normal. Competent criticism from others never came his way, and nothing is further from the truth than the idea that he lived in an atmosphere of adulation. He lived and behaved like a gentleman; and while his music, at its best and at its worst, gave abundant pleasure, it was produced in solitude. Nobody could help him.

We may then safely conclude that Mendelssohn's own dissatisfaction with the Italian Symphony is rather an objection to the laws of human growth than the recognition of defects that self-criticism and revision can remedy. Certainly in the first three movements every bar and every note is in the right place, except for one tiny oversight in the slow movement which only a mistaken piety would leave uncorrected. As to the finale, no defect is discoverable; but we can imagine that Mendelssohn could have wished to broaden its design towards the end. On the other hand, it is possible that the revising of it would have proved to be an arbitrary and endless business, leaving the movement neither better nor worse than before. Mendelssohn and Handel often show a merely restless inability to abide by a final settlement of their music. Much is omitted in modern performances of *The Messiah*: and one thing that is always omitted is the air 'Thou art gone up on high'. Yet Handel wrote six versions of this air!

The splendid opening theme of the Italian Symphony is famous for its brilliant scoring with an accompaniment of repeated chords in the wood-wind; a device to which some purists object. The only ground for objection is that few students can calculate how such things will sound, and that no poultry-yard can rival the consequences of miscalculation.

Ex. 1.

In a characteristically rapid tempo, but with the leisurely youthful phrasing that cannot be hurried however fast the motor may go, Mendelssohn works out a broad opening and a masterly transition to the dominant. His second group begins with a theme which is obviously in no hurry

Ex. 2.

But its rhythm is, like many underrated features in Mendelssohn's works, more subtle than it looks on paper. The first figure has two aspects. As first announced it begins on an accented bar. The unexpected long notes at its sixth and eighth bars prolong the phrase and bring its next clause into a different position, thus—

Ex. 3.

where the first bar is unaccented; so that the phrase is very different from the la-di-da affair made of it by misrepresentative quotation. Hence in the sequel the accent of Ex. 2 becomes reversed, as indicated by the lower group of figures. One of Mendelssohn's great romantic moments is the entry, soon afterwards, of the clarinet with an augmented version of Ex. 1, in C sharp minor. This quickly leads to a brilliant tutti, after which there is a quiet passage, important in its relation to the rest of the movement, leading back to the beginning. As this passage is omitted from the repeat, it is absolutely necessary that the repeat should be played, otherwise an essential part of the material will not be heard at all.

The development begins with a fugato on a new theme.

Ex. 4.

Here again the rhythm has two aspects. The theme is at first given with the accent on its second bar. As its entries become more crowded the accent shifts; and when the whole orchestra is treating the theme in a grandiose marching style, the accent has settled upon the first bar. By this time however the first theme, Ex. 1, has something to say, as it enters into polyphonic and melodic combination with this fugue theme in a most masterly imbroglio. The slow decline from its climax is another great romantic event; and the beginning of the subsequent crescendo leading to the return has left its mark on one of Brahms's most powerful passages, the return in the first movement of his First Symphony. (The cruel sport of snob-snubbing was a temptation Brahms could never resist when he heard sneers at Mendelssohn.)

In the recapitulation Ex. 4 is inserted into the second group; there, accented on the first bar, it replaces the romantic incident of the augmented first theme in the clarinet. The coda drifts into a quicker tempo and makes brilliant use of the passage that was omitted on the repeat before the development.

Parry was puzzled to know why the slow movement was inspired by Naples, and certainly it needs no illustration from the Bay, or from Vesuvius, or from any of the things that we are told it is worth dying to see. But there is no difficulty in tracing the main idea of this movement to a religious procession which we know that Mendelssohn did see in the streets of Naples. He might have seen it in any other Italian town: the weather would have been the same, and the rest of the background would not have made much difference. The wailing introductory figure is just such an intoned litany as Berlioz uses on a larger scale in the 'Domine Jesu' of his *Requiem*; and the rest is eminently processional and picturesque.

Ex. 5.

&c.

The combination of violins and flutes at the repetitions of the tune is one of the most delightful *tours de force* in all modern orchestration—modern is the word for it, since it is a paradox on any orchestral hypothesis. Verdi, substituting voices for violins and adding a third flute, gave the device a more literal interpretation in the 'Agnus Dei' of his *Requiem*. But the wonderful thing about Mendelssohn's idea is that it seems quite normal. The effect is so like an organ that the movement has become a favourite with organists who want to make the organ sound like an orchestra.

A second theme in the dominant major—

Ex. 6.

&c.

introduces a note of human wistfulness into the austerity of the litany.

The graceful movement that has the function of a minuet is more than pretty. The trio, with its dominant major key and its solemn horns, is beautiful with that depth that can be sounded only by a poet who knows that solemn things must be said with the lightest touch if they are not to become blasphemous. Mendelssohn has here exactly the touch that he misses in later and ostensibly more serious efforts.

The main themes of the finale can be represented by their prevalent saltarello rhythm.

Ex. 7.

W. S. Rockstro, a copious contributor to *Grove's Dictionary*, who knew and used the correct technical term for everything in music, no matter how familiar the thing or how sesquipedalian the term, has told us that, while the two principal themes of this movement are indeed saltarellos, the eel-like legato running theme which is a prominent feature in the development—

Ex. 8.

is a tarantella. The victims of tarantula-bite cannot even stop to jump in their dance.

Be this as it may, the finale of the Italian Symphony is a high-spirited romantic movement, with all the tendency of romance to vanish mysteriously round the corner. Haydn had ended two of his greatest quartets with a finale in the minor mode when the first movement had been major. But he could not bring himself to make the finale end unhappily at last. Mendelssohn, whose finale is here as unlike other things as the rest of the symphony, remains in the minor to the end. It would be an exaggeration to call its humour sardonic, but it is admirably free from either sentimentality or callousness. One detail, very amusing as Mendelssohn puts it, became magnified into a downright offensive feature in the finale of Saint-Saëns's G minor Pianoforte Concerto. The comparison is useful as a touchstone for the difference between an early work of genius and a piece of slick classicism.

SET IN GREAT BRITAIN AT THE UNIVERSITY PRESS, OXFORD,
BY JOHN JOHNSON, PRINTER TO THE UNIVERSITY.
PRINTED BY MERRITT AND HATCHER, LTD., LONDON.